Women's Club Football in Brazil and Colombia

Liverpool Latin American Studies

Series Editor: Matthew Brown, University of Bristol
Emeritus Series Editor: Professor John Fisher

Liverpool Latin American Studies, New Series 30

Women's Club Football in Brazil and Colombia

A Critical Analysis of Players, Media and Institutions

Mark Daniel Biram

LIVERPOOL UNIVERSITY PRESS

First published 2024 by
Liverpool University Press
4 Cambridge Street
Liverpool
L69 7ZU

Copyright © 2024 Mark Daniel Biram

British Library Cataloguing-in-Publication data
A British Library CIP record is available

ISBN 978-1-80207-362-1

Typeset by Carnegie Book Production, Lancaster
Printed and bound by CPI Group (UK) Ltd, Croydon CR0 4YY

Contents

Figures

Glossary of Terms

ACOLFUTPRO	The organisation representing all professional footballers in Colombia. Colombian Division of FIFPRO
CBF	Brazilian Football Confederation (Confederação Brasileira de Futebol)
clubes de camisa	Brazilian term for the best-known and most popular clubs
CONMEBOL	The South American Football Confederation (Confederación Sudamericana de Fútbol; Confederação Sul-Americana de Futebol); the continental governing body of football in South America; one of FIFA's six continental confederations
DI	discursive institutional theory
DIFUTBOL	División Aficionada del Fútbol Colombiano (Amateur Division of Colombian Football)
DIMAYOR	División Mayor del Fútbol Profesional Colombiano (Colombian Professional Football Division)
FCF	Federación Colombiana de Fútbol (Colombian Football Federation)
FENAPF	National Federation of Professional Athletes
FIFA	Fédération Internationale de Football Association (International Federation of Association Football)
FIFPRO	Fédération Internationale des Associations de Footballeurs Professionnels (International Federation of Professional Footballers)
marronismo	The practice of retaining players using illegal incentives/pay during the amateur era in South America
obrigatoriedade	CONMEBOL policy obligating clubs to open a women's team in order to be eligible to compete in the men's Copa Libertadores

Acknowledgements

As will become apparent throughout the book, this work has been shaped by the perspectives of women footballers across the continent. With this in mind I begin by expressing my gratitude to players from Santos FC and Esporte Clube Iranduba in Brazil, Deportivo Ita (Bolivia), Colo Colo (Chile), Atlético Huila (Colombia), Union Española (Ecuador) and finally JC Sport Girls (Peru).

Moreover, special thanks go to the three clubs where the majority of my fieldwork was carried out. For an extremely warm welcome during my ethnographic visits I thank all of the players and staff at Santos FC, Esporte Clube Iranduba and Atlético Huila in particular. Their affable disposition, kindness and willingness to help me whilst busy in their own every-day struggles stood out to me. For taking the time to carry out longer interviews the thoughtful contributions of Angelina Costantino, Karla Alves, Kelly Rodrigues, Maurine Gonçalves, Nicole Ramos, Rosana dos Santos Augusto, Sandrinha Pereira, Tayla Carolina Pereira dos Santos and Thais Picarte at Santos FC; Andressinha Machry, Camilinha Martins Pereira, Driely Severino, Duda Pavão, Giselinha Teles, Karla Yunesca Torres, Mayara Andreia Vaz Moreira, Monalisa Belém, Renata Costa (Koki), Rubi Pereira and Yoreli Rincón at Iranduba; and Carmen Rodallega, Daniela Narváez, Darnelly Quintero, Fany Gauto, Gavy Santos, Jennifer Peñaloza, Jorelyn Carabali, Levis Ramos, Maritza López, Nelly Córdoba and Paola Rincón at Atlético Huila respectively were all particularly useful.

It would be remiss at this stage not to acknowledge the forbearance of my three supervisors, Professor Matthew Brown, Dr Rachel Randall and Dr Edward King. Similarly, the wise suggestions of my PhD examiners, Joanna Crow and Brenda Elsey, provided excellent guidance in bringing this work to fruition. Their stimulating feedback often kept me going when I felt I was running on empty. I must particularly thank Matthew for going way beyond what is usually expected of a supervisor when the storms came. Similarly I owe a debt of gratitude to Professor David Wood for inviting me to the Level Playing Field event in São Paulo in late 2018. I should also take this opportunity to thank both the Society of Latin American Studies (SLAS) and the Bristol-Brazil fund for generous financial assistance without which the lengthy and meaningful ethnographic study I was able to carry out would never have been possible.

For making the necessary arrangements at each club I thank, in no particular order, Alessandro Pinto and Vitor Anjos at Santos FC, Cintia Valadares and Lauro Tentardini at Iranduba and Vanessa Díaz at Atlético Huila. I would also like to thank the wide range of instititutional figures who were interviewed for this book: Amarildo Dutra at Iranduba, Diego Perdomo and Carlos Barrero at Atlético Huila and Marcelo Frazão together with Aline Pellegrino at the Paulista Federation, Romeu Castro and Valesca Aráujo of the CBF and Katherine Pimienta, Carlos Lajud Catálan and Vladimir Cantor of DIMAYOR. In addition to this I would like to thank Albeiro Erazo, Emily Lima and Igor Cearense, the three club managers at the time of my visit, for allowing me to enter the normally private environment of club training sessions. Moreover, I also thank Vadão (sadly no longer with us) for taking the time to speak to me at length during the Copa Libertadores Femenina of 2018 in Manaus.

Along with this, I have benefited greatly from the expertise of a number of prominent journalists; particularly Camila Leonel of *A Crítica* in Manaus, Renata Mendonça with whom I was lucky enough to present at the Level Playing Field event at the Museu de Futebol in São Paulo and last but not least the Paul Weller of football journalism, Tim Vickery. Furthermore, some enduring friendships were made, not least with Aderbal Lana in Manaus, Fabio López de la Roche and Alejandro Villanueva in Bogotá and Juan Carlos Acebedo in Neiva. Additionally warm gratitude to Juliana Ottero and Bruno Rodrigues Pereira for such a warm welcome in São Paulo upon arrival. Similarly, I would like to thank Leticia Nunes, Helder Rivas Mariano, Naomi Moura, Jessica Collado and Bianca Lopes Barbosa for their encouragement and relentless optimism.

For his generous words and deeds I would also like to thank Jorge Knijnik in Sydney. For the experience of writing together I owe a debt of gratitude to two of the most influential writers on women's football on the continent: Silvana Goellner and Claudia Mina Martinez. Immense thanks also go to Francielly Rocha Dossin, Lee Mackenzie and also to Mary Ryder for offering to proofread the chapters of this work.

On a personal level, the mental distraction of playing (badly) in our intergender *pichanguitas* and faring (rather better) in the *tercer tiempo* in the pub afterwards helped keep me sane, especially during the long winter months. For numerous stimulating chats in *los jeiburi vol un abrazo para todos* in no particular order: the immense Martin Prestón (unplayable on his day and also a dab hand with the barbecue), el maestro Claudio Frites, el filósofo Hugo Parra, el capitán Alfredo 'Nica' Menéndez, el carnicero Francisco Palma, el ladrón de goles JP Rodriguez, Igor Cerna Labraña, Carlos Palma, el siberianista Diego Repenning, la mayor goleadora de la pichanga Rocío Almuna, el mago Josese Cruz Sanmartin, Ricardinho Valenzuela, the indefatigable Dana Gabor, Alice Willatt, el caballo loco Matías Rodriguez, Fernan Osorno, el niño Unai De Francisco, Paola Caro and Max Guarini among many others. For many other fruitful conversations about the book, all of which helped greatly, I also thank Narcisa Ruiz Carabali, John Keogh, Tony Patterson, Nick Morgan, Patricia Oliart, Francisca Irarrazabal, María Jesús Vega Salas, Victoria Rivera Ugarte, Alessandra Sciurello, Nancy Gonzalez Lainez, Ahd Othman, Barbara Castillo Buttinghausen, Barbara Foster Tejero, Silvia Espinal, Cristhie Mella Aguilera, Duygu Cavdar, Gözde Doğanyılmaz Burger, Selin Daştan, Eileen Sepúlveda, Leonela Jaramillo, María José Carvallo, Tamara Cepeda, Gaby Vázquez and Roberto Sacoto. Finally, I owe a particular debt of gratitude to Suzan Dean for allowing me to stay at her house on three occasions, accommodating my many comings and goings, and to my parents Yvonne and Michael Biram for their unconditional support in the face of my, at times, seemingly unfathomable decisions. Their patience has been tested many times but has never wavered. This is for you.

Foreword from Silvana Goellner

Belittling and even hostile attitudes towards women, *per se*, are depressingly common across South America. Often represented as second-class subjects, women are subject to multiple forms of gender-based violence, which prevent them from fully exercising their rights.

Although clearly there are differences between and specificities in countries, *machismo* and sexism are structural and deep-rooted in societies of the Global South. The repercussions of this are clearly discernible on the sports field, an area often so inextricably linked to national identities. In football, a sport that is of great importance on this continent, there is a chasm between the opportunities available for women and men both in terms of access to it initially and opportunities within the sport. Gender inequalities permeate practice within and without: in the sporting institutions and the grassroots which feed into them.

The marked lack of continuity at institutional level that historically marks women's football goes hand in hand with a very precarious and fragile structure that can be observed, among other aspects, in the non-professionalisation or semi-professionalisation of the athletes, in the media (in)visibility and in the absence of public and private policies directed towards their promotion. In addition to this situation, discourses and practices reverberate which objectify and sexualise the players' bodies in order to highlight a heteronormative representation of femininity which systematically marginalises anyone who deviates from these rigid norms. The greatest challenge, then, is to change this scenario. This requires a *modus operandi* of constant confrontation, especially with the institutions that govern football. Broadly speaking, these institutions are characterised by deeply patriarchal values which eschew any notion of a more democratic re-definition of power relations between genders.

Topics like these, essential to understanding women's football, are masterfully addressed in this book, which originates from a dense and meticulous research process developed both here in Brazil and in neighbouring Colombia. Doctor Mark Biram immersed himself in the culture and language of both countries, lived with researchers, sports leaders, athletes, members of technical commissions and journalists. In short, this work is rich in engagement with the day-to-day experiences of women's football. For that reason, the epistemological limits they each envision for this sport, from their distinct perspectives, shine through. In addition to the ethnographic work that allowed him to see club football up close and from the inside, he has also provided an innovative analysis of the inner workings of the representations media put into circulation, showing clearly how these discourses actually emanate from the sport's regulatory institutions and occasionally from the players' own voice and agency.

By triangulating different sources of data with a consistent and appropriate theoretical framework, the author presents us with an exemplary work which is insightful beyond the specificities of women's club football in South America. His analyses, even when anchored in this particularity, allow dialogues and comparisons with other ways of playing football and with other regions. They reveal how much, for women, football remains a space to be conquered fully since it remains, to all intents and purposes, a sub-category of the hegemonic male version. Knowing and accepting this reality is the first step to changing this history and rejecting the symbolic annulment of the histories, struggles and achievements of those who play football in its most varied forms of appropriation.

Silvana Goellner
Porto Alegre, February 2023

Introduction

In one sense, it is difficult to summarise many of the positive develop-ments in women's football since the bulk of the fieldwork for this book was carried out in 2018 and 2019. The sport is undeniably experiencing growth and there is some acknowledgement of this at institutional level. When I started my doctorate in late 2017 it would have seemed inconceiv-able that within five years the Brazilian Football Confederation (CBF) would agree to equal pay for appearances in the famous yellow (*canarinho*) jersey (Glass, 202). Moreover, it would have appeared equally unlikely that an ex-captain of the women's team would be entrusted not only with overseeing the women's competitions for the CBF, but also the men's (Dibradoras, 2020).

Cynics may argue that both of these developments represent strategic concessions of a sort. Women are seen to receive equal pay whilst representing the national team, but the great bulk of the footballers' income comes from lucrative contracts with clubs. Yet even in club football, there are signs of a pace of change that could not have been foreseen just a few years ago. At the age of just 17, América de Cali sensation Linda Caicedo has been reported to have been the subject of a €2 million bid from Spanish giants Barcelona (Gómez, 2022; Belas Trindade, 2023). If anything like this figure changes hands, it will surely be a landmark transfer for women's football – a figure that will make girls all over the world dream of the kind of financial security from the game that men have long enjoyed.

This, of course, is happening at the elite end of the spectrum, with the great majority of women players on the continent still unable to earn a full-time living from the sport. The recent developments in the women's game are, for the most part, welcome and of course long overdue. Nonetheless, this is not the moment to sound a note of complacency. As alluded to by Silvana Goellner, on a symbolic level women's football remains very much a sub-category in every respect. As elsewhere in the world, in Latin America women's football suffers by being a marked category – that is to say, it is women's football as opposed to merely football. This means the consistent usage of *fútbol femenino/futebol femenino* as opposed to the unmarked *fútbol/futebol*. Moreover, in South America the marked version includes the adjectival judgement *femenino/feminino* (translated literally as feminine), whereas alternative versions (which are not commonly used in any case) sound even less satisfactory to most of the players I interviewed. The great majority of players felt *fútbol de mujeres/futebol de mulheres* sounds even more like a subordinate category. Running counter to this, there is an increasing body of work on football that is conscious of the links between language and the sporting male hegemony, which for that very reason is resolutely gender-aware (for example Dubois, 2018). Sports and gender specialists Messner, Duncan & Jensen (1993, p. 127) argue that 'gender marking women's athletics renders it the other, derivative, and by implication, inferior'. This consistent gender marking has been picked up in a number of studies considering the media representations of women's football (Salvini & Marchi Júnior, 2013b; Cashman & Raymond, 2014; Mina & Goellner, 2015b; Barreto Januário, 2017; Barreto Januário et al., 2022). This is bolstered by the presence of masculine generics which I overheard on the training grounds – for example, *el Mister* to refer to authority figures, or using *los jugadores* when just one male player is partici-pating in a training session. On the other hand, it is worth noting that the particularities of football also offer some opportunities to de-stabilise gender norms. For example, whilst Wood (2018, p. 575) argues that the use of the name 'Marta' is a gendered marker of one player's status as a woman, the idiosyncratic naming conventions of Brazilian football also offer possibilities to undermine the feminisation of players. For example, as players told me on numerous occasions, Formiga (which translates to 'ant' in English) focuses entirely on the athletic performance of the player rather than emphasising her femininity or feminising her. It describes the way the player unselfishly works for the good of the collective, in the same ways ants work in a colony.[1] From the early pioneers of sports literature like Dunning and Elias to the first wave of sports researchers in Latin America, then, the central focus has been the multiple ways in which sport buttresses and foments what Connell (2005) labelled 'hegemonic masculinity'. As noted by

---

1 Formiga has the record for appearances in the Brazilian women's national team. She has starred at seven World Cups and every Women's Olympic tournament since 1996. The player's real name is Miraildes Maciel Mota. However as with Pelé (Edeson Arantes do Nascimento) the public is far more familiar with the nickname. Women players in Brazil appear to be designated by the same chaotic and idiosyncratic mix as male players: for instance, nicknames (Koki or Chú [women], Dunga or Kaká [men]), diminutive first names (Andressinha or Debinha [women], Ronaldinho or Jairzinho [men]), first names (Marta or Cristiane [women], Romário or Neymar [men]), first name and surname (Gabi Nunes or Andressa Alves, Thiago Silva or Roberto Carlos) or a mix of nickname and diminutive (Pretinha [woman], Formiguinha [man]).

Goldblatt (2016, p. 9), Baron Pierre de Coubertin founded the Olympics as 'the solemn and period exaltation of male athleticism with internationalism as a base and female applause as a reward'. This conceptualisation of the meaning of sport hinges upon the contingent social constructions of masculinity and femininity in a given period – and a growing gender awareness. Clearly, women's football offers multiple opportunities to undermine this type of discourse.

In the context of Brazil and Colombia, the linguistic struggle cannot be separated from the generally polarised political environment. In both countries there has been a notable stigmatisation of so-called 'gender ideology' (Muelle, 2017; Wasser & Lins França, 2020; Borba, 2021) that seeks to vilify movements like #NiUnaMenos (Elsey, 2018). The stigmatisation of a movement highlighting gender violence, femicides, sexual harassment and objectification gives a clue to the depth of misogyny and outright discrimination feminist movements on the continent frequently face.

This was clearly in evidence during the period that followed my visits to Brazil and Colombia. On 5 June 2020, Atlético Huila, then champions of South America, confirmed their non-participation in the Colombian Women's League in October 2020 (Díaz, 2020). To those unfamiliar with the inner workings of women's football in the country this decision was perplexing, to say the least. Founder members of the Colombian Professional Women's League in 2017, Atlético Huila finished runners-up (2017), champions (2018) and finally defeated quarter-finalists (2019). They represented Colombia twice at the continental championship the Copa Libertadores, becoming the first Colombian winners of the competition, in Manaus in 2018 (Bermúdez, 2019; Buitrago, 2020). By any reckoning, their three-year existence brought an unparalleled level of success in Colombian women's football that ought to have been widely celebrated both at national and continental level. Contrary to what the evidence above would suggest, the news that the women's team was to be 'discontinued' or 'temporarily shelved' in a bid to control the club's dire finances came as little surprise to me, having spent three months with the club in Neiva in early 2019. Outright hostility towards women's football from the club's board was manifest. The resolutely gendered attitudes of decision-makers in South American football mean that, regardless of incredible success and widespread interest from the public, there remains a deep discomfort about women playing a game that is still considered socially masculine.[2] Elsey and Nadel argue (2019, p. 2) that sport has historically been used in Latin America 'to naturalise gender differences in society more broadly'. Seen in this light, the accomplishments of Atlético Huila Women must have been seen to de-naturalise perceptions of gender difference in Colombia. Rather than expand a clearly successful project, it was brought to an abrupt end, with the

---

2 The women's team were greeted by thousands of locals when they brought the Copa Libertadores trophy home to Neiva.

women's team disbanded. Following the COVID-19 pandemic, a period when the second-class status of women footballers was manifest (Biram & Goellner, 2020; Biram & Mina, 2021), Huila re-formed the women's team, albeit with a much lower budget than the previous incarnation that had competed success-fully at continental level.

In the same month of June 2020 in Manaus, another of the three clubs I visited, Esporte Clube Iranduba, suddenly announced an enormous shortfall in funding attributable to their sponsors reneging on a sponsor-ship deal – a sum of money a small club needs in order to survive. In order to remedy this situation, the club needed to raise 900,000 Brazilian reais in a matter of days to stave off bankruptcy. They announced that they had started an online *Vaquinha* (similar to Crowdfunding), by which members of the public could make donations in order to save the club (Globoesporte.com, 2020). In a matter of days they had gone from being an alternative model that prioritised women's football over men's football to a club no longer financially viable. Iranduba, at that time, held national attendance records for Brazilian women's football, even outstripping the attendances of several top-division male clubs on several occasions (Padin, 2017). They had reached the semi-finals of the national championship and were considered a model for growing women's football.[3] Having had the immense privilege of carrying out ten months of ethnographic fieldwork at close quarters with both clubs, the resultant financial shortfalls felt entirely in keeping with players' worst fears about the fragile economic basis upon which women's football operates. Players were used to short, casualised contracts and always felt their existence was day-to-day rather than secure. In order to complete its commitments during the 2019 and 2020 seasons, Iranduba had to enter a partnership with a rival club, 3B, whose owner then became responsible for Iranduba's debt in the short term. The longer-term future of the Iranduba project remains unclear.

Out of the three clubs I visited, this left only Santos FC, one of the largest clubs in Brazil, still operating with reasonable comfort. Whilst it could be argued that there were a number of contingent factors behind the fall of these two previously significant players in South American women's football, my feeling is that structural disadvantages and a clear lack of support and policy directed towards smaller clubs meant the chronicle of a death foretold. It confirmed many of the worst suspicions I had about the threadbare infrastructure underpinning women's club football in South America. Moreover, it justified my decision to focus on the day-to-day travails of club footballers, provincial teams rather than wealthier clubs from the economic centre, and the decision to focus largely on the role of football's governing bodies (clubs, federations and confederations) rather

---

3 As per the social and economic order in the country, Brazil's 'centre' is actually in the south and south-east of the country.

than the heavy focus on the media that has characterised the scholarly literature on the topic so far. The media in a broader sense is also included in my analysis, but taking a step away from top-down analysis to try to account for the agency of other actors (in this case the players) in the shifting digital media environment.

Women's club football in South America appears riddled with contradictions. On one hand, in many countries record attendances (AS.com, 2017; Lima, 2017; SoyReferee.com, 2020) and television viewing figures (*Economist*, 2019) evidence the immense commercial potential of the women's game; on the other, (largely male) institutional figures have suggested that continuing with the women's league is commercially not viable. The income generated by women's football is relatively low, but then with clubs refusing to charge fans to watch women's football (in most cases) it is impossible for the women's game to generate income. In terms of representation, traditional discourses about *marimachas* (Oxford, 2019; Oxford & Spaaij, 2019)[4] remain prevalent, and yet very few women players are openly lesbian. The media is complicit in perpetuating this as they choose to highlight different narratives. Alongside the *marimacha* discourse discussed by Oxford (2019), new narratives of athletic femininity have begun to emerge. This book seeks to examine how the traditional media and elite discourses interact with narratives from players themselves. Moreover, in the ethnographic chapters (Three, Four and Five) my examination goes beyond the selective strategic (mis)representations of the women's game to produce a thick description of the reality at the three clubs in this study.

Why Brazil and Colombia?

Across the continent, women's football finds itself at an important moment of development. This is inextricably linked to a cultural moment that has seen widespread activism from movements like #NiUnaMenos (Elsey, 2018). This has fed into existing collectives and activist movements who have long promoted an activist agenda of *fútbol feminista* (Tato et al., 2022) The fact that Brazil has long been the only country from the Global South with a top ten position in the FIFA rankings for the women's game gives the lie to the many trials and tribulations and institutional neglect faced by the country's players. Whilst women's football is more established in Brazil than elsewhere on the continent, the country remains a key battleground in developing women's football in the Global South.

Colombia, meanwhile, provides a fascinating case study, given that the country's marketised football federation the División Mayor del Fútbol Profesional Colombiano (DIMAYOR) claims their women's league is the

---

4 A derogatory term used to designate a woman exhibiting behaviours traditionally thought to be socially masculine.

only professional women's league on the continent. This claim is contentious and is regularly disputed by ACOLFUTPRO, the official organisation representing Colombian women footballers, among others. At the time of embarking upon this project, the league had just been launched in 2017, albeit the degree to which the federation and clubs would make good on promises of professionalisation remained uncertain (Elsey & Nadel, 2019, p. 258). Colombia had regularly been competitive at international tournaments prior to the formation of the league (Mina et al., 2019) – begging numerous questions as to which factors are in fact influential in engendering a culture conducive to success.

The final chapter in this book – the survey – sets out the chasm in the development of women's football among the members of the South American confederation CONMEBOL (Confederación Sudamericana de Fútbol; Confederação Sul-Americana de Futebol). Since the inception of the Women's Copa Libertadores, the domination of Brazil has been relatively clear – Brazilian clubs have won ten out of thirteen times the competition has been run. Mirroring this, Brazil has won the Women's Copa America seven out of eight times. Indeed, in spite of threadbare support from their national federation, the Brazilian women's team reached both World and Olympic finals, competing against nations with significantly better infrastructure and formalised opportunities for women to play the game (Goellner, 2005a, 2021). Similarly, significant achievements by Colombian women players pre-dated institutional advances in their country. For example, the club's leading amateur club Formas Íntimas reached the final of the Women's Copa Libertadores prior to any advances with regard to professionalisation. Likewise, the Colombian women's national team defeated one of the world's leading teams (France) and reached the last sixteen of the Women's World Cup in 2015, before the creation of the Colombian Women's League by DIMAYOR (Biram & Mina, 2021). In light of this, bottom-up mobilisation – from players, smaller independent clubs and enthusiastic activists and sympathisers – is propelling the growth of women's football on the continent rather than often cumbersome institutions that are slow to adapt to a rapidly changing gender order. The tensions between federations and players foreground much of this book.

Why Santos FC, Iranduba and Atlético Huila? (Chapters Two, Three and Four)

A long period of institutional inertia has given way to forced change as (con) federations aim to show compliance with global policy prescriptions *vis-à-vis* gender equality (FIFA, 2016, 2018). Increasingly, the model for women's club football in Latin America in many cases mirrors the European model of incorporating it into larger clubs. This ties women's football, in many cases, into the same relationship of dependence upon men's football that characterises the current UK panorama (Dunn & Welford, 2014, 2016), which at present generates the majority of the income.[5] Following this model, where licencing depends upon the availability of infrastructure that generally only exists at larger clubs, these clubs are comfortably able to cover the turnover of a female team using a tiny percentage of overall turnover from the 'male' club, as and when the political will to do so exists within clubs. This 'will' only began to increase in the Latin American context with the onset of *obrigatoriedade* – the policy that requires teams to open a women's division in order to continue competing in the lucrative (male) Copa Libertadores. Nonetheless, closer scrutiny of the situation shows that many of the main players at the time of the policy being enacted were not, in fact, these large clubs at which the policy was aimed. For this reason, this book considers one club tied to the country's masculinised 'country of football' trope (Santos FC) against two other indicative cases, Atlético Huila of Colombia (where a men's top division club existed at the time of the research but where the club is better known for the achievements of the women) and Iranduba of Manaus (a club where women's football is unambiguously the main part of the club).

Each of these three clubs, then, has been affected in different ways by the policy. At Santos FC, the policy almost guarantees the existence of a women's team, as the size of the club dictates they would not countenance losing the chance of the men's team competing in the Copa Libertadores. At Atlético Huila, a club that has only once participated in the lesser Copa Sudamericana, the policy was met with ambivalence, doing nothing to dissuade the club hierarchy from outright disbanding the women's team in 2019. At Iranduba, a smaller independent club, the arrival of monied clubs from the country's footballing and economic 'centre' has meant an immediate struggle to survive. The following section sets out some of the particularities that make the three clubs well suited to a comparative study analysing the impact of policy prescriptions on women's football, from the perspective of women players.

Santos FC

Santos FC is one of the traditional *clubes de camisa* in Brazil. It is the best-known club in the municipality of Santos, São Paulo state.[6] Its identity is inextricably linked to the wider national identity of Brazilian football. The club was founded in 1912 but owes much of its fame and cachet on a global scale to a golden generation of players in the 1960s that included Mengálvio,

---

5 It is beyond the scope of this book to pinpoint the exact points at which women's football started within the larger clubs. Nonetheless, the traditional *polideportivo* structure of many clubs means women's football has been a fixture for a significant period – sometimes even defying the prohibition of women's football (see Elsey & Nadel, 2019, p. 109).

6 Santos FC is the best known club – but despite claims to the contrary the city has other clubs, such as Portuguesa Santista, that also have long-standing links with women's football.

Coutinho, Pepe and (best known, of course) Pelé. With these strong links to the country's masculinised footballing identity in mind, women playing for Santos FC represent a crucial symbolic incursion into a highly contested space. Indeed, women's football at Santos FC temporarily ceased between 2012 and 2014 when the president at that time cited financial difficulties, despite managing to triple Neymar's exorbitant salary (Goldblatt, 2014). Santos FC Women won the first two competitions for the Women's Copa Libertadores in 2009 and 2010, hosting the first of them at the club's traditional Vila Belmiro home. This stadium is rich in history but is considered dilapidated by the club hierarchy. For this reason, there is serious debate at the club over whether to base its games 100 kilometres away, in São Paulo. The women's team, however, is most readily linked with Vila Belmiro in Santos as much of the women's team's history has taken place there, such as victory in the first ever Women's Copa Libertadores. Santos FC, then, provides a crucial battleground for women contesting a space in an area inextricably linked to masculinity in the country's social imaginary. Moreover, it is an indicative case for establishing how larger clubs with a vested interest in competing in the male Copa Libertadores are reacting to *obrigatoriedade*.

Atlético Huila

The club is based in Neiva, which is the capital city of the province of Huila. It is located in the valley of the Magdalena River, around six hours by road from Bogotá in south central Colombia. Atlético Huila does not make the same symbolic claims as Santos, nor does it have any obvious link to its country's football identity. The club was only formed in 1990 and thus does not and never has belonged to the elite of Colombian football. Since 1990 the men's team has spent a number of seasons in the second division (where it remains as of 2023) but twice achieved more than might have been expected, finishing runners-up in the Colombian first division. The club began the refurbishment of Estadio Guillermo Plazas Alcid (the city's municipal stadium) in 2015. This remains in the early stages and has caused consider-able controversy owing to four fatalities and ten serious injuries occurring at the work (*El Tiempo*, 2017). Moreover, much of the (public) money set aside for the refurbishment has not been accounted for. When complete the stadium will have a capacity of 25,000 but at present only 2,000 specta-tors can safely attend each game. Citing financial difficulties the women's team has been discontinued and the refurbishment of the stadium has been temporarily suspended.

In spite of this, the women's team surprisingly rose to prominence when the women's professional league started in 2017, as the women's operation benefited from an outside benefactor, local businessman Diego Perdomo, who from 2017 to 2019 funded a team competitive at continental level. The lack of football tradition in the city of Neiva means that there is not the same accumulated social capital in the men's team. As a result, at the peak of the success of the women's team, both attendances (around 2,000 spectators for

Figure 0.1   Estadio Guillermo Plazas Alcid, Neiva, Huila

home games) and social media followings (30,000 followers on Twitter and Instagram) reached parity with those of the men's team. For these reasons, Huila lies somewhere between the two Brazilian case studies insofar as the women's team exists alongside (or perhaps better said, is imagined by the club's hierarchy as an addendum to) a relatively established male team, but without any of the symbolic and cultural capital of Santos FC.

Esporte Clube Iranduba da Amazônia

Esporte Clube Iranduba da Amazônia, more commonly known simply as Iranduba, was formed in the city of Manaus in 2011 with both a men's and a women's team. Early on it became clear to the club hierarchy that it would be considerably less costly and thus more realistic to plough much of its budget into the women's team. For this reason, it is important to note that institutionally the rise of Iranduba was coincidental rather than planned. As of December 2018 club president Amarildo Dutra prioritised the women's team. The club participates in many youth categories, from under-15s upwards. The club became particularly popular between 2017 and 2019 when it twice reached the later stages of the Brazilian Women's National Championship and broke Brazilian attendance records for women's football. Moreover, the women's team has won the Amazonian championship six times.

Iranduba is the smallest municipality in the metropolitan region of Manaus in the north-west of Brazil, with 48,296 inhabitants (Instituto Brasileiro de Geografia e Estatística, 2019a). Around a fifth of the Rio Negro sustainable development area, inaugurated in 2008, is found in this part of the region; however, it remains an underprivileged area relative to the rest of Greater Manaus with average salaries and GDP per capita particularly low within the metropolitan region (Instituto Brasileiro de Geografia e Estatística, 2019a).

For the third club to study, I wanted to choose one which operates outside the model that imagines women's football as an addendum to an established (male) club. In Brazil, a number of clubs either are known solely as hubs of women's football – like Sociedade Esportiva Kindermann – or have a women's team that is clearly more prominent on the national scene than its men's team – like São Jose or Ferroviária. Any of the clubs just mentioned would have made an excellent case study to complement Huila and Santos. I decided to choose this particular club as it challenges not only the model of women's football as a subdivision of the larger (male) club, but it also constitutes the most sustained challenge in women's football to Brazil's footballing centre – Rio and São Paulo states. Wishing to look at a club that challenges the footballing centre of the country, in some sense, owes much to my belief that the footballing centre reflects the wider socio-economic configuration of the country. There are examples of clubs from the north-east, like Tiradentes, which have fleetingly challenged the hegemony of the centre; however, Iranduba of Manaus has done this for a period of years. For that reason, along with the considerable support the club has generated in Manaus, Amazonas, I chose Iranduba to be my third case study, as a fascinating anomaly where women's football is the central most important feature of the club.

Contributions on/about the Global South have correctly noted that until now the history of women's sport privileges middle-class women from the global north (Saavedra, 2003; Engh, 2010; Nauright, 2014). This book makes a clean break with this narrative, adopting an intersectional approach that brings out other, crucial facets of discrimination. In this vein, Bowes & Culvin (2021, p. 4) argue that whilst the glass ceiling preventing women's participation has now been lifted, it sits at different heights for different women depending upon a range of intersectional factors. They argue that heteronormatively feminine women and those from the middle class and above receive significantly more positive media attention and that moreover barriers to participation are lower for them. This is reflected across a range of sports and international contexts where professionalisation is on the agenda but at best partially complete (Taylor et al., 2019, 2020; Garton et al., 2021).

Book overview

Chapter One considers two stories generated from the social media accounts of Colombian player Yorelí Rincón. Firstly, Rincón kisses her teammate and partner on the team bus after winning the Copa Libertadores in Manaus, and secondly she records a video explaining how Huila players will not receive any prize money or bonus for winning the competition. The first story is largely ignored for a number of reasons, whereas the second story is re-signified and re-packaged to present the player as greedy and belligerent. The chapter employs and sometimes problematises a theory of Argentine semiologist and media theorist Eliseo Verón. It calls into question top-down assumptions about how the media covers women's football. This is done using a framework that considers different phases of circulation. Verón defines these according to scale and where the interactions take place. The chapter recognises players' agency, as Rincón's activity triggers a positive resolution for the players, but it also acknowledges the uneven power relations that are merely reconfigured rather than dramatically altered in the digital era.

Chapter Two considers a range of institutional theory to explain changes and continuity within the institutional polity. It uses the flagship policy of CONMEBOL, colloquially referred to locally as *obrigatoriedade/ obligatoriedad*, along with material taken from interviews with a number of key institutional figures in both Brazil and Colombia, to explain how the gradual professionalisation of women's football is understood, elaborated and legislated for in Brazil and Colombia. In both cases the differences in national context are taken into account. It is argued that the development model being pursued by CONMEBOL is flawed insofar as it ignores the role of independent women's football clubs, instead encouraging the concentration of wealth and talent within a small number of clubs where male hegemony is hard to dislodge. Moreover, it argues that the conservative approach of institutions impinges significantly on the day-to-day existence of women's players.

Chapter Three considers the experiences of Atlético Huila Women players. Huila is an unusual case insofar as the women's team were significant achievers in comparison to the men's team. An outside benefactor funds Atlético Huila Women on a year-round basis (much longer than other clubs in the country), allowing the club in effect to compete on a continental level without spending any of its own budget. This arrangement works well until the women's club becomes so successful that its success is no longer conscionable to the club hierarchy. This chapter uses an intersectional analysis to explain how players are discriminated against from multiple angles. Moreover, in dialogue with Chapter Two I argue that a considerable gulf remains between the promises of a professional women's league from Colombian federation DIMAYOR and the lived reality on the ground for Colombian women players.

Chapter Four contrasts with the case of Huila, to some degree, in considering the experiences of women players at Santos FC, perhaps the country's best-known club internationally on account of Pelé. Santos FC is well resourced financially, but the situation of its women's team could not be more distant than the situation at Iranduba (described in the next chapter). I argue that the equal incorporation of women's football into Santos FC is significantly encumbered by an invisible and deeply rooted 'banal patriarchy' which pervades every level of the club. The invented tradition of Santos means that women's football is always considered an appendage to the main part of the club by its hierarchy. Nonetheless, even within a club such as Santos, gradual inroads are being made, with improved conditions and the achievements of women players being recognised. Rather than decide between the two models in Chapters Two and Five, it is argued that progress can be achieved in both environments as long as the fundamental differences between them are taken into account by policy-makers and other actors involved.

Contrasting with both the previous chapters, Chapter Five considers the experiences of women players at Esporte Clube Iranduba in Manaus. Iranduba is a radically atypical case, particularly in the era of *obrigatoriedade* with the larger traditional male clubs coming to the fore as described in detail in more detail in Chapter Two on football institutions. It is a club where the women's team commands a larger portion of the budget than the men's team. Moreover, the women's team has a much larger following as they are able to compete at the highest level in ways that, historically, men's teams from Manaus and the north-west of the country have been unable to do. For this reason, this chapter argues that from the periphery of the deeply masculinised 'country of football' the possibility of a women's team taking centre stage proffers a profound symbolic challenge to male hegemony. Whilst in recent times the club has run into serious financial difficulties, a concerted spell of three years challenging the Rio and São Paulo giants proved that another development model would be possible were there to be sufficient political will to implement one.

Chapter Six closes by foregrounding the opinions of players from across the continent. It uses an opinion-based survey I carried out in Manaus in November and December 2018 with 103 players from 8 of the 12 teams competing for the Copa Libertadores Femenina that year. The chapter takes a dual approach, first asking closed questions to players around their satisfaction with the organisation of women's football on a national and continental level, then (following most of the questions) giving players an opportunity to provide anonymised remarks around each of the questions. The data collected is from players based in Bolivia, Brazil, Chile, Colombia, Ecuador and Peru respectively.

CHAPTER ONE

Mis-representing the Agenda

The Case of Yoreli Rincón at the Women's Copa Libertadores 2018

Introduction

This book begins by sketching out the backdrop against which women footballers operate. It aims both to set out the agency that players have through social media and at the same time problematise the notion of digital media as a democratising force. Evidence from this chapter suggests that, if anything, the ubiquity of digital media has only exacerbated and consolidated already uneven power relations.

Victory for Atlético Huila at the Women's Copa Libertadores 2018 represented an unprecedented achievement for a provincial club, for Colombian football's most emblematic female player Yoreli Rincón, and for embattled women players fighting for the survival of the precarious gains made in recent years. In spite of existential doubt over the future of the Colombian women's professional league, a series of stoic displays saw Atlético Huila overcome numerous obstacles, not least beating two of the Brazilian favourites (Iranduba and Santos) on penalties in the semi-final and final respectively, to bring the continental women's title to Colombia for the first time.

After typically threadbare media coverage of the first round of the tournament, the triumph brought a rare moment of visibility for Colombian women's club football. Their victory saw the team trending on social media and greeted by jubilant crowds in their home city of Neiva (@HuilaSport, 2018). However, rather than using the moment to publicise the proven quality of Colombian women's football at continental level, the diverse sections of traditional media included in this study – largely television and newspapers but also radio programmes – tended to deflect attention from the players' victory by focusing disproportionately on a row over tournament prize money. Influenced heavily by players' concerns about the logic underpinning media coverage of women players, this chapter considers the downplaying of the performance of women players and the attempts to portray them as belligerent and inopportune in attempting to discuss the clear inequalities and contradictions in the way they are treated. Moreover, it calls into question the top-down assumptions underpinning work on media coverage of women's football to date by considering an increasingly heterogeneous range of actors who produce meaning via social media platforms.

Media representations paradigm

A great deal of the contemporary sociological work on women's football has analysed the output of traditional media – in particular television coverage of matches and newspaper discourse. Broadly speaking, a transition from the crass caricaturing of female participation found in early twentieth-century coverage of women's football (discussed in Bonfim, 2019; Brewster & Brewster, 2019; Santillán Esqueda & Gantús, 2010) towards the gender-bland sexism (Musto et al., 2017) identified in more recent coverage is in keeping with the progress presented by institutional narratives in the 'official' era that began with the 1991 Women's World Cup of the Fédération Internationale de Football Association (FIFA) – then marketed as the FIFA Women's World Championship so as not to threaten the reputation of the other World Cup. Scholars have identified tendencies that have character-ised coverage – for example, how match action is consistently described in polite but lacklustre and often sexist terms (dos Santos & Medeiros, 2012; Salvini & Marchi Júnior, 2013a; Mina & Goellner, 2015a; Gutiérrez Sánchez, 2015; Morel, 2019). In both Colombia and Brazil, coverage has been shown to conform on a superficial level with notions of gender equality, whilst suppressing any notion of female athletic performance, and notably falling short of the hyperbolic overexcitement that characterises coverage of male football. This polite but banal, uninspiring presentation was charac-teristic of both print and broadcast media coverage of the Women's Copa Libertadores 2018 in Manaus during my research. It is a strategy that serves to deny women a symbolic space in a domain that is discursively portrayed as eminently masculine.

Similarly informed by the male gaze is the trope that eroticises and sexualises women players in order to market women's football (to men). Pfister (2015) details how this objectification is a recurring framing device used to portray women footballers in the German press. This is echoed by similar tropes of athletic femininity across a range of global settings. For example, Cashman & Raymond (2014) describe the overt and covert objectification of the Mexican women's national team; Christopherson et al. (2002) and Jones et al. (1999) explain how a heteronormative femininity is central to representations of the US women's national team; and finally Ravel & Gareau (2016) recall how model Adriana Karembeu was used for a promotional campaign 'French football needs more women like Adriana'.[1]

---

1 Adriana Karembeu is a Slovakian model, married to ex-French international Christian Karembeu.

Tropes of athletic or heteronormative femininity are reproduced and even actively encouraged by institutions. Indeed, ex-FIFA president Sepp Blatter infamously suggested that 'tighter shorts for women players could be a step towards making the game more marketable' (quoted in Christenson & Kelso, 2004). Sports companies have got in on the act – despite the availability of thousands of Colombian women footballers, Colombian model Paulina Vega was chosen to star alongside men's player James Rodriguez to promote a women's version of the Colombia national team shirt specially designed by Adidas (Marcos, 2017). This is symptomatic of the promotion of an idealised type that speaks not to the diversity of women players but rather to the male gaze from positions of power.

There have been attempts to account for the presence of social media in the existing scholarship. For example, Pegoraro et al. (2018) consider how Instagram is used overwhelmingly by players to highlight athletic performance rather than more superficial marketing aspects. Similarly, Coche (2016) and Hayes Sauder & Blaszka (2018) consider how the US federation and its players respectively use social media to generate interest in women's football and individual players.

Given the social significance afforded to sport, this locates women playing as particularly significant. In this vein, Messner (1988) considers the female athlete as 'contested ideological terrain', placing prevailing notions of sporting masculinity into dialogue with newly emerging discourses of sporting femininity. Responding to this, an emerging body of literature has come to consider how sportswomen perceive and represent themselves on social media (Thorpe et al., 2017; Toffoletti & Thorpe, 2018). In this vein, in the Latin American context Garton & Hijós (2017) examine the degree to which sportswomen conform with the recent shift in media discourse towards athletic femininity. This chapter considers traffic in the other direction – that is to say, to what extent does the media have to take account of the discourse and narratives of players?

In Colombia, much of the analysis around the Colombian professional league has come from Claudia Mina Martinez, who has considered many of the particularities of the Colombian case, from the extreme market rubric of its federation to the gulf between the achievements of the country's players and the level of commitment to the national team shown by its federation (Mina & Goellner, 2015a; Mina et al., 2018, 2019). Mina Martinez uses a mixed methodological approach, analysing media representations and juxtaposing this with interview material with players. An increasing body of literature suggests that social media is becoming a new site of struggle where women's football battles for legitimation (Antunovic & Hardin, 2012, 2013, 2015; Coche, 2016; Garton & Hijós, 2017). Nonetheless, this occurs on an extremely unequal footing as individual players often struggle against the full force of the industrial-scale media–sports complex that buttresses male hegemony (Curran, 2002; Rowe, 2013, 2015). This social media environment has opened up new opportunities to interact with fans and to build new strategic relationships as is suggested in this book. In this analysis, Twitter has been identified as the main forum for these interactions to take place (Gibbs & Haynes, 2013; Coche, 2016; Hayes Sauder & Blaszka, 2018). Clearly, whilst social media clearly offers potential for women players to raise their profile, it also brings the attendant problems of online abuse (Lavoi & Calhoun, 2014) particularly in the context of a history of the oppression and discrimination women's sport has faced. Almost all the players I interviewed during fieldwork highlighted the frequency with which they receive abusive communication – so clearly the flipside of social media's potential must also be considered. Research taking into account the growing voices of sportswomen appears particularly pertinent bearing in mind the extent their voices have largely been excluded from conversations about the transition from amateurism to professionalism in the past (Taylor et al., 2020).

Nonetheless, there is a clear *lacuna* in the literature to date. Top-down tropes from traditional media do not exist in a vacuum and neither do they go entirely unchallenged. The relationship between the use of social media by players to promote the women's game and how this is interpreted and reconfigured by traditional media remains relatively untouched. By considering them as separate entities the crucial interactions between the traditional media and social media are neglected. Moreover, to date there has yet to be an engagement with the notion of off-the-field scandal being used as a mediatic diversion to avoid covering women playing football. Many casual observers would be aware of Megan Rapinoe's Twitter spat with Donald Trump, or perhaps even her solidarity with Colin Kaepernick on taking a knee during the US National Anthem in 2016, but it is far less likely that they would know which club team Rapinoe plays for in the United States and even less still the fact that she was injured for most of the season before being awarded FIFA's World Player of the Year for 2019. This chapter argues that structural forces avoid focusing on women's athletic performance and place disproportionate emphasis on constructing narratives that characterise women players as belligerent; these discourses are rooted in misogyny and a reluctance to allow women to occupy a space that has long been solely male.

This chapter engages with and problematises media theory, which tends to be dismissive of the role of the internet in the changing the nature and scope of media representation. It engages in particular the prolific and influential output of Argentine semiologist Eliseo Verón (1982, 1997, 2013, 2014a, 2014b). Verón was a semiotician, sociologist and anthropologist of considerable importance, particular in the cultures in which much of his work on the media and mediatisation was produced in the French- and Spanish-speaking world. Verón's model of mediatisation considers traditional media and internet-based media as two distinct systems that often interact separately. Moreover, he considered the internet to represent, rather than a paradigm shift, merely 'una mutación en las condiciones de circulación de los fenómenos mediáticos' [a mutation in the conditions of circulation of mediatic phenomena] (Verón, 2013, p. 429). However, it appears clear that the internet in general and social media in particular, in their contemporary form, have effected profound changes upon the way traditional media operate (Scolari, 2015). I argue here that a *lacuna* in the current literature, particularly in the area of women's sports, is the way that journalistic practices are shaped, more than ever, by stories emerging online. Evening television news audiences have more than halved over a 20-year period in the USA and western Europe and sales of printed newspapers have more than halved during a similar period (Kamarck & Gabriele, 2015). The data for Latin America shows comparable shifts which have caused various publications to cease publishing altogether or to migrate to internet forms and adapt to the preferences and consumption patterns of an online audience (Suenzo et al., 2020). This phenomenon has been described as digital convergence (Dwyer, 2010; Turow, 2011). It has engendered intense debate about the democratising (or otherwise) potential of social media, with optimistic interpretations hailing the transformative potential of a many-to-many model of communication, supposedly empowering previously disenfranchised groups (Shirky, 2011). Conversely, bleaker interpretations maintain that the transition to online media has brought increased manipulation with concerted, targeted advertising based around particular demographics (Marwick & Lewis, 2017; Bradshaw & Howard, 2018).

Instances of different media actors in dialogue with each other – for example when social media posts are incorporated into newspaper journalism or radio broadcasts – have been referred to as hypermediations by an eclectic range of media scholars (Carey, 2007; Park et al., 2010; Palmer, 2012; Verón, 2014b; Scolari, 2015; Zayas, 2020). Generally, within this body of theory – when mediatic systems collide – there are multiple interactions that vary in scale, intensity and reach (Verón, 2013; Scolari, 2015). In theory, in favour of recognising the mutual circuits of influence (Martín-Barbero, 1983) at play in the creation and dissemination of meaning, the emergence of hypermediation theories has in some measure contributed to narrowing the very debates they seek to encourage.

It is clear that media outlets now depend to some degree upon social media providers like Facebook and Twitter to direct traffic to them. In spite of this dependence, in a sporting context there is widespread consensus that traditional media remain the key shapers of opinion (Messner et al., 2010; Cooky et al., 2010; Goldblatt, 2019). Nonetheless, that is not to say that the agency of other actors – in this case women football players – should not be accounted for.

There are a multitude of interactions between what Verón understands as the same mediatic systems – for example, the radio commenting upon the latest newspapers, or television programmes or social media users commenting on one another's content. These interactions within the same media system are referred to in *La Semiosis Social* as intra-systemic (Verón, 2013). On the other hand, the relationships between two distinct systems are categorised as inter-systemic (Verón, 2013), to take note of the way meaning often mutates and distorts on a scale that is quantitatively and qualitatively unprecedented. Verón's work considers firstly the status of enunciators, secondly the type of intervention (whether it is further production, or the reception of the previous discourse, or both) and finally the reach and capacity to construct collectives. This approach has been insightful in bringing linguistics and semiotics into dialogue with more traditional approaches to media studies. Nonetheless, at the present conjuncture, the fundamental question is – how can we conceptualise contemporary circuits of mediatic influence that operate intra- and inter-systemically in multiple directions through time and space? Clearly, this type of analysis, by definition, will only constitute the unique interpretation of the researcher subjectively constructing interactions considered of fundamental importance. As Verón acknowledges in much of his work, our analysis ought not aspire to exhaustivity. It inevitably only produces vignettes of a far larger panorama as a complement to other theoretical frames (Verón, 1987b, 2013, 2014b). The ethnographic chapters of this book (Chapters Three, Four and Five) tend to this need by offering the 'thick detail' (Geertz, 1973) of the day-to-day existence of women footballers and problematising many of the assumptions and discursive tropes perpetuated and disseminated by the mass media.

The trajectory of two Instagram posts from Yoreli Rincón will be examined first, in terms of how they were received, reconfigured and (re)presented by traditional media. The data for this study, then, is taken from a period spanning from 2/3 December 2018, Instagram posts made by Yoreli Rincón in the immediate aftermath of the Atlético Huila Women's Copa Libertadores triumph, to 20 December 2018 when, in the aftermath of Huila's victory, the president of one of the club's rivals, Gabriel Camargo of Deportivo Tolima, made derogatory remarks about women's football. In addition to visual and textual analysis, analysis draws upon empirical data gathered in a period of ethnographic research during three months in Neiva with Atlético Huila women from February to May 2019, and during the three-week Women's Copa Libertadores tournament in Manaus in November and December 2018.

Yoreli Rincón

Yoreli Rincón has a pertinent backstory both as a footballer and as a public figure. Rincón realised early that she wanted to play football professionally but saw no formal opportunities to earn a living doing so in Colombia. The only way for Rincón to forge a professional career was to move abroad early. At the age of 18, she migrated to the interior of São Paulo state in Brazil to play for XV de Piracicaba. This proved a springboard for opportunities in leading women's leagues in Sweden, the United States and then Norway. During this period, Rincón and a number of her contemporaries who honed their talent in the US university system gained a reputation for overachieving at national team level. In the absence of significant institutional support in their own country they helped Colombia reach two Copa America finals and even the last sixteen of a World Cup in Canada 2015. Rincón, as the standout player with the most impressive international trajectory, often found herself as the spokesperson for Colombian women's football and for the growing clamour to create a national league. This status as a pioneering Colombian female player who has played professionally abroad has helped her amass a social media following that is considerable compared to many other women players: 86,000 on Twitter and 232,000 on Instagram.[2] This agency has been a mixed blessing for Rincón as her role as spokesperson has brought her into direct conflict with football institutions responsible for the appalling treatment of women players in the country. She has consistently been a dissenting voice, highlighting the chasm between the marketing of DIMAYOR's women's professional league and the continuing amateur conditions that women players face, such as short, non-officialised contracts, pay below the national minimum, lack of adequate health cover and substandard training facilities, among other issues. Rincón herself claims that she has been vetoed by the Colombian Football Federation from appearing in national team games since July 2019 (Futbolred, 2019; *El Tiempo*, 2019b).

Wider conflict between players and federation

Conflict between Rincón and the federation, along with hostile media coverage, dates back to the beginning of her career in 2012 when she was also omitted from the team for the London Olympics on spurious grounds (*El País*, 2012; Semana, 2012).[3] She was not the only player punished for speaking out. Teammate Daniela Montoya even provided audio proof of having been vetoed from appearing for the Colombian national team after going public about the federation's failure to pay the players at all after their run to the last sixteen of the 2015 World Cup in Canada (*El Tiempo*, 2019a).

This background of outright hostility towards outspoken players can be situated historically in a context of uneven and often hostile relations between players and institutions and as a consequence of widespread corruption among sporting authorities on the continent. Indeed, other South American players like Carlos Caszely, Socrates and Diego Maradona have all received harsh treatment from the media and/or their clubs for taking supposedly political positions on issues those at director level habitu-ally opine about (de la Parra, 1989; Peinado et al., 2013; Florenzano, 2010; Downie, 2017). Colombian sportswomen who have not directly challenged

---

2 The only women's player with a larger following is Nicole Regnier (400,000) – a player consistently foregrounded for her appearance, clearly against her will (*El País Cali*, 2014). The second most followed player for Huila is Liana Salazar, who has around 10,000 followers. To place this public reach into context, the two highest-profile male players in the current squad, James Rodriguez and Radamel Falcao, each have around 17 million followers on Twitter.

3 Rincón was left out of the squad for supposedly not being match-fit – though she continued to be selected consistently at club level during this period without showing any signs of such.

authority in the way Rincón has, for example Catherine Ibargüen and Mariana Pajón, have consistently been treated much more sympathetically.[4] Their endeavours are less high-profile than football and do not encroach or impinge in the same way upon the symbolic male sporting hegemony. This point was corroborated in the North American context by Jones et al. (1999) who found that female athletes' performances in sports that are not seen to encroach upon the male identity are emphasised and praised.[5] There is a clear tension, in the Colombian context, between the way the traditional media protects and polices the traditional link between football and masculinity and a discernibly gendered discourse of national identity, which has notably incorporated football in recent times (Watson, 2018, 2022). This has contributed to a fractious relationship between the media and female players, with Rincón in particular habitually portrayed as querulous and belligerent.

The way hostility to players like Rincón and Montoya manifests itself is sometimes blatant and sometimes more nuanced. It is certainly located within the habitual *modus operandi* of media coverage which tends towards scandal. Indeed, referring to the historical development of the British media, Curran (2002, p. 92) points to a shift towards 'the easy arousal of sensationalism as a strategy to maximise sales'. This chapter problematises the notion that traditional and digital media are separable or distinct systems by considering the economically driven drift towards scandal, exacerbated in the digital era by the desire to provide clickbait online. Scandal, as a sales-maximising technique, is deployed with a dual purpose in the case of Colombian women's football. Firstly, it serves as a pretext not to cover any actual women's football. By disproportionately covering scandal rather than actual games, a female performance of gender out of sync with Colombian social representations is avoided. An excellent Colombian study suggests a perceived incommensurable sexual difference between men and women in social representations of sport (Vélez, 2001). In this environment then, for women to play football, *per se*, constitutes a subversive act that undermines the credibility of 'the collective societal agreement to perform, produce and sustain discrete and polar genders' (Butler, 1990, p. 140).

Secondly, given the stark imbalances of influence between players and traditional media, the latter are able to construct narratives that serve to discredit those threatening the status quo: for instance, the subject of this chapter, Rincón, is portrayed as belligerent and unreasonable. For this reason, a sustained analysis of the coverage of Rincón explains how the player has

---

4 Catherine Ibargüen is a high-, triple- and long-jump athlete and Mariana Pajón is a BMX cyclist.
5 This would seem to account for the relative social acceptance of the US Women's National Soccer Team, though this acceptance, as yet, does not translate into equal pay (Das, 2020).

become a lightning rod at the centre of ongoing debates about the contestation and reproduction of heteronormative, gendered visions of what women's football means in Colombia.

Post-match celebration video

On the team bus in Manaus after Huila's remarkable victory Rincón is sitting with teammate and partner Jaylis Oliveros. Various members of the team are celebrating with drinks, singing songs and relaxing after the tournament. With the caption 'Disfrutemos que nos atrevimos soñar – somos campeonas continentales' [celebrate our daring to dream – we are continental champions], salsa blaring in the background and a celebratory beer in hand Rincón kisses Oliveros and exclaims 'vamos a brindar que somos campeonas continentales' [let's drink a toast to being continental champions].

This video travelled from social media to mass media, as Caracol gave it a short television slot, reposting it on Twitter and on their website (@GolCaracol, 2018; GOL Caracol, 2018) together with a brief summary of Rincón's comments. A number of other well-followed social sites followed suit (Pereira, 2018; Pulzo, 2018; Sánchez, 2018). One provincial newspaper takes the retrograde stance that 'figuras públicas deben dar ejemplo de ética y moral' [public figures should set an example of morality] (La Piragua, 2018). This is explicitly homophobic as it is unlikely a call for morality would have occurred if a man and woman had kissed in the video.

From empirical observation during fieldwork it was clear that the club hierarchy felt that Rincón's open show of affection for a female teammate had the potential to damage the image of the club. Equally, they were grateful that traditional media did not embrace what they considered to be a non-story. I will argue in Chapter Two that there is a top-down push towards presenting a unidimensional, heteronormative athleticism for women's football. Indeed, the advertising campaigns for FIFA World Cups and national leagues consistently show this. From Sepp Blatter's much criticised remarks about 'tight shorts', on a (slightly) more nuanced level there has been a continuation of its logic which can be found in almost any promotional material for tournaments or in the decisions about which players to interview pre- or post-match. There is a consistent evasion of the issue of players' sexuality, particularly in South America. From earlier portrayals of *marimachas* the present iteration of women's football in the mainstream media is reluctant to touch upon the subject, even while it is highlighted by the players themselves or by international commentators.

It is worth considering the reasons, given traditional media's predilection for scandal, for the omission of a lesbian kiss between two female football players. During informal discussion during fieldwork a deeply unsatisfactory hypothesis floated was that traditional media might be respecting the privacy of individuals. More realistically, the agenda-setting choice made by the media in this instance is far from coincidental and is symptomatic of the male-dominated media and institutional polity. Having demonstrated how a singular focus on one issue was used to attack Rincón, the reasons why structural conditions did not allow the hostility to continue in this instance are illuminating.

The most plausible explanation for the omission of Rincón's post-match kiss with Oliveros is simply that lesbianism destabilises the matrix of heteronormativity. In theorising this matrix Judith Butler argues that gender is discursively constructed through a 'grid of cultural intelligibility' (1990, p. 208). Within this understanding gender is a performance that serves to reproduce itself. Within the matrix a masculine male is assumed to be heterosexual as would also be a feminine female, for instance in Rincón's case.[6] The unreality of the continuing media taboo *vis-à-vis* lesbianism in football is symptomatic of the symbolic importance of sports to male hegemony. The short biography of Rincón underlines her importance as a figurehead in the launch of Colombian professional football. For that reason, it is inconceivable, in spite of all other (unfair) criticisms levelled at her, that the media present her as a lesbian player. Nonetheless, the lack of media coverage did not prevent the issue going further. Whether on this occasion Rincón chose to 'subvert and resist the construction of heterosexual space' (Caudwell, 2002, p. 35) is unknown. Rincón and Oliveros certainly helped legitimise and create a space for other lesbian players. It is established, then, that the non-story around Rincón and Oliveros kissing had little to do with a respect for privacy and much more to do with the heteronormative vision of the media and institutions. This story largely escaped the international community and thus in a sense the heteronormative vision of the media and institutions was not openly problematised, but it seems likely that in the future similar occurrences may disrupt the hegemonically promoted image of women's football.

There were no stories about this incident and thus the story remained limited to local coverage until an extraordinary outburst from Tolima president Gabriel Camargo some 17 days later. In an interview with Caracol Deportes, Camargo was asked about the progress of the women's league, in which Deportes Tolima participated in 2018. His provocative answer was the following:

> Eso anda mal – eso no da nada ni económicamente ni nada de esas cosas. Aparte de los problemas que hay con las mujeres son mas tomatragos que los hombres. Preguntan a los de Huila como están de arrepentidos de haber sacado el título y de haber invertido tanta plata en el equipo. Es un caldo de cultivo de lesbianismo tremendo. [It's going badly, it's doesn't give anything back, economically or otherwise and apart from those problems the women drink more than the men. Ask the Huila directors how much

---

6 Openly gay male footballers remain few and far between. Robbie Rodgers of LA Galaxy was one of the first to come out during his career. Justin Fashanu, a black gay English footballer, came out after his career before committing suicide.

they regret winning that title and putting so much money into the team. It's a breeding ground for lesbianism.]

Camargo's comments do not cite Rincón personally, but do cite Atlético Huila's victory together with a supposed culture of alcoholism and lesbianism.

Now, considering their initial reluctance to even touch the inconvenient taboo of lesbianism, the traditional media were forced to engage with the topic. The only saving grace from the media perspective was that Camargo's comments could be portrayed as abstract, making no particular reference to anyone. In this way, they were able to dismiss his remarks as an unfortunate exception. In this vein, a clearly serviceable story of Latin American *machismo* travelled quickly, appearing in the Spanish, British and Brazilian mass media among others (ABC Fútbol, 2018; BBC Mundo, 2018; Mendonça, 2018b). All of these were quick to condemn Camargo and explain his outburst in terms of an aberration linked to the inherently *machista* culture of Colombia. Bizarrely, given the openness to feminism displayed in other sections of the newspaper, Colombia's leading daily newspaper *El Tiempo* reported Camargo's comments in neutral terms with barely a word of admonishment (*El Tiempo*, 2018a). Here there is a clear compartmentalisation of the ideology of the organisation, which is instructive. Within football coverage, inextricably linked to tropes of male identity in Colombia, coverage remains deeply defensive, of largely male football institutions. *Machismo* within a football institution must be admonished; but the lesbian kiss that triggered the outburst remains somehow taboo – an area where media outlets are not prepared to go, particularly in the case of two sportswomen playing the most hegemonically masculine sport.

Mediations of the prize money episode

During interviews with players a recurring theme was that Huila were playing to save the professional league from extinction. A sense of hyperbole notwithstanding, the existential threat the players perceived to their liveli-hoods undoubtedly fuelled an extraordinary effort against more established Brazilian opponents in the Copa Libertadores.[7] In the immediate aftermath of the tournament, the unbridled joy of an unfancied provincial outfit becoming champions spilled over into anger, expressed by the team's figure-head Yoreli Rincón.[8]

According to media reports, after just two years of competition the players faced the threat of the Women's Professional League being dissolved (Galindo, 2018; Prieto, 2018). The legitimacy of the league depends largely

---

7 Brazilian teams had won eight out of eleven times the competition had been run, beginning with two Santos victories in 2009 and 2010.

8 Rincón, as the best-known player, is often mistakenly referred to as the captain. In fact, Colombian international teammate Gavy Santos, often mis-spelt as 'Gaby' in the media, captained the team.

upon the cooperation and commitment of Colombia's professional football clubs, who in theory are able to offer the infrastructure, pay professional salaries and operationalise the women's game using professional marketing departments.[9] In the first year, women's teams travelled to games without adequate medical staff or physiotherapists. The non-payment of players was a consistent problem and Colombian businesses were reluctant to sponsor women's teams (Galindo, 2018). After two years a number of these clubs had been unwilling to make the financial commitment to paying for a women's team, disbanding it quietly. This struggle transcends the economic sphere, involving the considerable symbolic social capital that football has in the formation of identity. In this way, the history of the Colombian women's league dramatises a disjuncture between the corporatised global vision of gender equality promulgated by FIFA and the deeply embedded, masculinised, cultural meanings attached to football at a local level. Plagued from the outset by this inherent contradiction, the league has suffered from insufficient length, being scheduled at times that make attendance prohibitive (during work hours) and generally from being undermined at every turn by those purporting to support global policy prescriptions encouraging gender equality.

When Yoreli Rincón took to social media after the Copa Libertadores tournament negotiations of 'the hypermediatic circulation of meaning' (Verón, 1987b, 2013, 2014b) began in ways symptomatic of the effects of social media downplayed (or explained as changes of scale) in the hypermediations literature. Post-tournament Rincón made two social media posts (@yorelirincón, 2018a, 2018b) which were subsequently reproduced on Twitter, Instagram and Facebook among other social networks, circulated globally and were re-signified in traditional media discourse in Colombia. Firstly, she published a video revealing that the CONMEBOL prize money received by Atlético Huila would not reach or be spent on the women's team at all. This situation is symptomatic of the precarious nature of women's football in Colombia and beyond. Male players' contracts would not only run for much longer than those of women players, crucially they would also include clauses regarding bonuses for winning a tournament like the Copa Libertadores. The club might receive the prize money if a male team wins the Copa, but contractual stipulations would oblige them to distribute significant bonuses to players. To exacerbate the problem, the fact that the salaries of Atlético Huila women were fully covered by a third party, businessman Diego Perdomo, made the players feel that the club itself had not invested in the women's team and thus did not deserve the prize money.

In his earlier work, written prior to the emergence of social media, Eliseo Verón argued that social events only occur when the (traditional mass) media

---

9 According to sources at Santos FC in Brazil, the cost of running a women's club is less than 1 per cent of the club's overall budget.

construct them as such (Verón, 1982). Seen in this way, the post made by Rincón in Caracas Airport only became an event in the Verónian sense when traditional media reconfigured its meaning to suit their agenda, as will be shown later in the chapter.

The media coverage of the prize money feud did accelerate a settlement. Within a short period, Perdomo clarified to the media that each player would receive a bonus for winning the tournament, though details remained private. Subsequent to this, agreements were made with each player. Rincón was correct in alleging that the CONMEBOL prize money would go to Atlético Huila (men), despite the fact that the club's hierarchy had not contributed to the salaries of the women's team. They depended upon a third-party benefactor to cover the women's salaries, and after a disagreement with that benefactor (Perdomo), the club simply disbanded its women's team rather than use Atlético Huila (men's) money to continue the operation.

Initial mediations of prize money scandal

Atlético Huila, and all the other teams in the tournament, returned from the Copa in Manaus on ordinary scheduled flights, rather than the charter flights customarily used for male players (RedGol Chile, 2018; RT, 2018). In the case of Atlético Huila this necessitated a lengthy double stopover, with several hours in the Venezuelan capital Caracas and then another in Bogotá before they could return to their base in Neiva. From Maiquetía Airport in Caracas, Rincón, with time on her hands, recorded a video which she uploaded to her Instagram stories, a format akin to Snapchat insofar as it means videos are only available for a short time (usually 24 hours) before becoming inaccessible. Owing to the incendiary nature of the post, it was quickly captured and saved by a number of users who reproduced it on other media sites – an example *par excellence* of what media theory calls hypermediations or what could be described as internet posts that become 'viral'. The substantive content of the message from Rincón is reproduced here. The message was posted at some stage on 4 December 2018, though the format does not allow the exact time to be specified.

> Quería agradecerles infinitamente por todo el apoyo que nos han brindado, todos los buenos mensajes, las felicitaciones y el orgullo que han sentido por nosotras, por el Atlético Huila, por Colombia. Somos campeones continentales pero no crean que a las campeonas femeninas también les da premio. Por ser campeonas nos ganamos $55,000, la cual nunca va a llegar a nosotras lastimosamente. Eso llega al Atlético Huila masculino, quiénes tienen un presidente diferente al nuestro presidente Diego Perdomo el femenino. Sí tendremos un reconocimiento que nos da nuestro presidente Diego Perdomo. Pero es del bolsillo de él. [I want to give my heartfelt thanks for all the support you've given us, all the positive messages, congratulations, and the pride you've felt for us, for Atlético Huila, for Colombia. We are continental champions but don't believe that the female

champions also received a prize. For being champions we earned $55,000, which will never come to us, sadly. That will go to Atlético Huila men, who have a different president from ours; Diego Perdomo for the women's team. We will receive some reward, given to us by our president Diego Perdomo. But it's from his own pocket.][10]

At this stage the message was only available to Rincón's followers on Instagram. Despite the uneven power relations Rincón was clearly aware of her agency and it is beyond any doubt that the message was fully intended both to reach a wider audience and to exert pressure on the club and the national federation to ensure a fair settlement and to explain the lack of professional agreements in women's club football. In this way, from the beginning Rincón was aware of the mediations and mediatisation that would ensue, both nationally and internationally – as the following sections show.

First phase of social media circulation

The intended circulation on a wider scale began with a tweet from a provincial fan site (@futbolsinlimi, 2018).[11] This phase in media theory is a 'change of scale' (Verón, 2014b). Verón refers to an immediate shift, both qualitative and quintive, in readings of the original discourse. By this he refers to the demographic of the audience changing and with this a multiplication of new readings based upon the amount of knowledge the new readers have. For example, a new reader of the text elsewhere in Latin America might not know who Rincón is, or that Atlético Huila (men) do not pay the salaries of the women's team, or that there is a third-party benefactor involved. This provokes an immediate and abrupt decontextualisation of future processes of reception and resignification (Verón, 1982, 1987b). The loss of context goes beyond knowing background details. In a Verónian sense, it also refers to the original time and place when the video was recorded, coloured by the euphoria, emotion and fatigue of the moment, and influenced by surroundings (here, being in a run-down airport terminal late at night surrounded by teammates who have just become continental champions, trying their best to sleep on a concrete airport floor).

In addition, the change of social media platform is also consequential. As a photo- and video-sharing service Instagram is viewed differently to Twitter, which has long been used for (pseudo-)official statements by companies, organisations and individuals. The concise format of Twitter is key to re-signifying meaning. With only a certain number of words

---

10 This video can be found at the following link: https://www.vanguardia.com/deportes/ futbol-local/yoreli-rincon-denuncia-que-no-les-daran-los-premios-ganados-en-la-libertadores-OCVL452185.

11 Fútbol Sin Limite is a football site based in Pereira, Colombia. It has approximately 75,000 followers and largely shares memes, videos and articles related to regional football, but also some material on national football.

available inevitably meaning is lost and a small chunk is emphasised (Verón, 2014a). The post from @futbolsinlimi foregrounded the idea of the players not receiving any prize: 'Muchas felicitaciones han recibido las chicas del Atlético Huila, pero lo triste es que este premio no será para ellas' [Huila's girls have received lots of congratulations, but the sad thing is that they won't receive the prize]. This constituted a mis-representation of Rincón from the beginning. Her original post stated that the team would receive some recognition from Perdomo, but this nuance was immediately lost in this first re-tweet. Rincón was keen to highlight the disconnect between the Atlético Huila (men's) hierarchy and the women's team but this detail, too, was lost early on. Whether intentional or not, this important loss of context had profound effects for the later stages of re-signification. Given the brief nature of Rincón's original intervention, there is no clear articulation of the women's precarious, third-party-outsourced, marginal status within Atlético Huila – assumed knowledge, which some of her followers might have had but most people do not. Allied to this, the Twitter format, with its overarching logic of generating re-tweets and follows, took precedence over elaborating on the minutiae of the problem. It needs an easily consumable narrative to be produced, which had consequences further down the line.

Already, the agenda of Yoreli Rincón – to highlight the discriminatory treatment of women's football and the way in which the outsourcing of women's football has occurred within clubs perceived to have fully incorporated it – was guaranteed not to figure in further negotiations of meaning. This omission is particularly pertinent as it is a salient issue on a continental level. For example, in Colombia Independiente Medellín entered a partnership in 2019 with the long-time dominant amateur club in Colombian women's football, Formas Íntimas, meaning the professional Medellín club could lean on existing infrastructure (training facilities, connections in the women's game and expertise) rather than commit to any serious investment themselves. Similarly, Brazilian giants Corinthians, a club with considerable demotic tradition, initially entered into a partnership with Osasco-based Audax, again sharing the 'burden' of developing women's football internally. This partnership has now ended with both Corinthians and Audax operating separately in the top flight of Brazilian women's football. Similar outsourced arrangements at arch rivals Palmeiras and Belo Horizonte giants Cruzeiro have characterised the lip service major clubs have at times paid to the need to create women's sides (Mendonça, 2019a) – an issue, to some degree, provoked by the ham-fisted application of *obrigatoriedade*.

Confirmation of the distortion caused by the paraphrasing of Rincón's original video is found in the polarised responses, which reflect how readers generally inferred that either CONMEBOL prize money would immediately be awarded as a bonus to Atlético Huila's male players, or concluded that there was no story as tournament prize money always go to the club rather than the players. In the latter interpretation, social media users, who were already reading others' interpretations, saw Rincón as simply having misunderstood the rules of the game. A new video saying this was shared a day later by two other accounts, whose interpretations further consolidated the emerging polarisation. For example, 'deben decirle a la señorita que Huila es solo una institución con equipo masculino y femenino – la plata siempre va a la institución' [they should tell the girl that Huila is just one institution with a male and female team – the money always goes to the institution]. Beyond the patronising 'señorita', this comment was essentially true – what it lacked is any understanding of the context that Rincón was trying to highlight. From these tweets onwards the news reached national and international traditional media, effecting, as the Verón literature suggests, far greater changes of scale.

In this vein, the post first reached the Anglophone world when freelance journalist Carl Worswick re-tweeted it.[12] Again embedding the original post from Fútbol Sin Límite, he added an English-language translation of some of Rincón's words: 'Atlético Huila star Yoreli Rincón claims the $55k prize money the women's team earned from winning the Copa Libertadores on Sunday will go straight to the Huila men's team. None of it will go to us, it's unfortunate but that's women's football'. Inevitably, the way Worswick foregrounded the money going 'straight to the ... men's team' suggests it goes directly to the male players rather than to the directors of the club to administer as they see fit. By suggesting the money would go to the men's team rather than to the directors of the club, a reductionist dichotomy is then invoked, pitting the men's team against the women's. In due course, a response bemoans 'the appallingly bad men's team benefitting from the amazing women's team's victory'. From Worswick the tweet then followed the usual pattern of re-tweets by members of the public and other sports journalists, ensuring that the news reached the English-speaking traditional mass media further down the line. Worswick's tweet was re-tweeted 67 times, which is significantly more than any other post he made that week. Future understandings were certainly influenced by this. These include RT's focus on 'every penny being handed to the men's team' (RT, 2018), and the emphasis that 'the money will be given to a men's team who didn't even qualify for the Copa Libertadores' (Grez, 2018).

This concluded the first phase of dissemination of the news generated by 'social media' around the prize money for Atlético Huila. Within a matter of hours, the post had crossed language barriers and reached key social media users, paving the way for what is referred to in media studies as hypermediations. The later works of Verón refer to interactions on the internet as not being just another form of media. His work is characterised by a recognition of a 'nueva gramática y nuevas reglas de producción y reconocimiento' (Verón, 2013, 2014b). Allied to this the ease with which 'sensationalism' (Curran, 2002) travels is also fundamental to the case at hand. In the example

---

12 Worswick has written extensively for *The Guardian* and *World Soccer* and tweets at @cworswick.

of women's football, weighing the amount of coverage of the two fabricated 'scandals' in this chapter against the immense difficulty in generating any large-scale interest in the actual tournament, it is easy to see the media prejudice that women's football faces.

Second phase of circulation – 'hypermediations' of clarification and explanation
Verón suggested that people's everyday behaviour in the public sphere is essentially a 'performance' because they are 'acutely aware that what they say and do is actively being mediatised in some way' (Verón, 2013, p. 292). This observation appears more relevant than ever and certainly pertinent to the case at hand. The narrow framing of the issue is key to this phase of the reproduction of meaning. Without any attempt to contextualise Rincón's grievances, a series of institutional figures were given the opportunity to explain the 'real' situation regarding the Women's Copa Libertadores prize money. This version of events foregrounding the views of institutional figures is the one that reached a mass audience – this is the 'hypermediated' version of the Rincón story. The institutional view stripped away many of the nuances to tell a simplified version that defended the football authorities against the complainant. In basic terms it held that a tournament had taken place, the winners of the tournament received their prize money, as at any other tournament, and thus that Rincón's grievances were baseless. Without access to the background information about the internal politics of Atlético Huila, this appeared, superficially, to be wholly reasonable. Hypermediation in this case meant a change of scale. That is to say, the news reached a far greater audience. In social media news is condensed to a length digestible by Twitter, for example. Clearly the protagonists each deployed the *nueva gramática* Verón discusses, and in their public pronouncements they put on a performance to show the values that the audience expects of them (Verón, 2013).

Revealingly, during the 'hypermediation' phase, none of the other Atlético Huila players were asked for their opinion by media outlets, nor were any other 'professional' footballers operating in Colombia at that time. Both other professional footballers and the Huila players did also tweet their indignation and try to give the necessary context – but by this time they were drowned out by larger media outlets with much bigger followings. In this vein, given the imbalance in power relations, this phase of the debate was entirely framed around the narrow issue of whether or not players or the club ought to have received the prize money. Almost mirroring a well-known political science maxim, the traditional media agenda here encouraged 'very lively debate around an extremely limited spectrum' (Chomsky, 1998, p. 43), thus creating the illusion of healthy debate – space for the supposedly oppositional viewpoint that women players ought to receive their prize money directly rather than the club, in this way obfuscating more substantive debate. The wider issues that Rincón tried to highlight – that is to say the marginal position of the women's team outside the club proper and funded by a third-party benefactor – were now buried. As explained fully in Chapter Two, incorporating women's teams properly within the clubs represents a threat to male sporting hegemony. A common response to *obrigatoriedade* has been to pay lip service to it whilst keeping women on the outside of the clubs. By skirting over, or not even mentioning, the extent to which Huila's women players exist on the fringe, the nature of Rincón's point was misrepresented to the point at which significantly fewer people would sympathise with her.

The arguments put forth by institutional figures in this phase, then, disingenuously presupposed that the women's team was a fully incorporated part of Huila and centred upon the notion of merely following due process with the prize money being filtered down from CONMEBOL to the national league and finally to the winning team. The assumption of this fully incorporated status within the clubs, gender equality in FIFA's own terms, provided ideological cover for the claims of football institutions to have made more progress on gender equality than lived reality suggests – as will be shown in more detail in Chapters Three, Four and Five.

To begin this second phase, Diego Perdomo was interviewed by Deportes RCN, a national broadcaster (Deportes RCN, 2018). Unlike the short clip upon which Rincón was being judged, Perdomo was allowed several minutes to provide detailed background about how he had come to be involved with women's football, before explaining the misunderstanding. Once described as a man whose 'passion, diligence, competitiveness and management and hunger to win led Huila to a continental title' (Bermúdez, 2019, p. 9), Perdomo is habitually portrayed in traditional media as the man behind women's football. Underlining his non-economic motives, he pointed out to Deportes RCN that though he was derided by colleagues for getting involved in the unprofitable venture of women's football, he did so 'porque genera una pasión bonita' [because it generates a nice passion] and also because the president of Atlético Huila (men), Juan Carlos Patarroyo, 'no tenía tiempo, estaba enredado con el Huila' [didn't have time, he was busy with Huila]. With those comments the scene was set, and the women's team imagined as a pleasant side project that the president of the 'real' Atlético Huila did not have time (or money) to administer. Exemplifying 'la terquedad de diferenciación de género' [persistence of gender differentiation] that characterises Colombian attitudes to sport (Vélez, 2001, p. 44), the interview moved on to Rincón's complaint, to which Perdomo, the sole outside funder of Atlético Huila women, stated unchallenged that: 'aquí no hay equipo femenino ni equipo masculino. Fue la tergiversación de una jugadora. El dinero llega al Atlético Huila' [here there is no female and male separation. The issue was misrepresented by a player, the money will go to Atlético Huila.] The interview underlined the convenience with which the arrangement was used to suit the needs of the club's hierarchy. As players wishing not to be named explained to me during my work at Huila the club is one when it comes to glory and claiming prizes, but two different entities when it comes to paying salaries and expenses.

Almost simultaneously, to the point of seeming a coordinated strategy, the president of DIMAYOR, Jorge Enrique Vélez, appeared on Caracol's VBAR Radio Show (VBAR Caracol, 2018).[13] Inevitably, among the first questions was the prize money controversy to which the same officialist trope was deployed without challenge: 'no es un tema de equipo femenino y masculino, no queremos guerra entre mujeres y hombres' [this is not a male and female issue, we don't want a war between men and women]. With this remark, Jorge Enrique Vélez firstly reiterated the official line, insisting that equal status existed within the club, and secondly, by stating that the institution does not want a war of the sexes, clearly insinuated that the instigator was Rincón and that she did want such a war. By turning fire on Rincón, Vélez essentially engaged in gaslighting (blaming the victim). He went on to state that 'CONMEBOL le da al equipo que tiene la licencia y luego las decisiones administrativas son del equipo' [CONMEBOL gives the money to the team that holds the licence, and then they take any administrative decisions]. Once again, the media re-signification prioritised the institutional line, using a female presenter to create an illusion of balance. The female presenter lightly suggested that some people might side with Rincón, before asking Vélez a leading question that allowed him to reaffirm the correctness of the institutional process, emphasising Rincón's supposed lack of understanding. Having clarified the official line Vélez attempted to discredit the agency of Rincón, striking a condescending tone and stating that 'la niña pidiendo plata por internet' [the girl asking for money over the internet] was unbefitting and even suggesting it should be contractually 'prohibido hacer declaraciones monetarias públicas' [contractually forbidden to make public statements involving money]. There are precedents for these kinds of relations between institutional figures and dissident players – particularly at times when clubs and institutions held the upper hand over players via extremely dubious contractual arrangements.

Indeed, as a collective the players all felt that they needed to win the Copa Libertadores in order to save the beleaguered women's league from being discontinued. Whilst this felt like a case of hyperbole symptomatic of the fetishisation of winning, it would appear that it did give them extra leverage in the dispute. Whilst the line of questioning from the VBAR Caracol presenters was particularly friendly, not challenging Vélez at any point, the victory of the Atlético Huila women, allied to the scandal about the prize money, forced his hand to some degree, into confirming there a league would be held the following year.

To allow the club an opportunity to clarify the situation, Atlético Huila's general manager Carlos Barrero was also interviewed. He explained:

estamos dando los dos primeros pasos primero para preguntar en definitiva cuánto es el premio segundo del cobro del mismo. Desconozco igual

---

13 This was also tweeted to Caracol's 3 million followers (@VBarCaracol, 2018), marking the point at which the story reached a mass audience.

le pregunté al presidente y me dijo que desconocía hasta ahora cuál es el arreglo que haya hecho el ingeniero Diego lo realizará de ahí que vamos a esperar de todas maneras yo pienso que son conjeturas que no vienen al caso y que por supuesto todo el mundo entiende que quién gana merece el premio. [we are taking the first steps – first to define how much the prize is and second to claim the prize. I asked the president (Patarroyo) and he told me that he still didn't know what the arrangement that Diego has made with the players was, but anyway I think that these are unnecessary accusations and that of course everyone understands that the winners deserve their prize.]

Barrero admitted to not knowing what agreement had been made between Perdomo and the players. This demonstrates the club's distant relationship with the women's team. Moreover, it directly contradicts the official claim that the women's team is incorporated within the club at the same level as the men's team. These remarks, which undermined the official line, were given no prominence by national media.

This subphase of explanation was brought to a close when an anonymous *El Tiempo* article (*El Tiempo*, 2018b) summarised a number of the interventions I have just discussed in a single article intended to explain the story from the beginning.[14] Titled 'Insólita queja de Yoreli Rincón tras ganar la Libertadores femenina' [Strange complaint from Yoreli Rincón after winning the Women's Copa Libertadores], emphasis was placed on the belligerence of the player. In the first paragraph they cast doubt on her claims, reporting that 'se quejó en un video de que, supuestamente, el premio que le entrega la Conmebol al club va para el equipo masculino' [she complained in a video that, *supposedly* (my italics), the prize from CONMEBOL would go to the men's team]. *El Tiempo*, once again, embedded the original social media post from Fútbol Sin Límite, and also quoted from the Vélez radio interview with VBAR Caracol, notably 'las palabras de la niña son desacertadas' [the girl's account is wrong], without even reproaching the tone of the institutional response. Instead, *El Tiempo* once again repeated the official line:

El procedimiento de la entrega de los premios en dinero en los torneos internacionales es que la entidad organizadora le gira el valor a las federaciones a las que están afiliados los clubes y luego estas se encargan de enviarlo a los clubes. En el caso del Huila, el club es el mismo: el femenino no está aparte del masculino. [The procedure for distributing prize money in international tournaments is that the organising entity passes the money to the federations to which the clubs are affiliated who then pass it down to the clubs. In the case of Huila, the club is unified: the women's team is not separate from the men's one.]

---

14 *El Tiempo* is Colombia's most popular newspaper. It has 6 million Facebook and 7 million Twitter followers respectively, meaning its reach is considerable.

Once again, this has a twofold purpose: first to exonerate football institutions of any wrongdoing by re-stating the official procedure and second to discredit Rincón's claim and by extension Rincón herself. Whilst juridically the Huila women's team is part of the institution Atlético Huila, the editorial makes no mention of the peculiar two-president arrangement, whereby the second president, with no directorial influence over the club, funds the women's team's salaries separately.

In order to consolidate its discursive discrediting of Rincón the (anonymous) editorial draws a comparison between bonuses received for representing clubs and national team bonuses:

> En los campeonatos nacionales de FIFA el procedimiento es igual. La entidad gira a las selecciones participantes. Los jugadores, por lo general, arreglan un premio con su respectiva Federación antes de participar, independientemente del dinero que se reciba por llegar al torneo. [In FIFA national team tournaments the procedure is the same. The entity hands down the prize to the competing teams. The players, generally, have arranged bonuses, on top of their pay for participating, with their respective federation before the competition in question.]

By focusing tenaciously on money received on top of players' salaries and drawing attention to how even those representing the nation receive bonuses,[15] the editorial is insinuating there is a level of greed in Rincón's demands. This one-sided interpretation is backed up by *El Espectador*, which also embeds the original video from Fútbol Sin Limite in its online version, and also immediately dismisses Rincón's allegation in the first two sentences of its first paragraph:

> La jugadora del cuadro opita, que se coronó campeón de la Copa Libertadores Femenina, señaló que el premio económico se iría a las arcas del equipo masculino. Al llegar a Bogotá aclaró que, de hecho, el club le dará el dinero al plantel. [The Huila player, who was crowned champion of the Women's Copa Libertadores, stated that the prize would go to straight to the men's team. Upon arriving in Bogotá she clarified that, in fact, the club would give the money to the team.] (*El Espectador*, 2018).[16]

The chain of events and interactions that have been described thus far are reduced in the above article to a single sentence; the article exaggerates the de-contextualisation of time and space to which Verón (1987b, 2013, 2014b) refers, giving the impression that Rincón changed her mind during the course of the flight home and dropped her irrational complaint upon landing. The

---

15 The Colombian women's national team, in particular Daniela Montoya, complained at not receiving any bonuses from the 2015 Women's World Cup and was subsequently vetoed by the Colombian Federation.

16 *El Espectador* has just over a million followers on each social media platform. 'Opita' refers to people from Huila province.

article goes on to explain in similar terms Rincón not understanding how the award of prize money works:

> a pesar de la indignación de Yoreli Rincón, este tipo de premios general-mente son para los clubes, gracias a ellos se sostienen y le pagan a sus empleados, sus técnicos, deportistas, administrativos, etc. Eso mismo lo hacen los clubes masculinos. Los premios a los jugadores se dan siempre y cuando hayan pactado un arreglo con los dirigentes, o ellos mismos accedan a darles una bonificación por el rendimiento. [Despite Rincón's outrage, these type of prizes are generally received by the clubs, it is the clubs who pay for their livelihoods, they pay all the technical and adminis-trative staff, and the players. That is exactly what happens with the male clubs. Bonuses go to the players when they have a pre-agreement with the club's owners/directors, or they award one for excellent performance.]

El Espectador's article ends with a factually incorrect declaration, concluding that Patarroyo would give the players all the prize money, when in reality Perdomo awarded them an improvised bonus after the victory and following Rincón's successful complaint.

By the end of this phase of explanation, multiple processes of re-signification have taken place and the debate is framed in such a way that the public's responses are confined to a narrow debate about how and to whom prize money ought to be distributed, and to visceral opinions about Rincón. The ensuing divisive debate ensures that the websites receive high traffic and also serves the purpose of avoiding any serious scrutiny of the institutional status quo.

Third phase of circulation – conciliation and resolution of conflict

Whilst it is difficult to mark definitively the end of one phase and the start of another, a clear discursive change towards conciliation and harmonious resolution of the conflict is notable at the post-tournament press conference broadcast in Colombia by DIMAYOR's commercial partner WIN Sports.[17] In some sense the identified phases overlap as, for example, *El Espectador* referred briefly to the next step, which marked the resolution of the conflict (by incorrectly suggesting that Huila rather than Perdomo would be covering the bonuses). The post-tournament press conference streamed live from Manaus, on the day after the tournament, lasted 20 minutes and covered a number of issues. Nonetheless, it was used by traditional media, largely, to signal a harmonious end to the mediated conflict.

Nonetheless Rincón, once again, took the opportunity to address a roomful of largely male journalists and underline the magnitude of the players' achievement:

17 Half of WIN Sports is owned by Colombian channel RCN and half by American channel DirectTV. In 2018 they had announced a pay-to-view premium channel, ensuring revenue streams for DIMAYOR and an unprecedented number of Colombian games to be shown live.

nunca en la vida había visto a tantos periodistas aquí para el fútbol femenino. Es un placer para nosotras ver a todos ustedes haciendo un reconocimiento a la mujer futbolista de Colombia. [I've never seen so many journalists together for women's football. It's a pleasure for us to see you all together, recognising women footballers in Colombia.] (Yoreli Rincón: Soñamos la Copa Libertadores y aquí la tenemos | WIN Sports, 2018)

Inevitably, she is immediately pressed to explain how the prize money saga has been resolved and she replies:

creo que es más que merecido por estas veinte jugadoras … es lo que queríamos en un principio. [I think it is more than what these twenty players deserve … it's what we wanted from the beginning.] (Yoreli Rincón, WIN Sports, 2018)

To this, teammate Liana Salazar adds her support and emphasises the collective nature of the struggle and the complaint made:

si quiero invitarlos a todos los medios a que no le den palo solo a Yoreli porque realmente fuimos todas y somos un equipo y como equipo asumimos estas cosas. [I would like to invite the media not to slate only Yoreli as really we agreed all of this collectively as a team and as a team we face the consequences.]

Salazar's comments are skirted over or repeated extremely briefly in articles referring to the conference.

The first part of my summary showed how an Instagram video from Rincón gained significant traction on social media, forcing traditional media into covering it. Those media attached particular salience to the official procedures for distributing prizes, assuring the public that due process had been followed and that all was in order. Instead of considering the wider context of Rincón's complaint in a spirit of investigative journalism, the traditional media ensured the terms of debate were narrow, thus circumscribing debate. It argued that what became the prize money scandal was sparked by an intentional attempt by Rincón to highlight the plight of women's football. Recording the video in a dilapidated area of Caracas Airport, where her teammates were forced to sleep on a concrete floor, Rincón's video explicitly highlighted the perpetually second-class conditions women footballers have to face in comparison to their male counterparts. This choice certainly gave extra purchase to the claim being made, ensuring the scandal went as far as it did.

Chapter Three considers another social media post from Rincón that had a much lower media uptake. Considering the media's agenda-setting role in presenting women's football in a manner that lined up with the hegemonic institutional vision of the sport, it is argued that this earlier post was strategically downplayed and/or ignored as it does not fit within the hegemonic institutional vision for women's football.

Conclusion

The media representations paradigm within academic work on women's football accounts largely for how male hegemony is protected by marginalising female participation in women's football or covering it in ways that portray it as banal or as a sub-category of the men's game. The mass media clearly provide an important pillar underpinning the social masculinity of football. This explains, to some degree, why media has been a central theme in recent research globally (Mourão & Morel, 2008; dos Santos & Medeiros, 2011; Rial, 2013a; Silva, 2015; Pfister, 2015; Mina & Goellner, 2015b, 2015a; Ravel & Gareau, 2016; Goellner & Kessler, 2018). This is largely explained in a top-down fashion presupposing highly uneven power relations. This chapter does not dispute the power imbalances at play, but wishes to nuance existing accounts of mass media coverage by accounting for the agency of players themselves. Moreover, it opens debate about the complex inter-relationships that go towards making each 'story'. The phase of 'hypermediation' is characterised by a systematic and intentional distortion of events. In spite of this, Yoreli Rincón successfully managed to represent the collective interests of Colombian women footballers. Her achievements are laudable but came at a cost for Rincón who, as a result of this story, became (even more of) a lightning rod for resolutely hostile media coverage and arguably was further singled out by the federation as a trouble-maker.[18] The reaction of traditional media to Rincón's activism has not been to highlight the precarious lived experiences of Colombian women footballers but rather to depoliticise collective struggle and also polarise debate by emphasising a constructed, individualistic portrayal of Rincón as greedy and impudent. By closing ranks and refusing to discuss the substantive issues facing women's football, traditional media shows a distinct tendency towards compartmentalisation and most of all towards policing the status quo of male sporting hegemony. A certain level of media engagement with feminist issues is permissible or even desirable whenever it does not interfere with perhaps the most important symbolic area of male hegemony.

In the case of the lesbian kiss, for example, the story was closed down as it had the potential to open up a wider discussion about the sexuality of players and the unidimensional way the game is envisioned, represented and marketed by largely male football institutions. By contrast, 'scandal' – as the media would have it – is cultivated in the case of Huila's CONMEBOL prize money as it places all responsibility for controversy upon Rincón and finds her to be in the wrong before even the most preliminary investigation into the structural conditions that engendered the issue.

Whilst the central findings of this chapter suggest the continued power of traditional media, there are clearly reasons for optimism as the agency

18 Since this incident Rincón has not returned to the Colombian women's national team despite starring for Internazionale in Italy.

*Figure 1.1   Yoreli Rincón being interviewed after Atlético Huila won the Women's
Copa Libertadores 2018 on penalties against Santos FC in Manaus*

of Rincón, and women's football online media, have exerted pressure on institutions and created a growing consciousness of the struggles of women footballers. Moreover, Rincón's interventions ensured a settlement for the players that was not stipulated in their original contracts. The danger of social media engendering individualistic logic notwithstanding, it also appears that Rincón used what little agency she has to represent the collective in the case studied. In this way, it is important not to be entirely dismissive of the agency of football players, even if claims players are now more powerful than the media (BBC Sport, 2019) seem somewhat premature. This chapter hints at the possibilities for change, but at the same time highlights the uneven power relations in which players operate. The collusion of media and institutions to highlight certain perspectives is abundantly clear. Chapter Two builds on this by sketching out the prevailing logic of football institutions (confederations, national federations, leagues). It explains how they police socially constructed gender roles, promote a women's football they want to be perceived *femenino* rather than *feminista,* and in order to do this ensure as little representation as possible for anyone who seeks to destabilise the status quo.

CHAPTER TWO

Football Institutions

Introduction

This chapter has two primary contentions that will be examined with particular reference to the CONMEBOL policy requiring teams to open a women's division in order to continue competing in the men's Copa Libertadores. I contend, first, that sexism, *machismo* and male hegemony have taken refuge in the logic of the market and second, that the rootedness of male hegemony within the hierarchy of clubs and national federations runs into clear tensions with FIFA's global agenda, where gender equality is at least nominally enshrined (FIFA, 2016, p. 22). I argue this means that gender equality is quickly watered down to a logic of inclusion at best and that, in addition, women's football finds itself in a situation where 'by being subordinated it comes to reinforce the hegemonic practice' (Louro, 1997, p. 30). Finally, a third argument in this chapter is that previous, inward-looking, academic incarnations of institutionalism that emphasise conservativism and stability have proved insufficient to account for the gradual changes that are being forced by a range of outside factors. Moreover, I argue that the relentless application of market logic to gauge the popularity of women's football is unjust insofar as women's football suffers from multiple structural disadvantages. For example, women's football still receives very little promotion in comparison to the men's game. Its competitions are allocated fewer funds and less space on the calendar, and thus far nascent women's divisions within major clubs reflect a need to comply with legislation rather than an attempt to promote women's football. Moreover, by tying participation in women's football to an economic sanction affecting the hegemonic male team, both the hierarchical relationship between men's and women's football and the prevailing market logic are reinforced.

To illustrate both these points I look in depth at CONMEBOL's flagship policy, colloquially referred to locally as *obrigatoriedade/obligatoriedad* and consider how it has impacted upon the gradual professionalisation of the sport at my case study clubs in Brazil and Colombia. I argue that uncritically declaring a quantitative increase in the number of large clubs with women's teams neglects a number of worrying continuities of the 'equal but different negative integration' (Williams, 2007, p. 183) of women's football. Furthermore, I argue that a model which ignores the role of development and independent women's football clubs risks replicating the concentration of wealth and talent within a small number of clubs from which male hegemony is hard to dislodge. As explained in the introduction, this will be achieved by applying discursive institutional (DI) theory. Discursive institutionalism considers a broad range of social, cultural and political factors influencing the formulation and enactment of public policy. In its most recent iterations, most prominently the work of Vivien Schmidt (2008, 2010), it questions the supposed neutrality traditionally attributed to embedded institutional values.

The term *obrigatoriedade/obligatoriedad*, then, has become shorthand in South America for the policy incentivising clubs to open a women's division by making it a prerequisite for entry in the ever more lucrative male Copa Libertadores. To place this in context, it is worth considering the respective money prizes for the male and female competitions. The winners of the 2020 male Copa Libertadores received US$15 million and the losing finalist US$6 million (CONMEBOL, 2021). Meanwhile, Ferroviária, the winners of the female equivalent won US$85,000, some 176 times less (CONMEBOL, 2021). Barriers to female participation have clearly been eroded in recent times. The new obstacle underpinning male hegemony is the deep-rooted assumption of the greater commercial appeal of the men's game. This overlooks the role of the cultural capital the men's game has accrued. Whilst this has occurred women's football has not been promoted, has been actively discouraged and in some cases has even been prohibited (Goellner, 2005b; Elsey & Nadel, 2019).

At this point it is worth pointing out that the main thrust of *obrigatoriedade* is incentivising teams to open a women's division, falling short of specifying that this must be professional. Firstly, this chapter will contextualise the policy in Brazilian, Colombian and global terms and detail how and when it came into operation. It will then outline the clear impact of this affirmative action before pointing out fundamental flaws and loopholes which mean that, in some sense, it has consolidated women's football as a sub-category tagged onto the men's game. To support these arguments, interview material with directors of the three clubs in my study will be used.

For the interviews of figures at each of the three clubs involved in my study (Santos, Iranduba and Atlético Huila), I decided to counterpose one figure actively involved in the day-to-day running of the female team with another figure important in the club hierarchy but not solely responsible for women's football. This insider–outsider approach seeks to present a realistic portrayal of the internal struggles within many clubs, problematising older characterisations of the homogeneity of institutions. For the interviews with institutional figures I focused upon those responsible for making policy regarding club competitions at both national and continental level. Whilst numerically few women occupy institutional positions, in each instance I sought to include those in influential positions.

Within football institutions, I interviewed Aline Pellegrino, coordinator of the Paulista Regional Federation, and Valesca Aráujo from the CBF.[1] Allied to this I interviewed Romeu Castro, coordinator of women's football for the CBF and women's football executive delegate for CONMEBOL. At DIMAYOR in Colombia I interviewed Katherine Pimienta, head of marketing, Vladimir Cantor, general manager and Carlos Lajud Catalán, the director of communications. For the clubs in my study, at Santos FC I interviewed general manager of women's football Alessandro Pinto and club marketing director Marcelo Frazão. At Atlético Huila I interviewed director Carlos Barrero and then-president of the women's team Diego Perdomo, and at Iranduba I interviewed club president Amarildo Dutra and director Lauro Tentardini.

Brazilian overview

For almost four decades Brazilian women were officially banned from participating in the sport (Franzini, 2005; Goellner, 2005a). This began in 1941 when the Conselho Nacional de Desportos (National Council for Sports) instituted Law 3.199. This legislation was fundamental in ensuring a highly gendered social order in years to come. One of its articles prohibited female participation in various sporting activities, including football. This was formalised by the prohibition of women from 1941 to 1979 in Brazil (Franzini, 2005; Goellner, 2005a; Elsey & Nadel, 2019). By prohibiting women from competing, the momentum towards growing participation was entirely severed, and was consolidated as an exclusionary and highly gendered concern. Moreover, women who played the game in the early days were either heavily criticised or ridiculed (Wood, 2018; Bonfim, 2019). Even now, by almost any definition or data, including the world governing body's own report (FIFA, 2019), professionalisation is distant on the horizon, despite struggles yielding notable gains in visibility and structure. Drawing on data provided by all the associated members, FIFA states that 15,000 women in Brazil play in competitions at some level. This compares unfavourably to 27,000 in Argentina and 24,000 in Venezuela respectively. These numbers reflect long-term institutional neglect by the CBF. Many of the positive changes, on the other hand, have been a knock-on effect of the coercion or policy prescriptions of FIFA and CONMEBOL.

In the contemporary context moves towards female inclusion in Brazil can be traced back to the first mentions of gender equality in FIFA official policy in 2016 (Soares, 2019). This notional equality was quickly watered down to a logic of inclusion (Elsey & Nadel, 2019, p. 10) albeit on a negative footing,

---

1 Aline Pellegrino was a central defender who captained the Brazil women's national team. For a detailed account of her fascinating career and perspectives see both Joras (2015) and Haag Ribeiro (2018).

as Williams (2006, 2007) has argued. Nonetheless, the shift to inclusion marks the definitive end of absolute male institutional hegemony over football and signals the onset of a long symbolic struggle over the manifest social significance the world's most popular sport carries. For illustrative purposes it is worth setting out the first explicit FIFA policy prescriptions on gender equality. Article 23 states that 'legislative bodies must be constituted in accordance with the principles of representative democracy and taking into account the importance of gender equality in football' (FIFA, 2016, p. 22). Further significant mentions of gender equality appear in Articles 2, 15 and 49 of the same document.

It is also worth outlining some of the more significant changes. Giving the job of manager to men is symptomatic of ingrained attitudes, so placing a woman in charge was a significant step. Following this, a cross-disciplinary panel (the Commission for the Development of Women's Football in Brazil) was formed by the CBF (Soares, 2019). The Commission met just three times and lasted less than three months. Emily Lima was dismissed after eight months in the manager's seat, judged ostensibly on a few friendly games without being given the opportunity to take the team to a major tournament. In September 2020 Aline Pellegrino and Eduarda Luizelli, two ex-players of note, were appointed to prominent CBF roles. Indeed, Pellegrino, formerly captain of the Brazilian women's national team, now coordinates women's football competitions after an impressive period in a similar position overseeing club competition in the most powerful state federation – the Paulista (São Paulo state). This, allied to other appointments such as those of Beatriz Vaz (to assistant coach of the team) and Valesca Aráujo shows some intent on the part of the CBF to redress the gender imbalance, particularly in the running of women's football. Furthermore, these women voice, from personal experiences, the multiple and complex challenges women's football faces in establishing itself.

The most significant policy for women's football, as alluded to above, comes not directly from the Brazilian federation but rather from the South American confederation CONMEBOL. In light of FIFA policy the confederation elaborated a plan to incentivise greater participation in women's football from major clubs. During interviews a number of federation officials, including Romeu Castro, Aline Pellegrino and Valesca Aráujo, were keen to emphasise that they felt that *obrigatoriedade*, the name most often used in the media, is a misnomer and a misconception that has been driven by media oversimplification. These institutional figures were opposed to the term, considering it damaging. Each felt that it was fair that if the clubs wished to continue participating in the (men's) Copa Libertadores, they should modernise accordingly. The policy also includes requiring clubs to have fully operational youth teams, for example. From a DI perspective, the general policy of CONMEBOL is the 'inclusion' of women's football in order to satisfy the requirements enshrined within FIFA's gender equality statute. Reflecting this need, the program of *obrigatoriedade* is foregrounded in order to ensure this inclusion happens. The underlying assumption, as DI behind the policy, is that inclusion, and not any push towards outright equality, will be socially acceptable at the current juncture.

Colombian overview

In Colombia, advances in visibility began with the national team in the first decade of the twenty-first century. Colombia won its first honour when its under-17 team won the South American championship in Chile in 2008. In the 2010 Copa America in Ecuador, Colombia finished second, securing its first appearance at a Women's World Cup in 2011 (Mina & Goellner, 2015b). Following this they went unbeaten at the Ecuador 2014 Copa America and reached the last sixteen of the Women's World Cup in Canada 2015. These events were influential in pressuring intransigent institutions into making some kind of concessions to acknowledge the remarkable progress achieved in the absence of any concerted institutional support. Embarrassingly from an institutional perspective, since the professional league began in 2017 Colombia's women have failed to make the 2019 World Cup and have performed less well at Copa America competitions than before the league was launched.

Demands for further progress exist in a constant tension with the persistence of highly gendered understandings of the sport at regional and national levels. In order to remain a member of FIFA and to receive funds from the FIFA Forward programme, federations need to show quantitative progress; however, this is often frustrated by a lack of female representation at both club and federation level. Policy continues to be rooted in gender differentiation despite policy documents from FIFA and CONMEBOL stating a commitment to gender equality. Despite this commitment, the women's professional league has not meant a growth in opportunities for players at youth level. Clubs largely provide a single, senior, women's team, meaning the development of youth players remains an amateur concern. Many players still develop at schools like the Carlos Sarmiento Lora in Cali or at an amateur club Formas Íntimas of Medellín.

In order to get a feel for the atmosphere of DIMAYOR it is important to consider how it came into being. The Colombian professional federation emerged in 1948 in Bogotá as a market-oriented alternative to the amateur leadership of Colombian football until that point, headed up by ADEFUTBOL in the coastal city of Barranquilla (Goldblatt, 2007, p. 278). Within its first year the organisation was temporarily suspended from FIFA due to escalating quarrels with ADEFUTBOL. At that point an extreme, market-driven, *modus operandi* was consolidated by luring star players over from Argentina and beyond, offering high wages since they were not liable to pay transfer fees as a rogue league outside FIFA. In this way, whilst in Brazil for example, the CBF and its regional federations oversee both professional and amateur football, DIMAYOR is a federation that by definition was born in opposition to an amateur federation, and is wholly committed to delivering 'professional' football.

The progress made in Colombia appears similarly linked to the global FIFA shift towards inclusion (FIFA, 2016). However, there are discursive nuances that are significantly different in the case of Colombia. As the evidence below suggests, *obrigatoriedade* has also had an impact in Colombia. There has been a shift towards larger clubs more likely to push to compete in the men's Copa Libertadores; smaller clubs pay less attention to the policy. Nonetheless, the Colombian federation DIMAYOR pushes the idea of a Year Zero: 2017, when their professional league came into being. Eschewing the idea that the league was a consequence of FIFA's embrace of gender equality, sporting director of DIMAYOR Vladimir Cantor explained that 'the women's league is a product that Jorge Fernando Perdomo wanted to launch'. DI tends towards historical explanations of how discourse is elaborated. In this case, the underlying assumption behind the Colombian women's league is rooted in the extreme market logic in which Colombian professional football was born during the 1940s. In this vein, the launch of the Colombian women's league diverges from those of others in the region. Market logic is more deeply entrenched than elsewhere and thus the policy core elaborated by DIMAYOR reflects this. Another factor contributing to the formation of the league was the level of performance of the Colombian women's team who, in the absence of a professional league, have performed remarkably at international tournaments (Mina et al., 2019). From a DI perspective this is not foregrounded as the achievement of Colombian women prior to the establishment of a women's league, and is inconvenient to the organisation that, by definition as the professional arm of Colombian football, wishes to foreground the achievements of the professional federation. A talented group of competitive players, with professionalised counterparts globally, existed prior to the emergence of an official league. At club level for example, Formas Íntimas of Medellín in particular had already reached a Copa Libertadores final in 2013, years before the Colombian professional league was launched.

Beyond this, despite a discourse that focuses relentlessly on professionalism, even DIMAYOR's head of marketing Katherine Pimienta admits that 'at the moment we still have clubs without professional women's teams but we are still in a period of transition'. As alluded to earlier, the binary structure of the organisation of Colombian football dictates that any endeavour from DIMAYOR is likely to be characterised as professional. This is aided by highly supportive mass media pushing the slightly nationalistic idea that Colombia has been more proactive than its neighbours, having already achieved professionalism. Professionalism in football has always been a slippery and elusive concept. In the British case, the transitional period between amateurism and professionalism is well documented (Taylor, 2016, 2017). Similarly, in Argentina it is well-trodden ground, nuanced by the concept of *marronismo* (retaining players using illegal incentives/pay during the amateur era; see Alabarces, 2002; Frydenberg, 2011) which takes account of the multiple ruses used to incentivise amateur players to sign on in the 1920s – mechanisms that persist to this day in women's football, as described by Gaby Garton in Argentina, who lists covering scholarship costs at university teams, and paying for accommodation, travel expenses and food (Garton, 2019).

One of the main discursive planks in constructing the success of the Colombian women's league has been a couple of isolated high attendances back when the league was launched in 2017. Hinting at what could be achieved with sustained rather than occasional promotion, the final between Santa Fe and Atlético Huila attracted an impressive 33,327 spectators. Pimienta explains 'in June 2017, we achieved a world attendance record for women's club football, which shows what a success it has been'. This is not strictly true. In May 2017, 35,271 spectators watched the women's FA Cup final between Birmingham and Manchester City Women at Wembley (BBC Sport, 2017). This attention to detail was further highlighted when the Colombian Federation, in a letter complaining about their failed bid for the 2023 Women's World Cup, alleged that the Colombian Professional Women's League had an *average* attendance of 28,000 (Núñez, 2020). The majority of games attract fewer than 1,000 fans and often take place in midweek at obscure venues during the mornings.

In Brazil a number of the larger clubs offer free entrance to women's games. I was aware that fans paid to see the Santa Fe and Atlético Huila record attendance at the Estadio Campín. Given the generally market-driven ethos of DIMAYOR I asked director of communications Carlos Lajud Catalán about the cost of attending Colombian matches, to which he responded 'I imagine that the majority of the tickets for women's football are free, but that is up to the clubs'. The indifference as to whether clubs charge for games suggests that, as a commercial proposition, the women's game is not really taken seriously by the organisation. Moreover, DIMAYOR regularly cites the commercial unviability of the women's game.

Clearly, promotion of the women's league is lacking (Mina et al., 2019). To explore this, I asked whether there were separate social media accounts to promote the newly formed women's league. Catalán explained that there were not: 'the leagues are promoted on just one account on Twitter, Instagram and Facebook in order to give equal importance to the women's league'. Nonetheless computerised searches reveal just 42 tweets historically containing women's league or similar searches, out of a history of 21,000 tweets as of January 2021 (around 400 tweets each month since 2017). During the season of my fieldwork, one match was screened weekly during the women's season, meaning around ten games annually, given the short length of the season.

Further gender differentiation is discernible in the two-and-a-half month calendar the women's game has been given. Vladimir Cantor argues that 'a three-month tournament makes it more exciting and competitive'.

Official FIFA discourse

FIFA's embrace of women's football has been tentative and gradual. What is now the Women's World Cup began life as the World Championship for Women, on account of FIFA anxiety about the brand of the (men's) World Cup being tarnished by association (Williams, 2019). The FIFA chronology has the 1991 China tournament as a Year Zero for women's football despite overwhelming evidence of over a century of female participation (Mourão & Morel, 2008; Nadel, 2015). After the 1991 tournament, a quarter of a century would pass before gender equality was enshrined in FIFA's statutes (FIFA, 2016). From a DI perspective, gender equality (nominally) serves as the wider policy and a quadrennial World Cup tournament, eventually given the same name and mirroring the frequency of the men's equivalent, 'a micro-level programme designed to legitimise and lend credence to the notion of equality being a reality' (Schmidt, 2008, p. 314).

FIFA discourse now even acknowledges that 'years of institutional neglect and a lack of investment have prevented girls and women from playing the game and from assuming roles in technical, administrative and govern-ance functions' (FIFA, 2018, p. 4). Predictably, they foreground the FIFA Women's World Cup as a major milestone. This is bolstered by the FIFA Under-20 Women's World Cup in 2002 and the FIFA Under-17 Women's World Cup that followed in 2008. They take the credit for 'the level of play dramatically improving' as a result of these tournaments. Nonetheless, the official 2018 FIFA document acknowledges women's football is 'in need of fundamental change' and lists a number of key global objectives. These objectives, taken from the strategy document, include 'developing and launching new international competitions for women's clubs, developing, monitoring and raising the standard of professional club leagues, doubling the number of youth leagues and finally female representation at executive committee levels' (FIFA, 2018, p. 6).

Reception of official FIFA discourse in Brazil and Colombia

In the context of Brazil and Colombia, the incorporation of gender equality into FIFA's statutes in 2016 has had significant effects, which have manifested themselves according to local understandings of the social significance of football. It is worth outlining some of the more significant changes. In Brazil, just months after FIFA incorporated gender equality into its statutes, Emily Lima was appointed as the first-ever female manager of the women's national team. The manager job within the game remains one of the last bastions of male hegemony, so the gradually increasing presence of women in management jobs is significant. In addition to this, the Commission for the Development of Women's Football in Brazil was appointed (Soares, 2019). In Colombia, women's football was brought under the auspices of DIMAYOR for the first time, leading to a women's professional league being formed in 2017. Much of this progress has proved ephemeral and/or precarious. For example, Emily Lima was abruptly dismissed after a few months, despite reasonable progress (Pires, 2017). This episode might be explained (by new institutionalist analysis) by reference to the way formal and informal rules interact. The commission appeared in response to the formal need to respond mimetically to the actions of other similar organisations globally (DiMaggio & Powell, 1983); however, the way in which it was quickly disbanded responds to informal rules in operation at a local level (Peters, 2019; Schmidt, 2010).

Much of what is to follow explains how the gender equality in FIFA's statutes became watered down to a *modus operandi* of limited inclusion in the Brazilian and Colombian contexts. Inclusion, of course, is a far more nebulous concept which affords institutions considerable room for manoeuvre. A recurring theme during fieldwork interviews was the need for women's football to develop 'unique selling points'. This demonstrated two things: firstly, the unwillingness to allow women's football to share what some interviewees consider legitimate hegemonic masculine space and secondly, how interviewees are, at least, aware of the need to commercialise women's football. Interviewees felt, or at least expressed the idea, that women's football would have little chance if ever placed in direct competition with men's football. When I interviewed Romeu Castro, who has a dual role both as an executive delegate of CONMEBOL and as the supervisor of both women's leagues in Brazil for the CBF, I asked about the historical failings of the Confederation. Castro's discourse mirrors the FIFA one. He follows the rubric of FIFA discourse in wresting the responsibility from the institution and explaining the transition in terms of a linear learning curve for society: 'in the 1980s we had players who suffered violence simply for playing the game, it wasn't easy. But we're overcoming prejudices bit by bit and society is changing'. Once again there are interactions here that chime with the explanations of distinct institutional frameworks. The reference to society changing is an acknowledgement that institutions respond not only to internal dynamics, as older institutionalisms would suggest, but also to what new institutionalists see as 'the transformative impact of small, evolutionary adjustments over time' (Lowndes and Roberts 2013, p. 40). Institutions make 'rational choices' (Schmidt, 2008; Lowndes & Roberts, 2013) based on developments in wider society, rather than depending on their own internal dynamics.

The rhetoric of difference can be traced back to official documents. For example, FIFA's women's football strategy speaks of 'adding unique dimensions to the women's game' (FIFA, 2018, p. 6). By suggesting that it is possible for the women's game to have unique dimensions, the strategy implies it must develop outside the male hegemonic version (Archetti, 1998; Alabarces, 2002). The academic literature attests to the persistent 'othering' of the non-hegemonic form (Louro, 1997). Female participation in various sports is inextricably tied to male identity tropes (Hjelseth & Hovden, 2014; Ezzell, 2009). These narratives oscillate between emphasising the importance of not imitating (or challenging) male physical hegemony and, in even more inimical form, invoking supposed psychological differences between men and women that are understood to affect the running of a club. For example, Romeu Castro felt that 'women's football should be treated as a different sport – as a female sport and not as the same as men's football. We need to avoid the route of simply imitating men's football because if we go down that road we'll always lose.' Essentialising his vision further he suggests that 'women's sport is extremely creative, maybe more creative, so we need to emphasise that artistic side and not the physical side'. This socially constructed femininity continues in ex-Atlético Huila president Diego Perdomo's analysis that 'it is different because they're women, they think differently and thus make different decisions. They are less rational.' Along the same lines, Carlos Barrero, a director of the now-defunct 2018 continental champions Atlético Huila suggests 'it's a different sport. It's more complicated to manage a women's team because of women's moods, which are naturally very different from those of men.' These remarks are less extreme iterations of the infamous remarks of Tolima president Gabriel Camargo that 'the women's league breeds lesbianism, it is not profitable for clubs, and the women drink more than the male players' (Vanguardia, 2018). Curious as to the reaction to this in my case-study clubs, I asked Barrero, who responded that 'he was partly right but he expressed it in a rather unfortunate way'. Barrero reiterated the assumption of it being impossible to make a profit from women's football, in spite of his team being the continental champions at the time of the interview. Recent work delving into early representations of women playing football on the continent date 'lesbian' characterisations back to the 1920s (Wood, 2018). On the other hand, it has been suggested the influence of the heterosexual male gaze is discernible in the Latin American context where there are now fewer short-haired players, with a long ponytail becoming the norm with the foregrounding of 'white blonde players' (Elsey & Nadel, 2019, p. 144). The latter observation certainly dovetails with a more global tendency to present women footballers in a way more likely to appeal to television and attract advertising and sponsorship.

The notion of the women's game being 'different' is institutionalised by a FIFA policy that places it at the level of youth football, *futsal* and beach football (FIFA, 2020a, 2018, p. 4). Moreover, there is a distinct lack of accountability emanating from FIFA and this is embedded at all levels. Whilst gender equality is enshrined within policy documents there is little monitoring of where exactly funds received by national federations from the FIFA Forward programme are spent (Elsey, 2018).

Referring back to global objectives promising the development of competitions with ever increasing standards for women's clubs, a fundamental problem has been the reluctance of clubs to open a female team. Further goals pertaining to creating youth leagues and ensuring female representation at executive committee levels appear hollow when the basic objective of having a women's team has been dodged, paid only lip service or been met and later reneged upon, as in the case of Atlético Huila who, even after winning the continental challenge, now regard a women's team as being an extra they cannot afford.

The context and implementation of *obrigatoriedade*

Clearly the emergence of the policy of *obrigatoriedade* firstly did not occur in a vacuum, and secondly was not solely at the behest of the CBF. Rather it is linked, albeit indirectly, to a global push for greater gender equality, exemplified by movements like #MeToo and #NiUnaMenos (Elsey, 2018). Conversely, the same deeply patriarchal organisations that have underrepresented women's football have systematically championed the men's game, buttressing its immense structural advantages and reproducing a gendered social order (Goellner & Kessler, 2018).

The positive impact: expanded women's leagues in Brazil

As Figure 2.1 shows, the policy has changed the panorama of Brazilian women's football. From just Botafogo and Vasco da Gama in 2013, almost all of the major teams now have an operational women's team. Moreover, as a direct consequence of the policy, the Brazilian women's leagues have swelled in numbers in recent years. There are now two female leagues, Serie A1 and Serie A2, with 16 in the top flight and an unwieldy 36 teams in the second tier.

| | | Year | | | | | | | |
State	Team	2013	2014	2015	2016	2017	2018	2019	2020
São Paulo	Corinthians				A1	A1	A1	A1	A1
São Paulo	São Paulo							A2	A2
São Paulo	Santos			A1	A1	A1	A1	A1	A1
São Paulo	Palmeiras							A2	A1
São Paulo	Portuguesa		A1	A1	A1	A2		A2	
Rio	Flamengo				A1	A1	A1	A1	A1
Rio	Fluminense							A2	A2
Rio	Botafogo	A1	A1					A2	A2
Rio	Vasco Da Gama	A1	A1					A2	A2
Minas Gerais	América Mineiro			A1		A2	A2	A2	A2
Minas Gerais	Atlético Mineiro							A2	A2
Minas Gerais	Cruzeiro							A2	A1
Santa Catarina	Internacional						A2	A1	A1
Santa Catarina	Gremio							A2	A1
Pernambuco	Sport Recife				A1	A1	A1	A1	A2

Figure 2.1   Participation of clubes de camisa *in the top two tiers of Brazilian women's football (Serie A1 and Serie A2)*

Serie A2 began in 2017, to accommodate the increasing numbers, allowing a system of promotion and relegation to be instituted. Whilst as of June 2020 there is no official CBF youth division tournament, under coercion the country has clearly moved closer into line with global and continental prescriptions.

Many of the major teams who joined the league did so with marquee signings of players with experience in Europe and/or North America. For example, Cristiane initially joined the new São Paulo team and Rosana dos Santos joined Palmeiras. With one or two notable exceptions, each of the large clubs has maintained its women's team since. During fieldwork it was felt that the incursion of the large clubs had pushed up wages, a trend much welcomed by women players who still struggle to make a decent living from the game.

Recent times have seen an increase in female representation in key positions in the Brazilian federation. As alluded to earlier, the promotion of ex-players such as Aline Pellegrino who can empathise with the realities of women footballers is a step that will improve the possibilities that the next affirmative action will make a meaningful contribution. Under Pellegrino the Paulista Federation increased exponentially the number of games available to watch, both online and on mainstream TV channels, and also brought numerous games to the municipal Pacaembu stadium in São Paulo, opening the tournament up to a much larger audience. The presence of women players on the federation(s) means more opportunities to promote the game and win over further sympathetic sectors of the public. In this way, a growing public pressure for informal *obrigatoriedade* may force institutions' hands.

The positive impact: the professional women's league in Colombia

In Colombia there have been two main tendencies. First of all, as with Brazil, many of the larger clubs have opened women's teams, presumably in order to protect the potential income from participating in the male Copa Libertadores. From just Santa Fe and América de Cali in the inaugural competition in 2017, now all of the major Medellín, Cali, Barranquilla and Bogota clubs participate.

Less encouragingly, during the COVID pandemic participation slipped to as low as just 13 clubs, and even prior to the pandemic participation did not seem to be growing at anything like the rate it has done in Brazil. This hints at flaws in the policy, insofar as only a handful of Colombian men's clubs regularly participate in the Copa Libertadores, leaving the great majority indifferent to the punitive threat of expulsion from the competition. On one hand, the emergence of the Colombian women's league is the result of the same process of coercive isomorphism described above. On the other, local understandings mean that policy- and decision-making are influenced by numerous factors beyond merely complying with the social pressure exerted from elsewhere.

	2017	2018	2019	2020
Santa Fe	x	x	x	x
Millonarios			x	x
América de Cali	x	x	x	x
Deportivo Cali			x	x
Junior de Barranquilla		x	x	x
Independiente de Medellin			x	x
Atlético Nacional		x	x	x
Atlético Huila	x	x	x	
Deportes Tolima		x	x	
La Equidad	x	x	x	x
Envigado FC	x	x		
Cortuluá	x	x	x	
Total number of teams participating	18	23	20	13

Figure 2.2   Participation of selected clubs in Colombian Women's Professional League since inception in 2017

The launch of the Colombian league can be broadly linked to the unacknowledged assumptions tied to the economic paradigm in which Colombian society operates. It has been argued that the Colombian democratic model centres upon efficiency and the market, delegitimising the role of citizenship and state intervention (Mejía Quintana & Jiménez, 2005). Actors' decisions and social attitudes are foregrounded, or at least influenced, by this ingrained but often unacknowledged market fundamentalism more than they realise. Following Schmidt (Schmidt, 2008, 2010), an organisation as blatantly mercantile in its orientation, policy and discourse as DIMAYOR is only likely to change significantly once the paradigm of wider society changes or, as Schmidt has it, 'when the Kuhnian paradigm expires because it has lost its explanatory potential – ideational change will result from external processes and events that create a receptive environment for new ideas'. In this regard, the last Colombian election fleetingly hinted at this, with the end result being a (re-)consolidation of the social, economic and cultural assumptions underpinning the prevailing development model.

This said, the *modus operandi* of DIMAYOR and the Colombian Federation is clearly not only profit but also the protection of their own institutional hegemony and the hegemonic values of masculinity that they embody. This means women's football finds itself at an *impasse* where it cannot generate profit without much more promotion and investment and cannot attract the latter due to not generating profit. Whilst wishing to conform to global standards of gender equality (or some nebulous notion of inclusion), any substantive progress immediately comes into tension with the Colombian development model and the rootedness of deeply gendered attitudes to football and even in some cases misogyny.

Policy loopholes

This section of the chapter evidences how, taken at face value, *obrigatoriedade* has brought about improvements both in quantitative and qualitative terms. Numbers alone, however, are not enough to guarantee success. As Santos general manager of women's football Alessandro Pinto argues

> the success of *obrigatoriedade* will be governed largely by the level of seriousness of the major clubs. Inevitably all the clubs will now open women's teams – but will they just pay lip service to it or will they do it properly? Women's football has already accrued considerable cultural capital at Santos, this is not the case at some of the other large clubs.

By incorporating women's football into major clubs and opening up the potential to draw upon the considerable fanbases each club has, the policy has the potential to move women's football forward substantially. This sub-section will now highlight areas where the policy could be tightened up in order to accelerate the progress that women players need now and not as a gradual trickle effect of piecemeal concessions. For the purpose of analysis, an English translation of the policy is provided here:

> The solicitant must have a women's first team or be associated to someone that has. Also, they must have at least one youth category or associate themselves to a club that does. In both cases there must be proof of technical support with all the necessary equipment and infrastructure for the development of both teams in decent conditions. Finally, it is required that both teams participate in their respective regional and/or national leagues authorised by the respective member association. (FIFA, 2016)

Outsourcing

It is worth noting that in the first sentence FIFA states that it is sufficient to 'be associated with' another women's team. This first loophole has been used to outsource the responsibility to create a women's team. For example, upon the launch of the policy, Corinthians of São Paulo immediately entered an agreement with Grêmio Osasco Audax, another club on the periphery of São Paulo, which had a functioning women's team. Audax had been created just a year before this agreement and had already put the hard yards into developing youth players, making facilities available and so on. In this way, Corinthians kept its women's team, in a sense, at arm's length from the men's team as the women's team would use the Osasco facilities belonging to Audax.[2] In a similar fashion, Palmeiras, the richest club in Brazil based on its spending on the men's team, entered an agreement with the Prefecture of Vinhedo, some 75 kilometres outside São Paulo, allowing the women to

---

2 Corinthians has since taken full control of its women's team and established itself at continental level, winning national and international trophies.

use the facilities there rather than use the club's own facilities. There are examples of this occurring across the continent – for example in Colombia where Independiente Medellín satisfied the requirement by joining a deal with Formas Íntimas, a long-successful women's team from the same city, who also already had facilities where the Independiente women could train. This trend of 'being associated to someone who has' women's football is a direct consequence of the wording of CONMEBOL's policy. Outsourcing the women's team is a clear signal that it is a sub-category, that they only comply with the requirement because they have no other choice. The practice is light years away from recognising gender equality. It is a begrudging inclusion of women that is telling of the predominantly male hierarchies of Brazilian clubs and their deeply gendered understandings of the social meanings of the sport.

Women's youth categories
Similar to what has been described above, the policy also stipulates that clubs must have 'at least one [women's] youth category or associate themselves to a club that does'. Without wishing to repeat what has been set out above this immediately opens up the possibility of outsourcing the development of youth players rather than carrying it out within the club itself. In this way, the clubs remain hegemonically masculine and women's football is relegated to a sub-category at arm's length. Players spoke of growing up playing street football and only finding a club at 15 or 16 years old. Without multiple young women's teams starting from an early age, with the full commitment of the large clubs, the current semi-satisfactory situation looks likely to continue.

In stipulating that just one women's youth team is necessary rather than legislating towards the full incorporation of women's football on equal terms, there is a clear danger that the policy itself is, in fact, helping to reproduce structural inequalities. Major clubs have innumerable young men's categories beginning with under-7s which eventually feed into the club's senior team. A number of Brazilian women players have commented about how their background is in street football since the necessary facilities to develop in a more structured way are not provided. By allowing teams to have just one young women's team, which may be an under-17 team for example, many women players will continue to be denied the development opportunities that they clearly need.

Contractual arrangements
The most significant absence from the policy is any mention guaranteeing professional conditions for players. By 'professional' I refer to the conditions enjoyed by male counterparts where they are employed on year-round contracts (thus avoiding much of the precarity inevitably brought about by much shorter contracts), eligible for health benefits in the case of injury and registered with legally recognised *carteira assinadas* (legally binding contracts) that entitle the contractee to a notice period, unemployment benefits, paid holidays and maternity and paternity leave, among other benefits. There

have been reports of informal agreements between players and clubs that fall considerably short of these minimum standards. Once again, by leaving to chance any mention of professional conditions and merely stipulating that a women's team must exist, CONMEBOL policy has left players open to these kinds of abuse. There is an increasing awareness of these practices in the media where clubs have, to some degree, been held to account and been forced into giving concessions. An example of this is the COVID-19 situation, during which institutions gave financial support to women's teams (Biram & Goellner, 2020; Biram & Mina, 2021) without the necessary accountability for how the money was used (Mendonça, 2020a, 2020b).

The Colombian women's league was marketed aggressively as a professional league. It is telling that the word 'professional' is ubiquitous in every media or institutional mention of the league. If it really were professional, the label would be redundant, as it is with the Colombian men's league, the Premier League or Serie A for example. A recent report from ACOLFUTPRO, the organisation representing male and female Colombian players, stated that only 3 out of 18 clubs had formal contractual arrangements with women players, only 11% of women players had contracts lasting for longer than 6 months and over half were on short-term contracts lasting less than 3 months (ACOLFUTPRO, 2020). This owes much to the season itself only lasting between two-and-a-half and three months, a structural factor that meant almost all of the women players were out of contract at the onset of the COVID-19 crisis and thus ineligible for help emanating from CONMEBOL and FIFA, and distributed by DIMAYOR.

This sub-section has focused on the minutiae of the policy and how clubs have interpreted and implemented it in its present guise. The following sub-section considers how the policy has affected the wider panorama of Brazilian women's football – for example how it has affected clubs best known for their women's team and who have done much, under the radar, to advance women's football in the country.

Wider consequences of obrigatoriedade

There are a number of wider theoretical and discursive issues attached to the way CONMEBOL has sought to promote women's football on the continent. As alluded to in the introduction, by coupling the promotion of women's football with entry to the lucrative men's Copa Libertadores, women's football is placed in a relationship of dependence, ultimately, on the male team being a realistic candidate to compete in the Copa Libertadores. Firstly, mirroring Europe, this essentially means ever-decreasing circles of wealthy clubs, rather than an opportunity genuinely open to every team in each country. In this way, the mechanism to incentivise compliance is problematic insofar as many teams are unlikely to reach or even aspire to compete in the Copa Libertadores. Moreover, by making the primary incentive to open a women's team economic, women's football becomes bound up in a relationship with an increasingly marketised polity that tends to overlook structural imbalances.

Serious concessions need to be made to redress a history of discrimination. If not, it is likely that women's football is ultimately defeated by the very same logic being used to promote it – that of the market.

By making opening a women's team merely a means to an end – to compete in men's continental competition – women's football is clearly sub-categorised as an extra activity tagged onto the main one. The policy has been lauded as progressive (de Alencar et al., 2020), but this neglects the extent to which it buttresses the status quo of women's football existing on the fringes of men's football. The next sub-section examines how challenges to the country's dominant centre, both in a sporting and an economic sense, have been set back by *obrigatoriedade*.

The centre and the periphery

Much can be discerned about the social, economic and political power bases of a country from the spread of football teams and the power that they wield within their national federations. In Brazil, the so-called *clubes de camisa* are powerful to the point of building a '*clube dos 13*' to challenge the power of the CBF. These clubs come from São Paulo (4), Rio de Janeiro (4), Belo Horizonte (2), Porto Alegre (2) and Bahia (1). In Colombia, a similar football power base of large clubs in Bogotá (2), Medellín (2), Cali (2) and Barranquilla (1) dominates men's club competitions. Broadly speaking this spread of teams reflects the economic dominance of certain cities in the countries' social, economic and political life. The growth of women's football, in some sense, has offered an opportunity to redress this balance as clubs from outside this traditional power base emerged.

On one hand the Brazilian federation is aware of the symbolic power of football and thus of its need to push decentralisation as much as possible. Numerous women's national team games have been played in Manaus while a woman, Emily Lima, briefly managed the team. In Brazil's bid for the 2023 Women's World Cup the CBF made reference to Manaus (Amazon region) as the capital of women's football (FIFA, 2020b, p. 5). They broke all attendance records for women's football in the country – attracting 25,371 to the Amazon Arena for their semi-final with Santos in the 2017 tournament (Padin, 2017). As pithily summarised by Iranduba club president Amarildo Dutra

> there is a real injustice here as clubs who have done nothing for so many years now find themselves at the forefront of a new dawn for women's football in Brazil – there are so many teams like ourselves (Iranduba), Ferroviária, São Jose and Kindermann, for example, who deserve to be there – but this is not the model they are promoting.

The clubs he refers to are a record three times women's Copa Libertadores champions (São Jose), a renowned development club that has provided numerous players to the Brazilian national team (Kindermann of Santa Catarina) and 2021 Women's Copa Libertadores champions (Ferroviária).

This, clearly, mirrors what has happened in Europe and goes against one of the CBF's identified aims: to develop football in the provinces. Romeu Castro has commented on a number of occasions on how keen the federation and CONMEBOL are to bring the Copa Libertadores to Manaus. *Obrigatoriedade* is surely a setback for this project as ultimately it reinforces the centre rather than developing the periphery.

Obrigatoriedade informal?

This chapter does not take issue with affirmative action, *per se*, as an appropriate way to redress historical imbalances. On the contrary, it argues the policy falls short of including several guarantees for women's players *vis-à-vis* working conditions to incorporate them into men's clubs on a genuinely even footing with men's football. This would mean, among other aspects, sufficient women's youth teams, full incorporation into clubs rather than arm's-length involvement via outsourcing and the same facilities available as the men's teams. In any case, it is important to think beyond forcing teams to comply with the policy and to consider how women's football can be further established as a widely accepted part of social life.

Clearly, alongside the essentially punitive measures designed to ensure compliance with the policy, there is a greater and more important struggle to establish women's football in twenty-first century Brazil and Colombia. Indeed, outside the federation, it could be that an informal *obrigatoriedad* is starting to emerge whereby large clubs are seeing what others are doing and, so as not to lose face, are making some of the necessary arrangements to consolidate women's teams within their clubs. This is essentially what has happened with the major clubs of Europe – Real Madrid and Manchester United, for example, as recently as 2019 opened a top-level women's team as they felt growing pressure to match rival teams. Each club is a battleground with its own unique internal politics and nuances – meaning further investigation of club settings would be desirable. For example, periodic changes in club president can have an enormous effect on women's football – as in the case of Santos which disbanded its women's team between 2012 and 2014 coinciding with a considerable pay rise to hold on to Neymar (Goldblatt, 2014). Smaller clubs such as Huila are not moved by the threat of expulsion from a competition they have never played in nor come close to reaching. Similarly, clubs like Iranduba, whose women's team are considerably better known than the men's team, are not affected by the policy, other than the ripple effect on wages increasing their costs. What is clear is that a sense of being perceived as less modern or less malleable to societal shifts means that clubs will make progressive changes as and when they feel society demands them.

Conclusion

This chapter argues that, whilst quantifiable progress has been made as a result of *obrigatoriedade*, there is strong evidence to suggest it represents another addition to a series of global policies that treat women's football as a sub-category of the hegemonic version. DI is illuminating in explaining how certain programmes launched by CONMEBOL, the CBF and DIMAYOR respectively seek to legitimise the underlying assumption that only inclusion is actually required to satisfy FIFA, the global football body. Furthermore, particularly in the Colombian case, discourse around the professional nature of the league that was launched in 2017 is rooted in the historically extreme, market-driven rubric that has governed Colombian football for decades.

The numerical increase in teams participating in women's competitions is clearly laudable. Nonetheless, close attention must be paid to the detail of how these teams are formed, how they treat their players and to what extent they are actually embedding women's football within the club, at youth level for example.

This cultural capital develops over time and depends upon the sympathetic treatment of mass media in particular, but also the clubs who are responsible for promoting football as an inclusive game open to everyone. For this reason, it is of tantamount symbolic importance that a women's team is not located 75km from the much cherished traditional home of the club. Similarly, it is important clubs produce women's players from a young age within the club and its environs rather than just cherry-pick ready-made players who have managed to develop elsewhere in spite of a lack of formal routes. It is part of football culture for fans to have a particular affinity for home-grown players. Furthermore, the practice of outsourcing women's football to another entity or club sends out a clear message that certain clubs have paid only lip service to the policy rather than entered into the spirit of it. In this case, the wording of the policy 'must have a women's first team or be associated to someone that has' almost encourages the practice.

Finally and perhaps most importantly, the policy makes no stipulations regarding legally binding professional contracts. This omission, once again, buttresses a paradigm that continues to treat women footballers with disrespect, encouraging precarity and amateurism. It is assumed, perhaps, that given the enormous capital flows that men's football moves it may not be necessary to make specific mention of professionalism in legislation. In the absence of clear institutional guidelines, maybe professionalism will take root as a result of a more informal *obrigatoriedade*. In time the policy may cause a delayed domino effect as a critical mass of clubs seek to imitate the few clubs who have already provided year-round contracts and conditions that could credibly be described as professional. In this regard, even if, for numerous reasons, *obrigatoriedade* does not immediately trigger professional women's football, it may well inadvertently be a stepping stone on the way to doing so. For that reason, despite all its loopholes, the effect it has upon reinforcing the centre and marginalising the periphery, and its lack of contractual guarantees for players, the policy does provide something to build on and consolidates women's football as part of every major club in South America. The battle to turn sometimes negative inclusion into being equal partners in each club is a longer-term one which is already under way. Chapter One and this one, then, give a strong sense of the extent to which the odds are stacked against women players. Media consciously distort the intentions of players if and when they have the courage to protest against their treatment, as shown in the case of Rincón in Chapter One. Football institutions are almost entirely cisgender white men who ensure that a heteronormative agenda masks the diversity at play. Largely holding the levers of power ensures that the voices of women players are marginalised, to a great extent. The remainder of this book seeks to highlight the perspectives of players, in ethnographic chapters recording time spent with women's teams in Colombia (Chapter Three) and Brazil (Chapters Four and Five), before finally offering a holistic panorama of women's football in South America in the final chapter, which presents the results of a survey carried out at the Women's Copa Libertadores in Manaus.

CHAPTER THREE

Atlético Huila

The Champions of South America

Introduction

My first contact with Atlético Huila was at the Da Vinci Hotel in Adrianópolis, Manaus where the team were staying for the duration of the Women's Copa Libertadores in December 2018.[1] The club arrived in Manaus as winners of the Colombian league and left with the historic achievement of becoming Colombia's first winners of the continental women's championship. Despite this monumental feat, prior to the tournament the players told me they had very modest hopes about the impact such a victory would make. Their worst fears have been proved right – since winning the tournament the players have not gained the visibility of other Colombian sportswomen. Some 17 years earlier the Colombian sociologist Beatriz Vélez (2001, p. 39) lamented how masculine social representations of football had entirely escaped the attention of academics in the country. Conscious of the importance of the sport to the country's national identity she continued

> La carencia de estudios sobre el juego de género en el fútbol de Colombia, se hace más preocupante, toda vez que el balompié se identifica a la sola actividad que cohesiona el sentimiento de nacionalidad. [The lack of studies about how gender plays out in Colombian football is even more worrying when football has been identified as the only activity that unites us as a nation.] (Vélez, 2001, p. 40)

The decision to play down the considerable achievements of Atlético Huila, beyond any reasonable doubt, owes much to perceived encroachment on territory delineated as socially masculine in Colombia (Mina & Goellner, 2015b). Indeed, before Huila's victory the achievements of Colombian women footballers were consistently and systematically downplayed: these included two trips to the Women's World Cup, even reaching the second round

---

1 Atlético Huila stayed at the Da Vinci for the duration of the tournament with Santos FC, their rivals in the tournament, at the expense of CONMEBOL.

despite little institutional support (Mina et al., 2018, 2019). Two of the key players, talismanic midfielder Yoreli Rincón and defender Carmen Rodallega, both later told me the players had felt they had to win the tournament merely to safeguard the existence of the seemingly precarious Colombian women's league for another season. Paraguayan midfielder Fany Gauto agreed: 'fuimos con la mentalidad de tener que salvar el fútbol femenino en Colombia – aunque es absurdo la amenaza de acabarlo'. [We went there with the mentality of having to save women's football in Colombia – although it is absurd that it was under threat.]

In later chapters this book covers the Brazilian domestic season in the middle of which the Copa Libertadores 2018 in Manaus fell. In those case studies the teams involved are fully focused on winning their regional and national competitions, along with the most prestigious prize in South American women's club football. I went to Iranduba and Santos before the tournament, and I went to Neiva immediately after it, and so this chapter deals with an entirely different but equally valid period of the women's club football calendar – the long months of inactivity caused by inadequate and gendered provision for women's football. The Colombian Professional Women's League was launched in 2017, using FIFA Forward funds as a considerable step towards meeting FIFA statutes recognising gender equality (FIFA, 2016). From the beginning the implementation of this on the ground has been problematic for numerous reasons. This chapter examines the considerable gulf between the professionalisation of women's football claimed by the Colombian federation DIMAYOR and the lived reality on the ground for Colombian women players. My intention here, then, is not to cherry-pick the best moments, but rather to give an indicative sense of the day-to-day reality for players throughout the year. The way in which gender discrimination takes refuge in the logic of the market is foregrounded in much of this chapter, leaving women's football as a neglected sub-category that many refuse to acknowledge.

My initial contact at Atlético Huila, the affable head of media for the women's team Vanessa Díaz, looks slightly bemused as I run through the aims of my investigation into women's club football.[2] 'But wouldn't it be better if you came to visit us in Neiva when the women's league begins, so you can see the players in competitive mode and see just how good this team is?' she suggests. 'But when would that be exactly?' I ask slightly disingenuously, knowing full well from interviews with institutional figures that even DIMAYOR's officials have yet to define what they clearly see as a secondary priority at best. A decision will (have to) be taken soon – the fact it is being continuously deferred to a later date or emergency meeting speaks volumes. I've already seen, in Manaus, that Atlético Huila Women are an extremely well drilled, balanced

2 I later discovered Díaz reported largely to Diego Perdomo, an outside benefactor for the women's team, not officially part of the Huila hierarchy. Perdomo funded all the salaries of the women's team.

and adaptable team. Seeing more of this is not my fundamental objective. 'The season will be sometime in the first semester this time, they're saying', Díaz exclaims vaguely and hopefully. It's the first time I have heard 'semester' used outside an educational context. It appears to have become a serviceable euphemism used by institutional figures in Colombia to explain the woefully inadequate calendar. Arbitrarily, last 'season' had been held in the second semester of the year – the period directly preceding the Copa Libertadores in Manaus, meaning Huila arrived match-fit and ready for action, giving them a significant advantage over teams whose season had long since been concluded. The failure to expand the pilot four-month season, along with the lack of a fixed calendar for the Colombian Women's Professional League, speaks to the low priority Colombian authorities give to women's football. They are clearly paying lip service to it (exemplified by a half-hearted bid to hold the 2023 World Cup) rather than acting with any genuine conviction that there are structural and historical injustices that urgently need addressing.[3] The length of the tournament in its opening two years has been four months and three months respectively. This means many of the participating clubs cut their cloth accordingly, employing their women players for the minimum time necessary to allow for pre-season training and the possibility of reaching the knockout rounds of the Colombian Women's League. Upon being eliminated early, players' verbal contracts (which often are not even legally binding) can be cut short (ACOLFUTPRO, 2019, 2020).

As a result of these institutional conditions, from a 30-strong squad the continental champions find themselves down to the bare bones – just 13 players upon my arrival, supplemented by local players Daniela Narváez and Anyi Bonilla, promoted from Valkyrias, a local amateur women's club with whom Huila enjoys an informal but fructiferous relationship. This is the closest the club comes to having a youth division, an aspect crucial to developing players, which is sadly still lacking in Colombian football. This arrangement is barely formalised, however, and shows clear gender differentiation, considering the resources the club devotes to developing its own players for the men's team. Indeed, this problem goes far beyond Huila. The Colombian national women's team depends heavily on just two schools that produce younger players – the Escuela Carlos Sarmiento Lora in Cali and Formas Íntimas, until recently an amateur club from Medellín. Along with this the national team is supplemented by players who develop within the US university system – another factor for which the country's national federation cannot take any credit.

Much of the literature to date has made valid claims about the low level of media interest or pejorative coverage of women's national teams, both in Europe (Ravel & Gareau, 2016; Agergaard, 2019; Black & Fielding-Lloyd,

---

3 The first pilot season was held with the idea of enlarging the competition to cover more of the year. The exact opposite happened. The season has in fact become shorter each year.

2019) and North America (Christopherson et al., 2002; Burch et al., 2018; Pegoraro et al., 2018) and in the South American context (dos Santos & Medeiros, 2012; Ferretti et al., 2011; Mina & Goellner, 2015b). In Chapter One the prize money scandal after the Women's Copa Libertadores 2018 problematised the notion of one-way traffic in the production of meaning, showing how stories often begin online through the social media accounts of players themselves. However, national team football of a sufficient quality to arouse mainstream interest hinges upon a mutually beneficial relationship with club football, where players, in theory, stay fit and at a competitive level throughout the year. In the case of women's club football in South America, this relationship is hugely problematic. In Colombia this lack of continuity in the club calendar has been matched and exacerbated by the sparse or non-existent calendar of the national team over previous years (Elsey & Nadel, 2019, p. 252). Despite visible advances in national team women's football, such as equal pay in a number of nations (Glass, 2020; Taylor, 2020)and record television audiences (*The Economist*, 2019), it is my impression that the real story resides in the permanent state of limbo of women's club football, which prevents players from reaching their full potential in various ways.

With this in mind, part of the reason I chose to investigate the everyday experiences of Atlético Huila was the particularity, at the time I carried out my fieldwork, that the club trained all year round, while many of their rivals disband their women's team for months on end and only re-form a couple of weeks before the annual three-month tournament comes around. The wage bill for the women's team is bankrolled by local businessman Diego Perdomo, meaning they are one of only three clubs whose women's teams train all year round (Bermúdez, 2019). The other clubs cease to exist for large chunks of the year, before re-appearing to present a healthier picture than really exists at the onset of each three-month 'season'. I explain to Díaz then, that my intention is to produce as faithful a record as possible of the everyday experiences of women representing Atlético Huila. When she explains to me that these periods, characterised by uncertainty, are in fact the norm, that only reinforces my conviction that this should be, in fact, a fairly indicative period in the lives of women footballers. If players face perpetual instability, looking for offers elsewhere so they can begin practising their profession again as quickly as possible, then this should be on record as an issue that urgently needs addressing.

Locating Atlético Huila

Football in the provinces

Two of the three case studies in this book are located in places in which football is not an established part of regional identity. A footballing map of Brazil or Colombia would not traditionally include Manaus or Neiva, respectively. However, the emergence of women's football in these places has a common thread – the possibility of constructing a provincial, oppositional identity around antagonism towards the perceived centre of the country. The region of Huila has long been viewed as backward, in opposition to an enlightened elite in Bogotá – just five hours away by road but much more distant in the country's social imaginary. Restrepo (2012, p. 130) argues that the discursive hegemony of the centre and its accompanying undervaluing of provincial Colombia is discernibly buttressed by 'la política del chiste' which has *costeños* as lazy, *paisas* as *vivos*, *santandereanos toscos*, *pastusos* as stupid (*bobos*) and finally *opitas* (the region of Huila) as slow, in opposition to '*capitalinos ingeniosos*'.

The existence of this antagonism facilitates the growth of local interest (as argued for Manaus in Chapter Two). As many of the provincial and subtly racialised stereotypes refer to the rural nature of the province of Huila, it is perhaps for that reason that the name chosen for the team is that of the province rather than the more normalised practice of naming the club after the city. It is open to conjecture whether Atlético Neiva would have appealed to local pride in the same way. At various points in history the region produced more coffee than any other in the country (Ortiz, 2012), and yet the stigma which has Huilenses as 'gente sin iniciativa, mayordomos' persists (Restrepo, 2012, p. 134). Players were often aware of these nuances – though as per Chapter Two, the great majority of the squad were recruited from across the nation and beyond, meaning a period of adaptation to Huila.

The lack of invented tradition at Atlético Huila

Santos, discussed in detail in Chapter Four, could also be described in some sense as provincial, but has come to be of profound importance to the Brazilian football identity. Atlético Huila provides a counterpoint to the discursive weight of the invented tradition described in Chapter Four. Atlético Huila was only formed in 1990, meaning it has had less time to accrue the considerable cultural capital of many of its rivals. Atlético Huila women are a sub-category of the men's team, who have established themselves as a respectable top division team. They also differ from Iranduba, where the women's team takes social and economic precedence over a fledgling men's team. Even as continental champions, the Atlético Huila women's team have had to engage with the same unacknowledged assumptions as elsewhere – namely the sport is viewed as socially masculine and the women who play the game are viewed as inferior to and subordinate to the male players.

Promoting the women's team

In spite of these institutional and ideological obstacles, the Huila public have engaged with the women's team. My contact Vanessa Díaz explained to me at training how the social media accounts of the women's team have reached parity in terms of followers, engagement and posts with those of the men's team. Díaz is modest in omitting the extent to which her own endeavour and determination is responsible for this, rather than club policy. She created accounts solely to promote the women's team. It is telling that these women's-football-specific social media accounts had quickly amassed 30,000 followers, slightly more than the men's team as of April 2019. Of equal import, the club was quick to delete the accounts when the women's team was discontinued in June 2020. Interest in the club's success was consolidated by winning the Copa Libertadores 2018 in Manaus. Whilst many clubs have only one social media account, a practice which tends to marginalise women's and youth football, under Vanessa Díaz Huila opened separate accounts to promote the women's team. The players' recognition of this is clear from observing the close relationships between them and Díaz.

Arriving in Neiva

I arrive in Neiva on an overnight bus that takes in several police and military checkpoints. After a lethargic day, around 8pm on Friday night in Neiva I receive an unexpected WhatsApp message from the captain of Huila's team, Gavy Santos. Vanessa Díaz had passed on my number so Santos could contact me. This was over and above what Díaz needed to do, but she is obviously fiercely committed to the women's team and makes a real effort to help. The message is concise. Santos is exhausted from today's training, but is happy to meet for the first time in person tomorrow. She seems genuinely enthused that the club has a visitor and tells me there is a training game at 8am tomorrow at the Candido artificial surface, a municipal facility in the city centre, which I can watch (see Figure 3.1).

Figure 3.1   Atlético Huila Women at training camp

Visible and invisible realities

From my first days with Atlético Huila it is abundantly clear that day-to-day lived experience with the team paints a different picture to the media and institutional representations described in earlier chapters. The disconnect between those narratives and lived experience is stark. I arrive at the Candido synthetic pitch expecting to be greeted by the entire Atlético Huila coaching and back-room staff, as I was at the other two clubs. There seem to be two men's six-a-side teams playing on one side of the pitch. In the distance I glimpse the continental champions for the first time since being at pitch-side for their coronation as champions in Manaus. Or at least I see what remains of them. As they emerge from the changing rooms I already know that many of the heroes of Manaus are now elsewhere. It appears the coaching staff too are somewhere else, as only the players appear.

Inter-gender practice match

Despite being severely depleted as there are no matches to play at this time of year, a nucleus of the squad remains, key players without whom the club would never have won the continental championship. Those who are left behind, I would learn later, are generally the more senior players with fewer years of football left in them, or players with emotional links to the region. Captain Gavy Santos, for example, has set up her own football school for girls in neighbouring Ibague. Goalkeeper Maritza López grew up in a nearby town. At the present moment it needs those kind of circumstances or ties to keep a player at Atlético Huila as there is no official confirmation that a new Colombian women's season will even take place this year. Rather than depend on faith alone, a number of players have taken the proactive step of looking for a guarantee of football in another country. Those left behind wait, hoping each day that a date for the new season will materialise and trigger the arrival of players capable of defending the double they won the previous season.

It suddenly dawns on me that the training match will be against the men's team who were training frantically when I arrived. I enquire of one of the staff about the age and pedigree of the male players. I'm told implausibly that the grown men, who appear in their early to mid-20s, are all in fact under 15. They are apparently a successful youth team that plays in a local regional league. Nobody seems to know much more. Upon later questioning, official figures remain tight-lipped too, almost as if it wouldn't do for people to know that a women's team regularly trains and has success against a male team. These are just the kind of practices that, if made visible, have the potential to destabilise the matrix of male hegemony (Lugones, 2007; Butler, 1990). In *A Beautiful Game* Jean Williams argued (2007, p. 183) that US women footballers are represented by sex-appropriate characteristics. They ought to be 'wholesome, smart, ethical and collaborative'. This girl-next-door image of the players discursively denies them of their key sporting characteristic – namely being steely and competitive on the field. In this way, by differentiating discursively between characteristics 'appropriate' to male and female players, the heteronormative matrix (Butler, 1990) is held together. Practices like mixed gender football undermine this and thus are hidden away.

After the first ten minutes or so, the men's team take the lead. I'm told by a member of staff sitting alongside me at the training ground that a goal for the men was inevitable given the biological differences. The goal has come against the run of play – the men's team haven't been dominating the game, and scored on their first attack. At this point, I notice a young woman in a Huila tracksuit barking instructions at the women from the sidelines. I realise it is Jorelyn Carabali, a promising young Colombian international player who has recently suffered a horrific injury. During a training session she collided with a teammate and suffered a fractured femur, which has kept her out of action since April 2018. Carabali, like many of her teammates a product of the Escuela Carlos Sarmiento Lora, had been uprooted from her native Valle del Cauca at 19 to try and progress her career by playing at the highest available level. Watching the game Carabali is visibly frustrated. She yells comments at her teammates that seem far removed from the image of wholesomeness and gratitude projected upon women footballers like her. She tells her teammates not to let up for a second and to be 'duras con ellos' (tough on them). Soon enough they take Carabali's advice by flooring a couple of the men's team with fair but crunching challenges. Huila Women soon draw level and within 15 minutes are comfortably 3–1 ahead. Atlético Huila women claim every throw-in even when they know full well it isn't theirs, incessantly appeal to the referee for fouls, bookings and anything else that may be to their advantage. Whilst working within clearly gendered conditions, the players achieve the level of ruthlessness and efficiency you would expect from professional players.

Insofar as professionalism has been achieved in Colombia, it is found in the determination and resilience of these players, who turn out unsupervised to play a game like this early on a Saturday morning. In the absence of organised competition for much of the year these games are all the players have. The way they play the game reflects their determination to be as good as they possibly can, in spite of the structural disadvantages they have compared to a country that offers a regular club and international calendar. In fact, the way they are playing brings to mind the ruthless streak of the US women's national team – whom many of the players say they admire. Liana Salazar, for example, who has represented Colombia at two World Cups and the Olympic Games, says Megan Rapinoe is her hero as someone who 'siempre ha luchado por el desarrollo del fútbol femenino' [has always fought for the development of women's football]. Maybe the next generation of players will adopt footballers like Yoreli Rincón and others in this Huila side. In the same way as Rapinoe, the players have not only achieved on the pitch but have also worked tirelessly to improve the collective cause of women footballers in Colombia. Arguably, they have done this faced with far greater social stigma in an even more challenging social context than their North American counterparts.

The unnamed men's team, on the other hand, are now visibly irritated at being 'manhandled' (*sic*), as Joreyln Carabali puts it, though they don't look altogether surprised about the scoreline. Their women opponents are used to playing against the lexicon of football itself, as well as against another team, as the game's phallocentric language bolsters the heteronormative matrix that privileges certain characteristics for each gender (Butler, 1990, p. 41). Their embodied practice (rather than discourse) serves to contest the hegemonic masculinity and in turn to problematise terms like 'manhandled', and phrases like it. The despondent but knowing expressions of the male players betray a sense of *déjà vu* – these games are a frequent fixture and I later learn that the men are used to losing them, and that 'se portan bien por lo general, pero cuando se enojan, se enojan' [they behave well generally, but when they get wound up they really get wound up], as Jorelyn Carabali explained to me. I spoke to a couple of the male players after the game and they confirm that they frequently lose these games. The member of staff who had smugly declared that the physical difference was telling after ten minutes has long since disappeared. The second half brings more of the same with Huila women eventually running out 7–1 winners with the men's team down to ten players after a professional foul. Rather than slow up having won the game, the women continue mercilessly, as if every goal counted for goal difference. At this point I recall an anecdote from Beatriz Vélez (2001, p. 43) about the Fútbol por la Paz initiative. She recalled how women and men played exhibition games together with a number of fixed rules, such as that the first goal had to be scored by a woman player. She recalls firstly how the media applauded the exercise, choosing to exalt the image of women footballers in this context. However, they remained virulently opposed to women playing in any competitive context. Moreover, Veléz recalls a condescending attitude from the male players who would say after the first goal by a woman player – 'ahora si vamos a jugar en serio!' [now, let's play seriously!] My mind wanders to wonder how the media would explain the men being beaten so comprehensively.

The experience of this game on my first full day in town flies in the face of club and institutional representations of women's football. With a superior first touch, more accurate passing and even bullying the male team physically for large periods, Huila Women come out on top in every respect. The division of men's and women's football is defended vehemently by clubs and institutions. Indeed, women's teams are often presented as playing a qualitatively different sport from the men's game and it is an unacknowl-edged assumption that they would be unable to compete with their male counterparts. There are no serious injuries during the game and nor does there appear to be any greater risk of injuries than there is in an all-men or all-women game. Men and women sharing a pitch for a competitive game is certainly not on the cards in the near future, but this experience makes me think deeper about why, and further beyond the often-invoked reason of physical difference. The reasons for maintaining gender division in sports and leisure activities vary according to the particularities of each discipline, but even in an activity like chess, for example, a strict gender division is maintained. In this case, it has little to do with physicality and everything to do with protecting male hegemony. One similarity between chess and football is the overwhelming participation of men and historical marginalisation and derision directed at female participation.

At the conclusion of the game, I go over to meet the players for the first time and they welcome me by sharing their post-match snacks and drinks. They quickly change from the gnarly competitors who won the game to convivial hosts welcoming their new visitor. There is no formal introduction from anyone at the club so it is left to Gavy Santos to introduce me. Initially she is busy on the other side of the pitch, signing autographs for a group of around ten young supporters. The players are laughing and joking and Nelly Córdoba provides music from a beatbox that will become a familiar fixture in the coming months. The musical choices are eclectic – anything from old school salsa to urban and reggaeton, all of which seem to trigger choreographed comedic dancing from the more outgoing players, to much laughter from the rest.

An unintentionally damaging myth about women's football is that of saintly behaviour on the pitch. It is extremely common to hear how refreshing it is that women players don't simulate fouls or take advantage of grey areas in the rules in the same manner that men's teams do. For example, it is often argued that women players behave better on the football pitch (Evans, 2019; Casal et al., 2020), never try to get one another booked or claim throw-ins or corners when they know it not to be correct. Broadly speaking, this cliched observation is meant as a compliment to women's football as well as an opportunity to admonish the morally distasteful millionaires that some modern male players are perceived to have become. Nonetheless, this false dichotomy does, in some sense, reinforce a binary of competitive win-at-all-costs male players set against women players who naturally tend towards less competitive, fairer conduct. When men play football they are metaphorically going to war, as the pride of their nation or the region is at stake. By reducing women players to beacons of decency, this competitive edge is taken away and with it goes some of the interest that competitive sport generates. Furthermore, the notion of fair women players naturally not given to cheating or bending the rules is rooted in our social imaginary of what constitutes femininity. Merely by participating in competitive sports women are breaking with this binary. Watching them push every rule to the limit, claim every throw-in and corner regardless of whether it is theirs or not, and engage in psychological warfare with the male players, makes it abundantly clear that many of these stereotypes fail to stand up to scrutiny. This confirms Williams' findings in *A Beautiful Game* (2007).

Santos tells me she'll pass me the schedule for the following week when she knows it herself, reminding me acutely of the nomadic training arrangements of the first two clubs I visited. This, by now, feels unsurprising and even banal. I need to remind myself that, whilst these kind of practice are highly normalised, they are also discriminatory and reflect the gendered order that continues to prevail in football. The unwillingness of clubs to provide a stable home for women's teams is symptomatic of their attitude to women playing at all.

Gavy Santos kindly offers to drive me to training each day but explains she won't be able to do that next week as she hasn't been able to fill her car with petrol, since they haven't been paid yet. The way she tells me this leads me to believe the players' monthly pay is often late. This, it appears, is life with the continental women's champions, symptomatic of how even continental success does not bring the players far enough onto the radar to receive the courtesy of being paid on time.

One notable feature of the morning's activities worth remarking upon was the complete absence of any coaching staff. Presumably instructions for the game had been given at a previous training session, but the team was left to fend for itself. This meant that numerous experienced players, for example Carmen Rodallega, Jennifer Peñaloza and Gavy Santos, would need to tell other players what needed to be done when defending set pieces or organising the formation. There was enough evidence to suggest the players had the competence to develop into managers or coaching staff after their careers, if and when the doors were open for them.

The coaching team

At Atlético Huila the entire coaching staff are male, despite the club having a wealth of experience from a range of countries, settings and levels among its playing staff. The head coach is Albeiro Erazo and he is supported by physical trainer Robinson Ossa, physiotherapist Cristian Bustos, club doctor Oscar Sandoval and goalkeeping coach Javier Buitrago. Players are guarded with their views on this, for obvious reasons, with a male researcher such as myself and in the presence of the coaching staff. The anonymous survey material presented in Chapter Six suggests a clear preference for female coaching input.

Erazo provides a much-needed link between the all-male hierarchy of the club and the female players. He is not by nature authoritarian yet manages to command the players' respect with what they perceive as his homestead wisdom and humility. His daily repartee tends to involve imparting an anecdote or a joke from his youth in Gigante, a small provincial town in Huila province. Some of the players listen attentively while the usual suspects are already playing kickie-uppy or warming up in the background. Erazo is not a stickler for things like this and just lets it go. It is my perception that shared social class is a clear facilitator of the relationships. The great majority of players are from humble backgrounds and instantly relate to the calm homespun wisdom of Erazo. Indeed, watching the way players relate to those they perceive to be 'their own' underlines the importance of an intersectional approach that is not solely gender-based, but rather takes into account the crucial nuances of race and class that are at play (Crenshaw, 1990). This is enhanced by Erazo having suffered a stroke a few years earlier, which has significantly changed his outlook on life and has given him a different perspective, he says. The stroke has left him with motor skill limitations and with a slower speaking style. Rather than let this be a problem Erazo uses it to his advantage – he loves holding court with the players in his protracted, provincial Spanish, knowing the players relate to his humble beginnings and what he has achieved in spite of various obstacles. All of the players are acutely aware of Erazo's plight and indeed are inspired by him, they say. 'El profe es bien comprensivo, y siempre está pendiente de nosotros' [el profe is very understanding with us and always looks after our needs] commented Nancy Madrid during training. This is clearly the case, inverting in some sense the patriarchal relationship prescribed by clubs and more conventional male managers. The specificities of the relationship between Erazo and the players, whilst not horizontal exactly, evade some of the typical, patriarchal, hierarchical dynamics that are often present in women's football. It has been argued that aesthetically, structurally and culturally football serves as a prime site for the legitimation of men's power over women (Giulianotti, 1999, p. 298). The presence of an all-male coaching team suggests a continuation of this; however, the lived reality of how the players relate with the key authority figures at Huila suggests shifting attitudes. Players like Fany Gauto and Carmen Rodallega both expressed a desire to manage in the future, along with a confidence that they would be equipped to do so. It is open to conjecture how they would manage. A perfect storm of coincidences created the circumstances by which Erazo manages by consensus. Whether the players may wish to imitate this or use a more conventional, authoritarian style is an interesting question for the future which may be linked to destabilising male hegemony.

'Los sacrificios que nos tocan' [The sacrifices we have to make]

Earlier in the chapter I discussed the exacting standards the team imposes upon itself. By the same token, the lack of a professional calendar, a sub-categorised status within clubs and the precarious contractual conditions are also emphasised across the book. One day, midway through a training session, one of the players arrived late to training on a motorbike, having made the 30-kilometre trip from USCO (la Universidad Surcolombiana). She exclaimed wearily 'los sacrificios que nos tocan' before quickly getting ready and getting involved in the training session. This made me think about the ways in which the players themselves bridge the gap involved in achieving a semblance of professionalism despite unfavourable circumstances. Players have actively sought out places to develop at youth level, often meaning uprooting at an early age. Upon arrival they are often forced to live communally in cramped conditions on a short-term basis, and then move from club to club and city to city, sometimes numerous times in a calendar year. Similarly, in the absence of economic security (given the precarity and low-pay on offer), players have shown determination, living a kind of double life to continue pursuing their dreams. They have continued to study alongside playing football. Furthermore, they have withstood societal prejudices and in many cases managed to become a footballer in spite of very substantial odds. The following section considers some instances that came to light during the period of fieldwork.

The lived experience of the professional league

Unlike the experience with Iranduba and Santos, who train relatively close to their respective stadiums, the training facilities of Atlético Huila are some 40 kilometres from Neiva in rural Campoalegre. From the centre of Neiva to the training facilities it was necessary for me to travel each day on the official team bus with the players. This allowed me to get to know the level of comfort players had for travelling to training and a chance to chat in a more informal context before training began. When I say the official team bus, it is probably worth adding that it is considerably older than the brand new equivalent that the men's team have. In an incident that seems par for the course, on one occasion I was recruited to help push-start the rickety team bus. I could hear mutterings in the background that this never happens with the men's team bus. Another player wondered if it would start at all. The players, however, were not at all surprised. It took seven or eight staff and players to get the bus moving again – triggering wild cheering and a few minutes of singing. This is the life of women footballers, one of them told me. Another quipped that this is not true – they actually play in a *professional* league, causing more eye-rolling and laughter. The players are acutely aware that the nomenclature 'Colombian *Professional* Women's League' does not necessarily mean exactly what it says but rather hints at a discursive battle to convince the public that assertive action is being taken.[4] The institutional narrative, covered in Chapter Two, is that the Colombian Professional Women's League is the first of its kind in Latin America, providing a significant leap towards meeting global goals (set by FIFA) for gender equality. Colombian football is organised by two federations, DIMAYOR for professional tournaments and DIFUTBOL for *fútbol aficionado* (amateur football). For this reason, by definition, any tournament organised by DIMAYOR ought to be professional.

For the same reason, for the women's league to come under the auspices of DIMAYOR represented a significant step. From the moment the league started, headed by a savvy group of activist players like Yoreli Rincón, Daniela Montoya and Vanessa Córdoba, Colombian women players have consistently tried to hold DIMAYOR to account for the many loopholes and problems that have characterised the opening years of professional competition. Of course, definitions of football professionalism are slippery and open

---

4 It is redundant to say that, for example, Serie A, La Liga, the Bundesliga or the Premier League are 'professional'.

to numerous interpretations – in England (Taylor, 2001, 2005; Curry, 2004) and Argentina (Frydenberg, 2005, 2011), for example. In Argentina the grey areas between amateurism and professionalism have been labelled '*marronismo moderno*', first to describe the practice in men's football (Frydenberg, 2005, 2011) and latterly to describe the same struggle in women's football (Garton et al., 2021, 2022).[5] Nonetheless, in Colombia professionalisation has been linked to migration, nationalism and political upheaval, bringing about a uniquely marketised polity linked to national unity (de Souza Gomes, 2012, 2021). Professionalism in Colombia began with a pirate league outside FIFA in 1948, which offered lucrative salaries without much regulation or consideration for the welfare of players, social security and due process in registering players with the federation (de Souza Gomes, 2021). In a similar vein, a December 2019 report by ACOLFUTPRO, the Colombian sub-division of FIFPRO, noted that a third of women players had no contract nor social security cover, and many clubs had more amateur women players than professionally registered and contracted ones. There were even clubs that had only five officially contracted woman players. Allied to this, precarity in terms of contract length meant that players could be moving on after just three months (or even less if their teams were eliminated early). Information supplied anonymously to ACOLFUTPRO by women players explains that most clubs only contract them for the length of the Colombian Professional Women's League, meaning they are unemployed for eight to nine months each year. Added to this, it has been reported that as the Colombian Women's League operates on a knockout basis, upon not advancing from the group stage players' employment has been terminated by 'mutual consent' after just one or two months of the three-month 'professional season'. Finally, only 11 per cent of women players' contracts were longer than six months and the majority (58 per cent) were for only three months (ACOLFUTPRO, 2020).

The state of the team bus is symptomatic of the second-class status of the women's game and of the begrudging provision offered by clubs to accommodate it. The inclusion of 'professional' in the league's name is symptomatic of the way equality is watered down to inclusion (Elsey & Nadel, 2019, p. 12) or what Williams (2007, p. 183) calls the 'negative integration' of women's football under an 'equal but different' model. Players know that they are incorporated into clubs on deeply unequal terms and that they won't get a contract that offers them any life stability nor will they be treated equally within the club. As Jennifer Peñaloza puts it, 'jugar solo dos meses no es aceptable, la federación y los clubes tienen que hacer muchísimo más no simplemente cumpliendo sino comprometiéndose de verdad' [playing just two months a year is not acceptable. The federation and clubs need to do much more, not just doing what they have to, but showing real commitment.]

---

5 *Marronismo* refers to informal incentives offered to players that are unofficially tantamount to pay but escape sanction.

Double lives

As a basic requirement, a professional would need to dedicate themselves exclusively to their chosen vocation. The current state of women's football in Colombia certainly does not allow this. Nancy Madrid, the player whose late arrival to training began this section, is a typical example of a high-level player who is also taking a full-time university course. She is studying Physical Education at the USCO in Neiva. Madrid points out that it is a practical decision to both study and try to be a footballer, based on the understanding that being a women's footballer in Colombia brings no financial guarantees and thus continuing to study and safeguarding a future outside the game is vital. She is pleased at least to be exempted from writing a thesis for her bachelor's degree because she has become champion of South America in her field. She feels grateful for this, but balancing the two activities brings difficulties. In the worst-case scenario, missing a certain number of classes means repeating a semester and losing all the time she has put in. These are the challenges of the *semi-professional*.

Similarly, teammate Daniela Narváez is getting used to reconciling studies with training. On the bus home after training, she told me that her route into football was playing alongside boys. She explained that she was always a first-team player for the Huila municipality and felt well treated playing alongside male counterparts. Narváez was pleasantly surprised when the opportunity to join Atlético Huila women came, but noted that the demands of training in an amateur girls' club are hugely different from those of Atlético Huila. She joined at the same time as Anyi Bonilla, another Valkyrias player. Narváez wasn't as lucky as Nancy Madrid, and one consequence of her joining Atlético Huila full-time has been that she has had to forfeit a semester at university, where she studies engineering. This means, ultimately, that it will take her longer to graduate in the case she doesn't continue as a professional footballer. I asked to what degree she felt okay with this. She just shrugged and said 'pues, es lo que me toca, ¿que se puede hacer?' [well that's just the way it is, what can I do?] Players who are leading this difficult double life regularly use the bus ride to the training ground to have a short nap in order to catch up on lost sleep – no mean feat given the loud salsa music and the bumps in the road. Narváez has just turned 18 and thus has difficult choices to make about whether to dedicate herself to life as a women's professional football or to go for a safer bet through her university studies. This would be understandable, given she says that the 'tiempo de prueba sin periodo fijo no tiene garantías' [the open-ended trial period with the club comes with no guarantees]. This situation typifies the precarity which must discourage a great number of young women players. Narváez began playing at just 5 years old, like many serious players, and obviously genuinely loves the game. Clearly, the current institutional arrangements are not propitious for such a player to pursue a career in the game.

The issue of leading a double life came up in a discussion between a number of players on the bus. Nancy Madrid, normally a fairly shy player in the group setting, began by explaining how the situation came to a head in her case. She faced a particularly difficult dilemma when the club was about to travel to Manaus for the Copa Libertadores, between a place on the team and having to repeat an entire semester because a couple of exams clashed with the period of the tournament in December 2018. Luckily, at precisely the crucial moment, the university staff went on strike and thus the end-of-semester exams were deferred. This lucky coincidence meant that Madrid was able to travel to Brazil with a clear conscience, ready to take on the best players on the continent, rather than be penalised for missing her exams in order to do so.

The itinerant lives of women footballers

On the training ground I heard numerous regional references such as '*opita*' (Huila region) '*cachaca/rola*' (Bogotá), '*paisa*' (Medellín/Antioquia), '*chama*' (Venezuela) or '*costeña*' (from the coast). These labels, each loaded with the stereotypes mentioned earlier in the chapter, serve to provide a sense of identity to players a long way from home. The shared cultural references between the players give them a sense of familiarity. This is particularly important as players are often forced to relocate multiple times in order to find a salary and games.

After winning the Copa Libertadores in Manaus many of the club's star performers received offers to play elsewhere. In light of the unstable, shifting, three-month season on offer in Colombia players have nothing to lose, on the face of it, in listening to any offers whatsoever: nothing to lose economically and in terms of their playing careers perhaps. However, this neglects the brutal adaptation difficulties many players face when starting a new life in a country where they do not know the language or cultural references and in which they do not have any contacts.

Paraguayan midfielder Fany Gauto told me about the difficulties of 'comenzando de cero' [starting from nothing] in a new setting. When she was just 21 she relocated to Israel and felt daunted by the language and culture. Gauto recalls the move to Israel as a sink-or-swim moment – 'tuve que adaptarme super rápido y incluso me tocaba expresarme en inglés, que no era el primer idioma ni para mi ni para ellos' [I had to adapt really quickly, having to express myself in English which was neither my language nor theirs]. Despite the obvious culture shock this caused for a young player, it has imbued Gauto with the confidence she shows today. She wears Paraguayan nationality as a badge of honour, with a Paraguayan flag on her *tereré* container. The other players are generally accepting of this and even make occasional attempts to say words in Guaraní.

Two of the outstanding players from the Libertadores-winning team, Yoreli Rincón and Jaylis Oliveros, led the exodus by signing for Iranduba in Brazil. There they could continue playing football immediately, in the Amazonian championship in January, and look forward to a much longer season. Another leading figure, Aldana Cometti, left for Sevilla in Spain, where a much longer season runs from September through to May and where a great number of

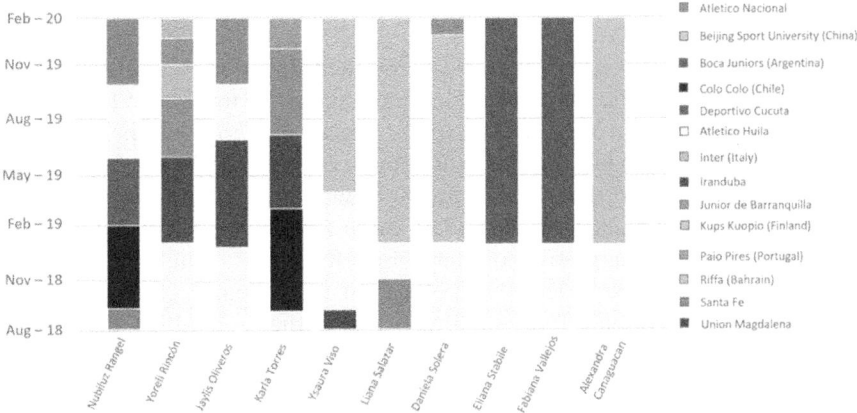

Figure 3.2   Indicative examples of player movement during fieldwork period

South American women players have moved in the last two or three years.[6] The less obvious moves were those of penalty shoot-out hero, goalkeeper Daniela Solera, who left to try her luck in Finland; and Liana Salazar and Ysaura Viso, who both moved to China. Eliana Stabile and Fabiana Vallejos returned to their native Argentina in order to continue playing competitive football. Clearly, with a World Cup approaching for the latter two players, months upon months without playing any competitive games made no sense and thus uprooting and moving away once again was the only option – in this case softened by going back 'home', at least. The way in which players engineer a full season of action by moving around is symptomatic of the structural problems and the lack of calendar synchronicity for women's football. Figure 3.2 sets out an indicative but not exhaustive list of some of the Huila players' movements during the period of my fieldwork (August 2018 to February 2020).

Within Colombia, it is notable how many of the Huila players are from either Antioquia or Valle del Cauca, and have been through the Formas Íntimas club in Medellín or the Carlos Sarmiento Lora school in Cali. The dominance of these amateur endeavours in the production of successful young footballers demonstrates the dearth of opportunities for young female sportspeople elsewhere in the country.

6 This mirrors the historical tendency for South American male players to move to Spain and Portugal, and to a lesser extent Italy, for practical and cultural reasons.

The real picture

This lack of opportunities clearly has a marked socio-economic dimension. Spending time with the players enabled me to come to understand the extent of over-representation of whiteness in the media and institutions. Within a neoliberal polity there is a marked tendency to emphasise players perceived to be more marketable to the national image of white *mestizaje* being promoted. As mentioned earlier, ex-FIFA president Sepp Blatter was keen to follow this type of promotion, suggesting tighter shorts for players might attract more (sexual) interest. More broadly in the case of Colombia, both Álvaro Uribe and Juan Manuel Santos have sought to brand the Colombian nation as a product to be sold internationally. This market logic is often discernible in attempts to promote women's football. On many occasions this branding has had markedly gendered layers to it. For example, it has been argued that Colombian beauty queens have been presented as natural national resources and as an antidote to the dated but hypermasculinised Pablo Escobar narrative (De La Torre, 2013). This gendered exportation of the country has spilled over into areas beyond the beauty contest, a wide array of other spheres promoting a neoliberal Colombia. I was in Colombia when the 2005 *Colombia es pasión* campaign began. This campaign was symptomatic of the ways in which a mixed nation is almost always presented in terms of a 'very whitened *mestizo*' (Wade, 2012, p. 38). More recently this type of branding has become all the more obvious with the increased usage of promotion on digital media. When the launch of the women's professional league is placed in this context it does not seem strange at all that from the beginning DIMAYOR has tried to present the league as something qualitatively different from men's football. Much of its publicity has tended to emphasise the whiter, idealised type of *mestizo* Colombian referred to by Wade – meaning more commercial opportunities for such players.

On the other hand, all the structural disadvantages women's football has are exacerbated by the very same logic that saw the 'pioneering' professional women's league introduced – one of conformation to a marketised vision of modernity.

On the training ground one of the more gregarious and considerate characters is Jennifer Peñaloza. Peñaloza was always ready to lend me some high-strength insect repellent and warned me several times that I would be eaten alive by mosquitoes if I didn't use copious quantities of it. 'The mosquitoes like *gringo* blood,' she joked to the rest, to uproarious laughter. She's another likable character and a fierce and determined player on the pitch. A constant across all the clubs I visited is the presence of players who have had difficult upbringings. As in the men's game, the demographic who play women's football is tilted heavily towards those from poorer backgrounds. All of the heroines in women's football could be said to be unsung – but there can be few for whom this is more true than Jennifer Peñaloza. She played in the inaugural Copa Libertadores in 2009 and has returned to contest it three more times, including a semi-final and a final for Formas Íntimas and latterly as a champion with Atlético Huila. Despite passing under the radar in ways that betray the heteronormative, racialised preferences of Colombian society, she is a player who was never going to be overlooked on footballing merit when the technical staff at Huila began putting together a team capable of challenging firstly for the Colombian title and later for continental honours.

The backstory of the player is symptomatic of the ills of Colombia's development model, which has ingrained structural inequalities and left the poorest sectors of society to struggle. Peñaloza grew up in the Belén *barrio* of Medellín. She was actively discouraged from playing football by her father, who was vehemently opposed to her playing. Nonetheless, with the support of her mother and her brother she began forging a career as a footballer. Her brother would watch her play and see her establish herself with Formas Íntimas. Formas Íntimas were the most important club in Colombian women's football prior to DIMAYOR's professionalisation. Many of the players who represented Colombia at the 2011 and 2015 Women's World Cups were developed by this amateur club, playing in the national team alongside a more privileged, whiter contingent who were based in North America. Peñaloza has thrived in Colombian club football but has been consistently overlooked by the national team. During the third occasion that Peñaloza participated in the Copa Libertadores, in Brazil, she received a call from Medellín and learned that her brother had died of an overdose. He had been suffering long-term depression and had taken his own life by swallowing 80 tablets prescribed for his mother's heart condition. Peñaloza immediately returned home from the tournament and, as a result, also sank into a depression and a cycle of drinking. She describes this period as the most difficult in her life and readily admits that she will never entirely get over the experience.

It is clear that Atlético Huila has given Peñaloza a new lease of life. Having come so close to the continental championship with Formas Íntimas, and having experienced personal tragedy during the tournament, there is no moment more cathartic than winning the Copa Libertadores with Huila. I asked her if she felt she had proved a point to anyone – to the managers of the national team, to those who run the league or whoever it might be. Peñaloza shrugs with genuine indifference. The meaning of the championship is profound to her: profoundly personal. As for those so removed from the struggle that has been her life, in her words 'no tengo que mostrar nada a nadie' [I don't have to prove anything to anyone]. Their reality and hers are like night and day.

When asked about who she looks up to we stumble upon the question of her own nickname – La Cuadradita. The nickname references national team midfielder Juan Cuadrado as a point of comparison. Peñaloza is clearly delighted at the comparison. She expresses how grateful she was to receive a congratulatory video from him and says that she would love to, one day, share a pitch with him. This implies that Peñaloza, like many players across the continent who I surveyed, is not entirely averse to the idea of mixed gender games. It is worth noting the relentless need to compare players with male counterparts, thus turning the attention back to male players and trivialising female agency. The same tendency is present in referring to Marta as 'Pelé in a skirt' or in numerous other comparisons to male players (Moreira, 2014). Similarly, the use of a diminutive can be seen to belittle the female player in comparison. I realise immediately, however, that in Peñaloza's mind these considerations are trumped by something far greater – a sense of having gone through the same rites of passage while emerging from the Colombian underclass. Peñaloza identifies significantly with the travails Cuadrado went through on the way to becoming one of Colombia's leading footballers.

There is a certainly a deeper reason for Peñaloza's affinity for Cuadrado, who had a similarly difficult upbringing to hers. Both were born in the state of Antioquia, a region of Colombia shaped by particularly marked social inequalities. While Peñaloza grew up in an underprivileged sector of Medellín's urban sprawl, Cuadrado grew up in a small village called Necoclí. His youth was marked by the familiar sounds of shoot-outs between narco-traffickers and paramilitary groups. Cuadrado would habitually hide under his bed when he heard the sounds of gunfire. One day, when he was only 4, Cuadrado hid, following the instructions of his parents, as a gunfight brewed up outside. His father, a truck driver delivering soft drinks, was caught in the crossfire and died of his injuries. Without his father, Cuadrado grew up very close to his mother. Peñaloza (or La Cuadradita as she would prefer it) also grew up extremely close to her mother, for the health reasons described earlier. Nonetheless, the example of Cuadrado certainly inspires her. She sees in his story the possibilities that football offers to turn a rigged social order on its head: the opportunity for those from the poorest *barrios* to be idolised and to be known across the country. The visible and invisible barriers that have meant that these possibilities for social mobility are significantly gendered are slowly being dislodged by footballers like La Cuadradita. Peñaloza clearly identifies shared class and race obstacles like those overcome by Cuadrado. These are areas where common ground can often be found between male and female players.

The story of Levis Ramos combines the deep social inequality experienced by Peñaloza with a further difficulty in accessing places to play, given the complete lack of women's football provision in the area where she grew up. Ramos is one of the few players who have come from the Caribbean coast, where the infrastructure for women's football appears most threadbare, perhaps because this is where there is most resistance to women competing (Llanos & Accorsi, 2002). She had a difficult childhood in Cartagena and was separated from her mother at the age of just 12. Around this time, despite significant social alienation, Ramos began playing football with male players. She never felt at risk playing with male players. The only significant barrier was the social pressure not to participate – they frequently told her that she should not be playing alongside them even though she always held her own.

All of this meant that Ramos' route into professional football was beset with difficulties from the beginning. To make it even more complicated, she had a child when she was still a teenager, who she was left to bring up alone. Owing to the lack of opportunities in her region Ramos had to re-locate, with all the adaptation issues this brings, in order to continue playing. She recalls vividly that just to be able to afford the ticket to Bucaramanga, where she had the opportunity to play, she had to 'pedir limosna' [ask for charity]. Nonetheless, she does not regret this move and considers it the moment when her football career really started. She goes so far as to say that without leaving Cartagena she would never have become a professional footballer. At the time I carried out my fieldwork Ramos was located in Huila with the team, while her son continued living with family in Cartagena, more than 20 hours away by road, until he could finish secondary schooling. This, once again, underlined to me the level of sacrifice being made by women players.

Sudden departures – 'thanks for everything'

The atmosphere on the team bus is jovial – it's now late April and the Colombian women's season has been confirmed to begin in the next few weeks – exact date as yet unknown, but at least it will definitely be happening, according to a new announcement from DIMAYOR. A mix of salsa and reggaeton blare out of a beatbox belonging to Nelly Córdoba and players frequently get up from their seats to dance provocatively to hoots of laughter from the rest of the team. Other players are more withdrawn, burying their heads in their mobile phones or covering their heads with a tracksuit top and attempting to sleep. The journey to the training camp some 30 kilometres from Neiva is usually fairly raucous, whereas on the journey home after training almost everyone either nods off or zones out exhausted. There is still joking on the way home, but the edge is a bit more blunted and less in-your-face.

Suddenly, the usual light-hearted atmosphere seems to disappear. The quasi-carnival spirit is replaced by a decidedly sombre one. Players look downcast and even bitter. There is conversation aplenty but it has taken on a suddenly serious tone. Whatever has happened, I realise that I am among the last, if not the last, to find out. In Colombian vernacular 'me quedé gringo' [I was behind the door or slow]. When a convenient moment eventually presents itself I ask Vanessa Díaz, who brings me up to date. She is clearly irritated and insulted by the way the club has handled things. It transpires that news reached the players by text message that the club has ended the contracts of three of their most experienced players – Carmen Rodallega, Jennifer Peñaloza and Darnelly Quintero – with immediate effect and thus today, 25 April 2019, will be their final session.[7] The three understandably decide

7 Rodallega is one of Colombia's most capped female players, Peñaloza played a pioneering role with Formas Íntimas and Quintero was part of the Copa Libertadores squad in Manaus.

it would be pointless to go through the motions of the training session now they are suddenly unemployed. At this point, a peculiar scene of awkward, impromptu goodbyes takes place and each of the players hug one another. They say goodbye to 20-year-old Jorelyn Carabali, who Quintero describes as 'la hija' [my daughter]. There is a due sense of sadness at losing three players so crucial to the national and Libertadores triumphs, with so little fanfare but also with a sense that the team have been here before. The players are beyond angry and the news takes the wind from their sails for the rest of the day's session and the rest of the week. I am speechless at the level of disrespect, given that these players are the first continental champions in Colombia's history. I can only surmise that those involved in the decision do not value the work and the effort the players have given. It appears, again, I am just about the only person surprised.

At this point, an unreal and absurd reversal of what I feel the roles should be occurs. Rather than my offering any words of consolation to the players I had shared so much time with, one of them – Carmen Rodallega – comes over and reassures *me* not to worry as this is not a problem. This happens all the time and they always find a new club, she says. Nonetheless, there is clearly a lingering feeling that something is not right here. The players know they have proved themselves to be the best in their country and have just won the continental title. Moreover, they continue to want to believe that this is a football league that offers professional conditions which will aid the players' development.

The club's callous goodbye to its continental champions is in tune with the disregard they receive from the Colombian state. Following recent sporting successes, the Cruz de Boyacá has been awarded to each of Colombia's ten medal winners from the London Olympics and Paralympics.[8] Two coaches of the Colombian national men's football team (Francisco Maturana and José Pekerman respectively) have received the Order de Boyacá merely for reaching the last 8 of the World Cup. Similarly, name players like James Rodriguez and Radamel Falcao have also received awards although their achievements in the Colombian national team shirt seem comparable to those of their structurally disadvantaged female counterparts.[9] Outside the sporting arena Tony Blair, Joe Biden and King Felipe VI of Spain have also all received the Order de Boyacá. The Order has yet to recognise a Colombian female footballer. Instead of recognition for bringing home the continental championship the Atlético Huila women face the annual doubts about the continuation of the short women's league (always couched in economic terms) and the consequent lack of commitment from Colombian clubs. Carmen Rodallega, Jennifer Peñaloza and Darnelly Quintero are all departing with

---

8 These were Mariana Pajón, Caterine Ibargüen, Oscar Figueroa, Rigoberto Urán, Jackeline Rentería, Carlos Oquendo, Yuri Alvear and Óscar Muñoz at the Olympics and Moisés Fuentes and Elkin Serna at the Paralympics.

9 The Colombian women's team recently emulated this achievement at the 2023 World Cup falling 2–1 at the quarter final stage to losing finalists England.

a bitter taste in their mouths, just months after the glory of Manaus. Their departure leaves Huila with just nine remaining players training – there will be a lot of close control practice using just a third of the pitch, I think to myself. From a self-centred perspective, I was disappointed because I had planned to interview all three players, but this appears a trivial concern and an unlikely prospect now. Much to my surprise, however, bearing in mind what has just happened, Peñaloza and Rodallega both again take the time to tell me they haven't forgotten I wanted to interview them and invite me to their house in the days before they leave.

Communal living and adaptation

I arrive in Los Cámbulos, a working-class *barrio* in Neiva close to the airport, in search of the players' house. Rodallega spots me from a distance and shouts me over. I thought that just Rodallega, and maybe her daughter Maria (who is also a footballer, aged 17), would be there. I learn that Maria Rodallega is in Cali with family undergoing trials to play for Deportivo Cali women. Meanwhile, Carmen Rodallega, one of Colombia's most capped women players, is temporarily residing in communal digs, sharing with enough players to make a very competitive six-a-side team.[10]

In order to economise and for the benefits of company away from home, I learnt that many of the players live together. Clearly the precarity of working outside most players' home cities, on contracts that only cover one-quarter to one-third of the year, means the players have to make do with conditions that are far from ideal. In one sense, there is an excellent sense of *camaraderie* between the players, but in another this is clearly not propitious to dealing with the multiple adaptation problems that come with living away from home. Sometimes this is the player's first experience away from home, as in the case of goalkeeper Paola Rincón, who was just 18 while I was in Neiva. At the other end of the scale, Rodallega is the most senior member of the club at 35 years old, and as of September 2020 is Colombia's most capped female player. Her age never shows on the training ground – she still moves at the speed of a player ten years younger and retains a remarkable level of stamina. Rodallega is admired by the other players on and off the pitch and commands their full respect. Moreover, her experience provides an excellent conduit between the male coaches and some of the younger players. The experience of communal living is another sacrifice even senior players make in pursuing a career as a professional footballer. Finding short-term accommodation is often left to the players – and it often falls upon senior players to make the arrangements, once again working in a surrogate role in the absence of proper provision from the clubs and football institutions.

---

10 This type of accommodation arrangement is common, with the clubs often arranging communal accommodation for players. This same practice contributed to the rapid spread of COVID-19 in March 2020 at Manaus club 3B.

Down to the bare bones

After these three players were 'let go', whenever I turned up to team events there would be much laughter about the form training could take with just nine players. One jokes that they could play 4.5 players a side. 'What do you think we will be practising today?' another asks. 'I would guess we'll be practising *espácio reducido* (reduced space exercises) in a third of the field,' another replies with a knowing look. Clearly, when later they are expected to put on a 'professional' spectacle this kind of disadvantage is not going to help. Close control in small areas of the field may improve but many elements of a full-size game are clearly lost.

Indeed, there is a sense within the group that the champions have now been effectively disbanded, and that when the new season begins it will be an entirely new start. Two of the nine now remaining are first-year professionals (Daniela Narváez and Anyi Bonilla) and one of the group is Jorelyn Carabali, who is returning from a long injury. At this point, another practice match is announced, against the men's team the Huila women so convincingly defeated just a few weeks before, when I first arrived. This time the men's team look notably older – perhaps eight to ten years older – yet when I ask how old they are I am told, once again rather implausibly, that they are an under-16 team. The men's team clearly were scolded after the first game and have regrouped, recruiting numerous new, older and more physical players. The arrogance from the first game is long gone, and this time it is all about winning. The men's team win the game this time, with more than a few dubious challenges that escape sanction in the absence of a qualified referee. I quickly lose interest and spend my time talking to some of the coaching team about what is to come. The coaches promise me there are some big-name players on the way.

True to their word, just days later a raft of new signings are announced. Using Diego Perdomo's contacts the club brings in a number of current national team players as of April 2019. The number of players coming in seems to be a statement to the rest of the league. Another possible explanation is that by continually moving the players on after short periods, there is less chance of the team having time to build a bond sufficient to allow them to collectively organise around the areas where they clearly face discrimination. Any notion of defending champions Huila having any advantage owing to stability in holding together the previous year's squad is certainly misguided. Five Colombians arrive – Manuela Gonzalez, Marcela Restrepo, Carolina Arias, Lizeth Ocampo and Kenia Romero – together with two Venezuelans who have played together briefly in Brazil – Cinthia Zarabia and Lisbeth Castro. A Puerto Rican – Delyaliz Rosario – returns for a second brief spell. Some clearly know each other from their national teams. Whatever the rationale behind the dramatic wholesale changes, so close to a tournament starting, immediately there is an entirely different atmosphere in training. My departure ends up coinciding with the onset of the new women's season which has just been confirmed. The club has once again brought in a number of players with international pedigree and is ready to appear in a tournament that will be promoted explicitly as being the 'Liga Professional Femenina' once again. On the positive side, the players' larking around, uncontrollable laughter and joking returns, and the sombre faces and existential doubts disappear again for a short while. It reminds me once more that all they want is to have a competitive team that can train properly, play the game they love and compete for the highest honours in their chosen field.

Conclusion

This chapter has examined the considerable gulf between the professionalisation of women's football claimed by the Colombian federation DIMAYOR and the lived reality of intersectional discrimination faced on the ground by Colombian women players. Many of the players have faced significant hardships in pursuing a career in football, which are intertwined with racial and class cleavages respectively. Nonetheless, it has been the players themselves who, with determination, resilience and sacrifice, have created and maintained the façade of professionalisation by continuing to perform admirably in national and international competition. Nonetheless, the potential to move the women's game in Colombia on to a new level can only be realised with greater economic support brought about by institutional change at the local and national level. This in turn would trigger further positive media involvement, something that is already occurring sporadically and arbitrarily at a few clubs – as with the exemplary work of Vanessa Díaz as head of media for the women's team at Huila.

Spending time with players it was clear that the role of inter-gender football, both in producing players at youth level and in the everyday training practices of teams, is an aspect that is treated as invisible by largely male-controlled media and institutions. It remains an unacknowledged factor because the implications of admitting its use would clearly destabilise the matrix of male hegemony. Furthermore, the importance of informal street football and/or football played at schools and universities, which emerges from the life histories of these players, serves once again to expose the lack of work done by federations in producing the players of this generation.

It is worth remembering that the panorama at Atlético Huila, as at Santos in Brazil (see Chapter Four), represents the best contractual arrangements available to women players (year-round contracts in most cases) rather than, as this chapter may have suggested to the uninitiated, the worst. That is why players are attracted to leave families behind in order to live and play in Neiva. In spite of this, women players still have to lead an impossible double life, for example trying to keep up with the rigours of university life whilst carrying out intensive physical training each year. Moreover, the level of commitment from Atlético Huila as an institution was negligible, with the club's success dependent upon one outside benefactor, and perhaps even more than this, upon the undervalued sacrifices of players themselves, and especially the experienced players whose contribution is much more than just playing the game.

Epilogue – success moves to Santa Fe

Subsequent to my fieldwork with Huila, in June 2020 Diego Perdomo left the club after a disagreement with the directors, and has since funded the Santa Fe of Bogotá women's team. This meant that Santa Fe could be one of only three clubs who were able (or willing) to continue paying their women's team during the COVID pandemic. Furthermore, it meant that the nucleus of the Huila squad moved to Bogotá with Perdomo, meaning Santa Fe benefited not only from a number of players of international calibre but also from the stability of players knowing one another on and off the pitch. Indeed, even the coaching staff from Huila largely made the move to Bogotá to join Perdomo's new venture.

The 2020 tournament was played entirely behind closed doors owing to the COVID pandemic, rendering many of the questions about how best to promote and attract an audience to women's football temporarily redundant. Even with Colombian football in a deep financial crisis, women's football continues to be played as the federation and league bodies realise how unpalatable it would be to their international reputation were they to renege on their commitment to the women's league at this stage. This commitment is not matched at a local level, where Atlético Huila and other clubs such as Cúcuta, Cortoluá and Deportes Tolima have decided to discontinue women's football indefinitely. The national league has a responsibility to comply with FIFA policies to grow women's football together. Moreover, its ideological commitment to presenting Colombia in a modern progressive light runs into clear tensions with what is happening on the ground – a continuation of amateurism presented as professionalism, precarity and the utmost disrespect for women footballers.

Following the Women's Professional League in 2020, a short eight-team event organised by the Colombian Ministry of Sport took place. A team representing the municipality of Huila, made up of largely amateur players who had never previously been involved with Atlético Huila, won the tournament wearing Atlético Huila official shirts despite the club having no input whatsoever into the venture. What happened at Atlético Huila was testament to the deeply embedded *machista* meanings attached to football within Colombia (and beyond). Arguably, however, the abrupt disbanding of a team who had recently been crowned as continental champions was only possible because of the relative size and importance to national identity of Atlético Huila compared to the team which follows in Chapter Four. Santos FC is one of Brazil's largest clubs. Moreover, it is quite possible that it is internationally better known than other Brazilian clubs wielding larger budgets and/or with bigger fanbases, on account of having been the club of Pelé. As the following chapter suggests, this profile is a double-edged sword for women's football: on one hand, it ensures that women's football could not be simply closed as easily as it was at Huila; on the other, the perceived hegemonic masculinity attached to the game's identity means that women's football is always treated as a secondary concern, a mere sub-division of the perceived 'true' identity of a football club.

CHAPTER FOUR

Mermaids in the Land of the King

Introduction

As I walk towards the Santos FC training ground I see several murals commemorating the rich tradition of the club and its importance in establishing Brazil as the country of football (Helal et al., 2001; Bocketti, 2016; Goldblatt, 2014; Kittleson, 2014). I am particularly taken with a quote from the great Brazilian poet Carlos Drummond de Andrade which says 'o difícil, o extraordinário, não é fazer mil gols, como Pelé. É fazer um gol como Pelé' [the most difficult thing is not to reach a thousand goals as Pelé did, but rather to score just one with the style of Pelé]. With Pelé unambiguously on a pedestal above all mere mortals, I wonder: what space is there for women to dislodge such mythology and establish themselves within the discursive tradition of these clubs? The question of how women's contributions to Brazilian club football can be recognised and incorporated into such hypermasculinised club discourses and traditions has been neglected thus far. Santos FC is an ideal case study insofar as it has both a significant but undervalued history of women's football and, owing to the Pelé era (see Figure 4.1), international recognition as an emblematic club in the country of football, which arguably exceeds that of other Brazilian clubs.

As I finally negotiate my way past security I am greeted by my contact: general manager (for women's football) Alessandro Pinto. He introduces me to some of the players who have arrived early for training. I meet Erikinha, Sandrinha and Kelly Rodrigues briefly as they warm up ready for training.[1] Just before the session begins, I also glimpse Rosana dos Santos Augusto. I momentarily feel slightly starstruck to see a player who has contested World and Olympic finals. With none of the reticence and apprehension of the other players she greets me in confident English and immediately enquires as to what exactly I am doing here. Rosana quickly disappears with the air of

---

1 Erikinha, Sandrinha and Kelly Rodrigues are three of the mainstays of the women's team. Each participated in the first Copa Libertadores Feminina in 2009. The tournament was held in Santos and Santos won it unbeaten.

Figure 4.1   Mural commemorating Pelé

someone not given to wasting time. I notice other faces I recognise – Maurine, a player with a similar international pedigree; and Ketlen who, despite little fanfare, has recently become Santos Women's all-time leading scorer and the first player to score 100 goals for them. This underplayed achievement reminds me that whilst it is well documented that the Santos of Pelé were the first Brazilian club to win the continental title (in 1962 and 1963), it is less well known that the Santos of Marta was the first Brazilian club to win the women's equivalent in 2009 and 2010 (Rial, 2013a).[2]

The identity of Santos the city is bound up with that of Santos FC. For that very reason, the discursive significance of Santos in the emergence of Brazil's gendered footballing identity makes it a particularly attractive case study. Indeed, beyond this, the way in which football dramatises wider cultural shifts (Da Matta, 1982, p. 40) is exemplified by Santos. The city experienced its formative boom years between 1820 and 1880 as a coffee port. At this point over half of the population were black slaves (Read, 2012). Without their labour it is inconceivable that Santos would ever have come to be Latin America's largest and most modern port (De Mello, 2008) and, by extension, without their labour Santos FC as one of the country's prestigious *clubes de camisa* would probably never have come into existence. In one sense, it took the generation of Pelé to finally invert the cultural stereotypes left behind by this legacy. For example, as late as 1950 black players were scapegoated for the country's losing the 1950 World Cup to Uruguay (Skidmore, 1974; Filho, 2003; Buarque de Hollanda, 2014).

Whilst racism and slavery are an ongoing struggle with no final victory in sight, football can certainly be said to have provided an arena in which

2 Marta Vieira da Silva is the only player to win the FIFA World Player of the Year award six times.

their residue can be contested. It seems conceivable that similar gradual shifts in the way Brazilians understand gender can be discerned via the optic of a deeply masculinised part of its sporting identity. Vibrant movements like #NiUnaMenos and #MeToo foreground clamours to re-define the gender order in more equitable terms (Elsey, 2018). This chapter examines the embeddedness of male hegemony within a large club and consequently considers how gender stereotypes are contested and reproduced. It is based upon three months of ethnographic fieldwork spent with Santos between October 2018 and February 2019 and presents several vignettes capturing episodes symptomatic of the strength of the masculinised invented tradition of the club and places them in tension with the everyday experiences of players. It differentiates between how, on the pitch and the training ground, the players, by definition, are sometimes able to challenge hegemonic representations by emphasising their athletic performance. This struggle continues off the pitch where players are still deployed to promote a gendered vision in keeping with the club hierarchy's sexualised branding of the club as Sereias da Vila. These narratives are challenged by players' own agency and by a burgeoning alternative media exemplified by Dibradoras, as covered in the Conclusion to this book.

The land of the king (King Pelé Training Facility)

Nearing the conclusion of the session at the King Pelé training ground (CT Rei Pelé in Portuguese) an animated discussion between back-room staff takes place, with players clearly within earshot. A congested and disjointed end to regional, national and continental competitions awaits. In just one week, the team will face Corinthians in an evenly balanced, two-legged final of the Paulista Championship 2018. With barely time to draw breath, Sereias da Vila then travel almost 4,000 kilometres to Manaus for the Copa Libertadores tournament in November 2018.[3]

Watching the hi-tech training session here, it is clear the infrastructure is on a different level to the other clubs I have visited. I am told the facilities match any available elsewhere in Brazil, and probably across the entire continent. Whilst a variety of cutting-edge training techniques are deployed, a number of drones fly disconcertingly above our heads, assisting the computerised devices attached to each player to monitor their individual daily performance across a range of metrics. The pristine surface of Santos' training pitch befits an ensemble of top-level professional women footballers, many of whom have accrued a range of experience nationally and in many cases beyond. The King Pelé Training Ground has three official full-size pitches. The first is the smallest, used largely for youth matches, with space for up to 5,000 spectators. The second intentionally has the same dimensions

---

3 Santos Women had won the Brazilian championship in 2017 to earn the privilege of representing Brazil at the continental tournament.

as the Vila Belmiro (Santos' stadium) while the third matches the size of
the municipal Morumbi in São Paulo. The impressive facility even includes
a five-star hotel at which the Santos (men's) first team often stay before
big games, and a sizeable, purpose-built space where journalists are able to
conduct interviews and press conferences with the players in a professional
environment. Beyond the training facilities, way in the distance is a steep
incline scattered with precarious tenement-style houses stacked one on top of
another. The view from the comfortable confines of a complex guarded by
numerous security staff typifies the stark social divide that characterises the
country and, in various and often unacknowledged ways, is foregrounded in
many of its social interactions.

An escalation in the initially good-humoured discussion diverts my
attention back to the issue at hand. Team manager Emily Lima and some
of the players appear somewhat irate. It appears that after just three days
training on the impeccable surface at the CT Rei Pelé, the women are being
moved on to make way for the usual custodians of the King's quarters –
Santos FC (men). I confirm I heard correctly whilst endeavouring not to
look too obviously aghast or surprised. With the quality of the facilities and
the number of pitches available there seems no rational reason why both the
men and the women could not train here simultaneously or, if necessary, be
scheduled at different times of the day. Nonetheless, the prevailing power
relations here seem still to not only negate this possibility but render the
suggestion of outright equality unconscionable. Football remains an area so
eminently masculine that this type of gender differentiation is often hidden
in plain sight, not even acknowledged by those perpetrating it, although
they surely know. The return to a status quo in which the women's team are
sub-categorised at the same level as children within the club is symptomatic
of this.

The land of the kids (Meninos da Vila Training Facility)

For the time being, it would appear, Santos Women are being moved back to
where I am told they spend most of their time – CT Meninos da Vila (Vila
Belmiro Boys' Training Ground). Whilst some of the players clearly recognise
this as a demeaning affront that trivialises their hard-earned status as professional footballers, there is also a common-sense resignation underpinned by
the club's own insidiously patriarchal self-presentation and organisation. I
have heard plenty, in confidence, about these facilities. The grass tends to be
a few centimetres longer than that at the King's ground. They warned me
the surface was full of bobbles, causing unpredictable bounces by the ball
and, much worse, a higher likelihood of incurring injuries.

Upon arrival I realise immediately that, if anything, my informants had
understated the case. The facilities at Meninos da Vila are rustic at best and
certainly not befitting of professional athletes. The training pitch has the kind
of surface upon which technical training on cohesive zippy passing is out
of the question. This inevitably further stymies the development of players

who often started later and with less infrastructure and facilities available than their male counterparts in the first place. Many of the players' touch appears a little more erratic than when they were training at the King's training ground. The exceptional players are still able to pull off the difficult touches – Maurine manages a perfect lob over the keeper at pace and then nonchalantly wheels away as if nothing happened. She tells me later, in an interview, that, like so many of her generation, she grew up playing alongside boys on far worse surfaces in her native Rio Grande do Sul.

Emily Lima, noting my downcast countenance, is quick to do what comes naturally to her every day in her job. She turns a negative into a challenge or into something that would have some value in the longer term. She tells me it is a good thing that I will see the full reality of Santos FC and not a falsely tamed experience designed to impress a visitor. Lima, I realise early on, is intent on ensuring that just this happens and she is always forthright and sincere about the things the club does right and those which she would change tomorrow, given the chance. The dissatisfaction with the situation at Santos owes much to knowing that it does not have to be this way at such a well-resourced club. These are political decisions made within the club and could be changed immediately were there sufficient political will to do so. The players play their part in keeping the club, regional and national hierarchies under pressure in numerous ways, but the final say still disproportionately rests with people distant from the reality I am witnessing. Despite undeniable strides made by women's football in recent years, in terms of priority at club level, professional grown woman players are placed on a par with boys as young as 11. I wonder what are the meanings and power relations that have naturalised and legitimised such obvious and violent gender differentiation? What are the players' lived experiences and impressions of this state of affairs? How have they contested it thus far, bringing us to the point we are at today?

At a quieter moment some weeks later Lima made an incisive passing remark that stayed with me. She noted that women's football is always seen as something additional, artificially grafted onto the deep-rooted tradition perceived and portrayed as all-important. My contention in this chapter takes note of this by exploring an unacknowledged tension at play – the way in which the agenda for equality is significantly encumbered by the rootedness of what I explain in the following section as 'banal patriarchy'. This tends to dilute any notion of outright equality into something far less radical and more akin to inclusion (Elsey & Nadel, 2019, p. 10).

Banal patriarchy

It struck me during my fieldwork that many of the deepest-rooted attitudes and practices at the club often manifest themselves in banal and often unperceived ways, akin to the concept of 'banal nationalism' elaborated by Michael Billig (1995): for example, the countless references to being bi-champions of the world on club merchandise and commemorated by

Figure 4.2   The façade of Santos' Estádio Urbano Caldeira, Vila Belmiro

two stars above the Santos club badge.[4] Billig's concept refers to everyday representations of national symbolism that contribute in often unacknowledged ways to buttress a shared sense of national belonging. This concept lends itself well to football fandom, which is also rooted in a perceived sense of collective identity. In this sense, this chapter registers less visible, everyday forms that are deeply ingrained and, in insidious ways, contribute more to upholding a gendered social order than more extreme or overt outbursts of sexism. Female participation in football, by definition, comes into tension with this patriarchy and in many cases, indeed, subverts it. Nonetheless the manifest power imbalances provoked by a lack of female representation in positions of power mean that banal patriarchy and the perceived masculine hegemony over club football can only be eroded gradually, particularly as much of the presence is often unacknowledged and unperceived.

The Santos FC invented tradition

To conceptualise the longevity the club discursively presents, Eric Hobsbawm's notion of invented traditions is also insightful in providing a further theoretical frame. It helps explain the selective omissions, inclusions and embellishments of the club's history. This discourse, clearly, is subject to analysis, contestation and re-shaping from a range of interested actors. As Hobsbawm (2012, p. 1) argues, 'traditions which appear or claim to be old are quite often recent

4 Similarly, for many years the Brazilian women's national team played with five stars above the club insignia, commemorating five men's World Cups. In the case of Santos' two 'World' championships, this in reality commemorates an intercontinental play-off that included only Europe.

in origin'. This is arguably the case with Santos FC. As of 2020 the club is 108 years old, having been founded in 1912 within hours of the sinking of the *Titanic*. Hobsbawm's conceptualisation of invented traditions incorporates 'traditions formally instituted within a brief and dateable period which establish themselves with great rapidity'. He continues to state that they are 'often of a ritual and symbolic nature, which seeks to inculcate certain values and norms of behaviour by repetition, automatically implying continuity with the past' (Hobsbawm, 2012, p. 2).

In this vein, much of the mythology dates back only as far as the period in which Pelé starred for the club, largely in the 1960s and 1970s, and not to a bygone era as club discourse would have us believe. This was concurrent and inter-related with the establishment of Brazil as the gold standard of men's football. Counting these friendlies, often against non-professional opposition in novelty matches, King Pelé scored over a thousand goals for Santos FC – a round figure often invoked to claim his superiority over other football legends (Goldblatt, 2014; Knijnik, 2018).

A section on the club website entitled 'muito além do futebol' [way beyond football] sets out a manifesto. The words constitute an attempt to express a creeping (corporate) social responsibility ethos in poetic form. The first verse begins as follows:

> Somos santistas, o time do Rei.
> Fabricamos sonhos e craques há mais de 100 anos.
> Com os pés no gramado, paramos uma guerra
> Com ousadia e alegria, globalizamos moicanos.
> [We are Santistas, the team of the king.
> We've made dreams and star players for more than 100 years.
> On the pitch we stopped a war
> With daring and happiness we globalise mohicans.]

The central discursive plank within Santos' tradition is always Pelé, as explained earlier. He is the player all others are measured against, be they the recent *moicano* Neymar referred to in the poem, or the Pelé in a skirt moniker used to trivialise Marta (Moreira, 2014). Moreover, this situates the tradition in a particular period (1956–74) that coincides with much of the mythology surrounding the national team and its *futebol arte* tradition (Knijnik, 2018, p. 28) but gives the lie to the longer tradition claimed in the manifesto. As Hobsbawm argues (2012, p. 2), the club tradition invokes attempts to 'structure parts of social life as unchanging and invariant'. That is to say, the figure of Pelé is used 'to legitimise a status or relations of authority' (Hobsbawm, 2012, p. 10) – in this case the elevated status of men in a hierarchical relationship that places women as a sub-category. Were there to be any serious political will to redress this, the club could do more to celebrate, as a counterpart, the most emblematic player in women's football history and her role in establishing Santos Women as a continental force. The poem then references the mythical day Pelé and cohorts temporarily halted the Biafran

War.[5] In defence of the poem, some gender awareness appears later when it names the fans as '*peixinhos*' and '*peixinhas*' (male and female fish), though this is only an acknowledgement of female fandom. This appears to delineate the limits of the acceptable incorporation of women into the club's mythology.

The obscured tradition – women's football at Santos FC

The previous section explained how the masculinised tradition at Santos FC is discursively rooted in a relatively short period whilst insinuating itself to have a far longer history (Hobsbawm, 2012). Similarly, the gendered tradition is accentuated by systematically obscuring the hidden history of women's football in Brazil, thus encouraging the misconception that the sport is something relatively new against a long tradition of men's football. A growing body of work recuperating the hidden history of women's football in Brazil (Franzini, 2005; Goellner, 2005b; Salvini & Marchi Júnior, 2013a) and elsewhere on the continent (Elsey & Nadel, 2019; Scharagrodsky & Peréz Riedel, 2022) emphasises these historical and structural injustices. Whilst part of the embellished tradition of the club is trying to elongate its glory period, realistically the main golden period of Santos, upon which its embellished tradition is based, occurred while women's football was prohibited and from 1964 onwards under military dictatorship.

Nevertheless, it does not take much digging below the surface to realise that Santos Women have accrued plenty of their own cultural capital which could easily be highlighted more if the political will existed within the club. Structural inequalities often mean that the club's significant women players spend less time with the club before flying the nest. Nonetheless, a significant step forward would surely be acknowledging the participation of women players and the significance of Santos in giving the Brazilian national team a base from which to build. From the team which reached Olympic and World Cup finals, Marta, Cristiane, Aline Pellegrino, Érika and Maurine gained valuable competitive and formative experience with Santos. This is to say, Santos could easily note the symmetry of having had arguably the best-known male and female player having played for them. Marta even achieved significant honours for the club forming part of the Santos squad that won the inaugural Copa Libertadores tournament.

Traditions, imagined or otherwise, accrue currency over a period of time. In 2020 it is abundantly clear that Santos FC is still imagined within the club as a masculine space to which, as Emily Lima suggests, the women's team is merely a precarious appendage. There are certainly precedents in the club's recent history that suggest Lima's analysis is not an opinion but a fact. In 2012, Santos Women were performing well on a national and continental

---

5 This myth of Santos stopping a war has been refuted in detail using sources from local newspapers and radio in Nigeria and beyond (Aiyegbayo, 2015).

Figure 4.3   The mermaid design, as used on the back of the Sereias da Vila shirt for 2018

level. They had won the 2009 and 2010 Copa Libertadores and finished third in the 2011 competition. They were reigning Paulista champions. The club's response to this success was to produce a raunchy calendar of the women's team, ostensibly to make the players 'more marketable' (Joras, 2015, p. 84) before proceeding to disband the team just three days after the calendar finished in 2012, coinciding with efforts to retain Neymar (Goldblatt, 2014; Knijnik, 2018). The commonly spun narrative around this is that the team was disbanded in order to fund Neymar's salary but, as Nicole Ramos pointed out to me, the salary of one male player could fund the entire female team. Seen from this angle, dispensing with one male player could have made the same contribution to retaining Neymar. It seems more likely that the decision to discontinue the female team at that point was an ideological rather than economic decision.

In spite of the club hierarchy consistently undervaluing women's football, it does have a particular pull at the Vila Belmiro, since the inaugural Women's Copa Libertadores was held in this stadium. The Santos women's team brushed aside rivals from across the continent, scoring 42 goals and only conceding 2 across only 6 games. Large local crowds flocked to these games as Marta, at that time, was the reigning world player of the year, with Cristiane also nominated in the top three in the world. It is lamentable that this accrued social capital is not celebrated more. It is symptomatic of the sub-categorisation of women's football and of the threat that having a second continent-conquering team poses to the deeply masculinised invented tradition of the club.

Each episode is coloured by the unacknowledged influence of the club's invented tradition. For example, even the club's own branding has sought to feminise the team as sirens or mermaids (see Figure 4.3), differentiating them from the hegemonic male version of the team. The gendering choice of

Sereias as the team name is telling. *Sereia* is defined in the dictionary as 'da mitologia nórdica, representado sob forma de metade peixe e metade mulher, ambos com cantos muito suaves que atraíam os navegantes para a praia ou para os rochedos, com o objetivo de matá-los; sirena' (Michaelis, 2020) or more figuratively as 'qualquer mulher muito atraente' [any very attractive woman] (Michaelis, 2020). In both definitions there is a clear focus on the physical appearance of women, so the choice of this symbol continues a long tradition of the objectification of women playing football (Bonfim, 2019).

Living and challenging the invented tradition

The following sections consider the players' experiences of women's football at Santos FC. They consider how the players' agency is gradually effecting changes, and also foreground the extent to which manifestations of banal patriarchy found within the club continue to throw up considerable obstacles. From their behaviour on the training ground to their involvement in formal and informal activism the players' presence consistently runs into tension with the invented tradition at Santos FC. This means the invented tradition is subject to constant (if gradual) modifications to take account of the presence of women players.

Women's Paulista Championship final

Upon my arrival, the team faced an important end of season challenge – the final of the 2018 Paulista Championship, predictably against Corinthians. The game typifies the vicious circle in which the women's game finds itself. There is definitely interest on the part of the public, but due to arcane federation rules the clubs are not allowed to charge entrance for nominally 'amateur' games. This typifies what young midfielder Karla Alves identifies as double standards between the male and female arms of Santos FC. She points out that many of the male clubs have large debts but 'a gente acha que são rentáveis' [people believe they are profitable]. She notes that the comparison of economic performance often made between the male and female teams is flawed from the beginning as the women's team is structurally straitjacketed by policies like this one. Nicole Ramos adds that

> com investimento a gente acredita que sim daría certo mas temos que brigar por nossos direitos. Sem brigar a gente não vai mudar' [with the right investment players believe women's football would work economically, but we have to fight for our rights. If we don't do this, they are not going to change.]

Anecdotally, when I spoke to some of the crowd that night, a good number said they would pay to attend the match and had been looking forward to it.

The players placed particular importance on this game, as it marks the end of an unwieldy tournament with two group stages, which were routinely dismissed as a 'phoney war'. Corinthians' and Santos' goal differences of +36 and +37, from a group of just seven teams, suggests two teams dominate the league and thus for most of the other teams there have been a lot of dead rubber games. The players complain consistently about this as they realise that the lack of truly competitive games is detrimental to their development. In this vein, Maurine, one of the leading figures in Brazilian women's football over the past two decades, notes that 'agora as jogadoras mostram menos debilidades básicas, mas igual a falta de balance competitivo ainda existe e causa problemas' [now the players make fewer basic errors, but still the lack of competitive balance is there and continues to cause problems]. The number of Brazilian clubs large enough to have a competitive women's team in the São Paulo region is certainly greater than two but, at the time I carried out my fieldwork, the dominance of Corinthians and Santos was a reflection of the lack of willingness among other large clubs in the region to open a competitive women's team.

The much-anticipated final was played over two games. The first was held at Santos' Vila Belmiro stadium and the decisive second leg at Parque São Jorge, part of the Corinthians training facilities. Both games were free to the public and attracted considerable crowds. The game in Santos attracted the larger crowd, 13,867 spectators.[6] This was a record for the Women's Paulista Championship. Players felt that this reflected improved efforts on the part of the club to publicise the game and the level of interest in equally balanced games. All over Santos in the week before the final there were posters and flags advertising the game.

During the half-time break, rather than concentrate on the game, some of the Santos substitutes are made to shoot numbered balls out into the crowd. Each number wins a prize. The prizes are tickets to a Santos men's game, a Santos men's shirt signed by the players, three visits to the King Pelé training ground, various club merchandise and then, almost as an afterthought, a signed Sereias da Vila shirt. Rather than taking the opportunity to promote solely the women's team at the Sereias game, the players are reminded once again that they are a sub-category of the club. It appears a small detail – perhaps going unnoticed by some fans – but the players' faces tell a story. Clearly, with the women's games legally obligated to be free, it is not possible to offer tickets for them as a prize. The occasion could have been used to celebrate a tournament that is much coveted by women players on the continent. Instead, this small detail concentrates on the tradition that fans are more familiar with a visit to the King's training ground and tickets to see the men play. The way the game is used as a sideshow with which to promote upcoming men's games detracts from the importance of the final. Nonetheless, Sereias da Vila would go on to win a joint-record fourth Paulista title, bringing them level with Juventus da Mooca and Ferroviária.

---

6 The Lei de Incentivo ao Esporte prevents clubs from charging for games in the Paulista Championship, as it attracts funding from a federal programme encouraging the practice of sports.

Sereias da Vila in the community and Recycled Lives

Like most Brazilian clubs Santos is involved in the community in which it operates. The following sub-section covers two initiatives – a visit to a non-governmental organisation called Recycled Lives and a project to promote girls playing football called Girls on the Pitch. Both in distinct ways are heavily gendered and both are telling of the way the women's team is imagined and cast by the Santos FC hierarchy. Early during my visit I was invited to accompany the players to an engagement with Vidas Recicladas (Recycled Lives). Vidas Recicladas takes in (often abandoned) street children for a period, and offers them wide-ranging psychological, emotional, social and economic support. Several women players were enlisted to visit a large home in the city of Santos, where interviews were carried out for television and photos taken for the press. Some players were more inclined than others to participate and say a few kind words. Others appeared a little overwhelmed by the experience. Most of the larger Brazilian clubs now have active Corporate Social Responsibility policies or are aware of the need for the club to undertake a social role within the communities in which they operate. From the players' perspective, visits like this are felt on a personal level particularly by players who have grown up in difficult circumstances.

Engaging in community work of this nature clearly has a function and gives something back to the community that makes Santos the large club it is. Nevertheless, I ask myself whether this particular activity is knowingly or unknowingly rooted in gendered thinking. Perhaps perceptions of traditional gender roles were taken into consideration when choosing to send the players to a home for orphaned children. Nevertheless, in the absence of sufficient exposure that highlights the women players as athletes, this type of work could be the only glimpse television viewers or newspaper readers see of the players – and thus inadvertently it could reinforce gender stereotypes rather than challenge them. In defence of the club, players were involved in a number of other events that were more directly related to their athletic performance and encouraged the notion of women as athletes.

Girls on the pitch (meninas en campo)

Clearly the problems regarding technical level go beyond the lack of major teams involved. The team's teen prodigy Angelina Costantino has become a regular at just 18. She points out how important it is to be able to develop technique from an early age. She was able to do this growing up, playing alongside male players, but there are scarcely any opportunities at all for young girls in Brazil. This feeds into the technical deficiencies identified.

In this vein, for example, I also attended an event where Santos FC signed a joint agreement with the University of São Paulo and the Girls on the Pitch project (Meninas en Campo) committing the club and its partners to help develop female players in the 11–17 age range.[7] Without doubt this positions Santos FC as a pioneer in offering provision for these age groups. Elsewhere, this type of initiative remains almost non-existent. This reminds me of several players' comments. Tayla, for example, casually explained she is the 'typical' example of a player who learnt her trade playing on the streets.

From one perspective I am clearly being shown a sanitised vision of Santos FC but from another it is clear that there is a progressive force that is pressing larger clubs like Santos into taking some of the steps necessary to grow youth team football for Brazilian girls. There is a possibility this type of initiative will have a snowball effect as competing clubs do not wish to allow Santos an easy propaganda victory. The instinct of clubs to compete and prevent their rivals from achieving something before they do may drive further positive action. In this regard, Santos were the first to get involved and were not cajoled or blackmailed into doing so. This reminds me that each club, even when they have an embellished tradition that systematically privileges masculinity, is influenced by progressive actors inside and outside who push quietly for this type of gradual progress. The project places emphasis on social formation as well as football, an aspect that has traditionally been much neglected during the growth periods in men's football. Beyond this, youth football is an area that is of fundamental importance given the backgrounds many of the players come from. A football career is relatively short and there are no guarantees of further employment after finishing as a player – particularly for women, who until recently have been systematically excluded from coaching roles in the game. Again, Santos uses the players to promote itself as a progressive institution. Carrying out work in the community is clearly a valid function, but nonetheless sending players to a children's home like Recycled Lives feels gendered and, more importantly, places the emphasis outside promoting the players' athletic performance – the area that truly undermines and/or destabilises male hegemony.

Undermining banal patriarchy

My time with the players on the training ground gave me the strongest indication of the plural realities of women's football, outside cliched representations. The remainder of this chapter considers how the players undermine the banal patriarchy the club presents. Through collective organisation and their everyday behaviour and athletic performance the players are gradually producing counternarratives that destabilise male hegemony.

Sereias on the training ground
Each morning on the training ground there is an atmosphere of joviality. These clear attempts to differentiate and present the women's team as

7 For more information see the website www.meninasemcampo.org.br.

qualitatively divergent from the men's team defend hegemonic masculinity (Connell, 2005). In the words of Butler (1990, p. 17), 'the cultural matrix through which gender identity has become intelligible requires that certain kinds of "identities" cannot "exist" – that is, those in which gender does not follow from sex and those in which the practices of desire do not "follow" from either sex or gender'. This explains the playing down of players' athletic performance. It explains why the club invites prize-winners to see the men train but not the women. In this vein, the following sub-sections of this chapter highlight how the everyday behaviour, self-image and aspirations of the players present a more heterogeneous picture of reality, breaking with cliched feminised narratives and thus, if given due attention, have the potential to de-stabilise dominant gender binaries.

From the outset, numerous players are larking around prior to the commencement of the training session. One of the players gleefully blasts a ball as hard as they can at the back of another player's head, to uproarious laughter. The lack of surprise suggests juvenile antics of this kind happen quite often. There are 34 players in an unwieldy Santos squad – a mix of highly established internationals who have plied their trade in other countries, players with a solid reputation within Brazil and hopefuls who aspire to break into the first team and make a career from the game. Many of these hopefuls have been uprooted from their home states to try their luck at Santos. There are clearly cliques within the group within which the more established exude self-confidence, while others know their future is far from guaranteed. Some of the veteran players take the time to help integrate the newer ones and offer them someone to confide in when things get difficult.

Whilst at the Copa Libertadores tournament in Manaus the players' training was based at the facilities of 3B. There we saw an atmosphere that was slightly different. The change of environment was a double-edged sword. The players each tried to feign the calm that is needed at a large tournament. Equally, the team genuinely enjoyed being away from home in a continental tournament. The players laughed and joked through the session. Notably, at the end they ambushed the club's press attaché Vitor Anjos. Four or five players grabbed him before taking out a razor and forcibly shaving off his moustache. Anjos struggled briefly, in between laughing, before realising he had little chance of breaking free, being overpowered by five or six players. A few minutes later he was left half-shaven, looking somewhat ridiculous. The players explained that this was an agreed penitence, part of a bet they had made with Anjos (and won). Anjos shook his head and tried to look surprised or upset. The players are prepared to stand up for themselves. This again seems to typify how distant the reality of the players is from the hyperfemi-nised club representations of the Sereias. Indeed, the everyday atmosphere with the players is more akin to the detailed description offered by Hunter Davies in his seminal text *The Glory Game* (1973), after spending a period of time with Tottenham Hotspur in the 1970s. The training ground performance is just that – a performance. It is not necessarily representative of how the players would ideally behave as individuals; however, it does represent the way they choose to present themselves on the training ground as a collective. They present themselves as tough, but with a sense of humour. In the case of some players, it is only when they are isolated in a different setting for interviews that they break with the matrix of behaviour expected on the training ground. Nonetheless, it is noteworthy that the tone for this expected behavioural pattern is set by the players themselves.

Nomadic sereias

One aspect of being Sereias da Vila that appeals to the players is that of being able to play at an emblematic stadium with an accumulated cultural capital in both men's and women's football. From interviews and participant observation it was clear the players have an affinity for the club's traditional stadium the Vila Belmiro – a compact, intimate ground where it is possible to feel the crowd close to the action, particularly when it is almost full, as it was for the Santos Women–Corinthians Women game. Maurine, in particular, recalls scoring the winning goal in the Copa Libertadores of 2010 at the Vila Belmiro. She recalls the stadium erupting as she scored from a final-minute free kick. Maurine does not say as much, but it is tacitly understood that such a goal would be famous had it been scored by a male player.

The affinity with the stadium is shared by Ketlen, Erikinha, Sandrinha and Kelly Rodrigues, who recall growing up watching Santos (men) on the terraces before also appearing in many of the women's team's greatest moments there. The chosen epithet Sereias da Vila, then, suggests the women's team are permanent residents at the Vila Belmiro stadium in Santos. Santos Women came into existence in 1997. They have played in several stadiums but following their triumph in the 2009 Women's Copa Libertadores, in which the final was held at the Vila Belmiro, they have become synonymous with the stadium.

The club's relationship with the Vila Belmiro is complex and for that reason it is worth contextualising. The stadium is the traditional home of Santos FC, having played host to a great many of the most significant games in both the male and the female teams' history. It is actually called the Estado Urbana Caldeira but is always known colloquially as the Vila Belmiro, after the Santos *barrio* in which it is situated. Playing in Santos takes on an extra dimension of meaning as Santos FC is the sole club representing the city. Rio has four major clubs, São Paulo has three and Porto Alegre and Belo Horizonte each have two. In those cities two or more clubs fight to symbolise their respective cities. In Santos the identity is not shared with any other club, and an identity based around Santos is of crucial importance to many Santos-born fans, who feel strong links to their home city.

On the other hand, in large part because the golden era of the club was in the 1960s, the club has national support with a particularly high number of supporters in São Paulo, probably greater in number than those at Santos. Against an increasingly commercialised backdrop in Brazilian football, where

Santos play their games has become a central dilemma *vis-à-vis* the future direction of the club. From the modernisers' perspective, the Vila Belmiro appears dilapidated compared to some of the stadiums built in Brazil for the 2014 World Cup. Moreover, it has a low capacity and fewer facilities than more recent stadiums and thus generates less income. This has led José Carlos Peres, as president of the club, to pursue avenues that are intended to modernise it and bring it into line with the managerialist tendencies of other clubs – most notably Palmeiras and Corinthians, who each have brand new stadiums close to strategic metro stations and public transport in São Paulo. In response to an ever more marketised environment, and on the pretext of catering to the club's sizeable São Paulo fanbase, Santos FC has moved various men's games to São Paulo's Estadio Pacaembu in an attempt to maximise revenue.[8] This has not always suited the manager of the (male or female) teams as it essentially means ceding home advantage to play in another city. In this way, the institution finds itself in a constant war between those who envision the club's future in economic terms, and those who are more interested in defending the tradition of the club, which largely lies in the Vila Belmiro. Tensions over the club's traditional home came to a head when President Peres exclaimed 'Vila Belmiro é um estádio puxadinho. Eu vou para a Vila Belmiro e fico angustiado. Não consigo mudar' [the Vila Belmiro is a dump. I go to the Vila Belmiro and feel uncomfortable. I can barely move.]

With this background in mind, allowing Sereias da Vila to use the Vila Belmiro for prolonged periods appears less an act of equality by the club, and more a symbol: allowing the women to use a stadium not considered to be fit for the male team. Indeed, over a period both teams have been moved around considerably, with the women also playing tournament games occasionally in the Pacaembu and even other venues like the stadium of Portuguesa Santista, the CT Rei Pelé training ground and further into the interior of São Paulo state. Emily Lima has been a constant critic of these arrangements, adding that the team have become accustomed to the quality and size of the Vila Belmiro pitch and arguing that it allows the team to play their passing game more effectively.

Later during my stay with Santos, which took place in two parts around travelling to Manaus to see the team play at the Copa Libertadores, the club brought in a well-known coach to revive the fortunes of the men's team: Jorge Sampaoli.[9] This change caused considerable friction with the women's team as one of Sampaoli's first acts was to insist upon only the men's team using the Vila Belmiro. Rather than intervene to ensure the women's team

8 The Estadio Pacaembu is an Art Deco stadium from the 1940s with a current capacity of 40,000.
9 Jorge Sampaoli has managed a range of major South American clubs in Ecuador, Argentina and Chile and has also won the Copa America with the Chilean national team.

were able to play at the club's stadium, President Peres claimed meekly that 'his hands were tied and that they had allowed Sampaoli his way as the *club* [my italics; read 'men's team'] desperately needed to win a trophy' (Cardoso, 2019a). Here it is tacitly understood that the priority and organising principle of the club is the men's team. The overarching aim is for the men's team to win trophies. Moreover, even the club president and ultimate authority claims to be unable to overturn the prioritisation of the men's team. This clear sub-categorisation of the women's team has meant a series of haphazard arrangements for the Sereias' games, making it difficult for the team to gain momentum or feel any sense of home advantage as they ended up travelling at least as much as the nominal away team.

Many of the players I spoke to were acutely aware of the double standards at play when considering the economic aspects of the game. Clearly, at large clubs like Santos the women's team is tied into a relationship of dependency where the money to fund women's clubs comes from the revenue of the men's club. Given the structural dependency and disadvantages, drawing any conclusions as to how popular women's football might be given the requisite support is problematic. Nonetheless, a commonly cited argument is the unsustainability of women's football. This transition from dealing with more overt social discrimination to seizing the pretext of market forces has been noted (Elsey & Nadel, 2019, p. 6). Indeed, when Sereias da Vila was closed in 2012 this very pretext was used. As an institution Santos FC, like all the other large Brazilian clubs, finds itself heavily indebted, stuck between two models that seem unsustainable: paying to be tenants at the Pacaembu or losing revenue at the Vila Belmiro.

The day-to-day struggles of players are certainly influenced by the wider political environment in Brazil. I get a strong hint as to one of the major barriers to tackling some of these instances of clear gender differentiation – the stigmatisation of so-called 'gender ideology' – within national political debate. Whilst talking to Karla Alves, one of Santos' young stars, she suggests that complaining about inequalities has become problematic and polarising in Brazil owing to the wider political malaise. Just a couple of weeks into my stay in Santos, Jair Bolsonaro comfortably won both rounds of the presidential election, which consolidated the country's lurch towards the right. The mere usage of the word 'gender' immediately triggers the visceral fears provoked by an unprecedented campaign of digital mudslinging.

The street football route to Sereinhas da Vila (youth teams)

The systematic privileging of male youth teams has only served to exacerbate deep inequalities of opportunity between male and female players. Conversely, the lack of official channels for girls to play football in Brazil has produced a generation of players who grew up playing street football rather than in any structured way. Santos and Brazil defender Tayla is just one of hundreds of players who have developed from street players into professionals. Tayla told me she began playing in the street at just 8 years old (younger than many girls in her country, according to official statistics discussed later in this section) and that she only began playing in a team officially at the age of 15. We can only speculate as to what the Marta generation might have achieved had they not faced a panorama of such stark institutional neglect and failure. Tayla, for example, has won contracts playing outside Brazil, and has made an excellent career from football in spite of, and not because of, the Brazilian institutions. Whilst the history of the prohibition of women's football during the dictatorship is now well known, policies that address its essential injustices have been gradual at best and in many cases non-existent. The perceived tradition, essentially male, has certainly continued at youth level, where opportunities have remained scarce for young girls.

There is a well-developed network of youth teams at any large male club with teams operating at under-11, under-13, under-15 and under-17 levels in most large clubs in the São Paulo region. The CONMEBOL *obrigatoriedade* policy stipulates that a (single) women's youth division must be in place but the devil is in the detail. It does not specify how professionalised or formalised this needs to be, nor the age group for which it must cater. Santos, in this regard, represents one of the more developed female youth teams in the country. This is a recent development. When I spoke to a number of players, they explained in a matter-of-fact way that their story was the 'same familiar story' that is true of so many other girls in Brazil. They grew up playing in the street as no formal outlets were available, and often until a certain age they grew up playing alongside boys. This is not to be confused with mixed gender games with proportionate numbers. This often meant being the only girl on a field of boys – with all the social stigma and immature bahaviour that comes with that.

Days later, on Sunday 21 October 2018, I head back to the CT Rei Pelé, this time to see a youth match between Santos FC Under-17 girls and a team from Guarulhos named Barcelona. The Santos girls' team are referred to as Sereinhas da Vila (Little Mermaids of the Vila Belmiro). Santos run out easy winners 9–0 (if my counting was correct – there was no scoreboard and no-one seemed sure or bothered). The general consensus seems to be that being part of the Santos youth ranks affords players a great opportunity to 'make it' professionally but that the problem with many of these games is a lack of competitive balance. There are approximately a hundred spectators, many of whom seem to be the families of the players. They all seem willing to chat. The general consensus appears to be that the under-17 Paulista girls' league could be vastly improved by limiting it to the four or five teams that are truly competitive. I checked back after the tournament to see that winners São Paulo had amassed a goal difference of +44 in eight group games. The *obrigatoriedade* policy, which came into force during my fieldwork in 2018, ought to force larger clubs to open at least one female youth division, which should result in an increase in standards and competitive balance. The Under-17 tournament is the only one involving professional teams in the state of São Paulo. The situation is generally worse in other states, rather than better. In this context, players are forced to dive in at the deep end, playing their first football in the 'professional' ranks of their respective clubs. Inevitably, this diminishes the quality of the spectacle, as players have not been through the entire cycle of development and thus do not reach their full potential, and in consequence it contributes to the sexist notion that lesser football ability is genetic or that women's football is of poor quality when the audience first glimpse female first-team games. Conversely, this bolsters male hegemony and acts as a justification for further de-funding of women's football, as it is deemed to be commercially unviable.

The lack of women's youth divisions is such that Natalia Pereira, a 9-year-old player in Santa Catarina province, attended trials and has been allowed to join the under-10 boys team there. A recent study shows the highest percentage of young Brazilian girls only begin playing sport between 11 and 14 years old, at which point their male counterparts have probably already played for several years in youth divisions of clubs or at least in school teams (Instituto Brasileiro de Geografia e Estatística, 2018).

Collective struggle on and off the pitch

Football, by its nature, offers varying levels of job stability dependent upon previous experience and accrued agency within the game. Goalkeeper and activist Thais Picarte is the first to admit that the conditions at Santos are superior to those at many other clubs in Brazil in this regard; however, she continues working tirelessly for players across the region. Picarte is a director for the FENAPF (National Federation of Professional Athletes) and is also the vice-president of SIAFMSP (the Union of Professional Athletes for São Paulo). Beyond this she is involved in the Guerreiras project. Guerreiras is an international movement aimed at fomenting gender equality and challenging discrimination by bringing together activists, academics and athletes (Aguiar et al., 2018).

In her work for FENAPF Picarte is engaged in the gradual struggle to professionalise Brazilian women's football. Despite rhetoric to the contrary, she is quick to underline how the Brazilian tournament, whilst improving, is still a long way from being a professional one. It allows amateur teams to compete, some of whom pay the players badly if at all. Picarte laments that only two teams – Santos and São Paulo – entirely register their players with the tax authorities, allowing them to accrue pension benefits and such like. Others tend to only register certain star players and then fill the rest of the squad with amateurs. This type of practice is clearly divisive and has the effect of diverting players from their common interest. Picarte is absolutely clear that the common interest must come first. She realises that whilst elite players can forge a more comfortable career outside Brazil, the great majority of Brazilian women players are subject to the conditions within the country. Picarte believes firmly that the debate in Brazil has moved on. She summarises that it is now much less about 'being a lesbian or not' and she argues that prejudice has taken refuge in the logic of the market. Contract terms have remained stagnant for two decades, she argues, with the justification always being the vicious circle that claims women's football does not generate sufficient income as it is never promoted enough to do so.

On the training ground there is appreciation of the type of work Picarte does, but also a barely disguised trepidation as to how such activism would be perceived were younger players to get involved. Similarly, players often cite the advances made by the Paulista tournament under the control of ex-Santos player Aline Pellegrino. Regarding union struggles, it is difficult to build the level of solidarity necessary with players, on one level, competing with one another for short, flexibilised contracts. Conversely, given the divisive contractual situation, the sense of solidarity between the players is all the more admirable. Many of the players know that they are ultimately playing a long game and that real change will come only with further representation from ex-women players and/or more allies on the boards of both federations and clubs.

Moving into coaching/formalising experience

From the first training sessions at the Rei Pelé one of the first players who looks out for me is Rosana dos Santos de Augusto. She has played alongside some of the best players in the United States, in Scandinavia and has won the European Champions League with the prestige women's club of European, if not world, football, Olympique Lyon. At international level she has played in a World and Olympic final for Brazil. Like many women footballers, during her experiences abroad she has gained a functional grasp of several languages and cultures. Conscious of the experience she has to share Rosana has already taken the Brazilian Federation's A and B licences and also possesses similar UEFA qualifications. Similarly, Emily Lima continues attending CBF coaching courses, even when she is the only woman on the course. By any objective measure, if Rosana were to achieve her aim of moving into coaching she would add a wealth of knowledge to the technical setup of any women's team. Other players clearly look up to her and treat her almost with deference. Were the opportunities to materialise, there is no doubt Rosana would be able to command the same respect that Emily Lima has from the players. There is a clear sense from the players that those who are familiar with the curious transitional state of women's football are best placed to negotiate its various complications and also to fight their corner in the frequent battles between club hierarchies and players.

Despite all this, the overwhelming majority of coaching staff remain male and predominantly, without this experience in women's football. This does not preclude them from making a valid contribution. What it does mean, however, is that at times players perceive in them an indifference to women's football. Almost all the players interviewed felt the lack of women coaching players was of grave concern. Rosana is teaming up with Emily Lima for at least a third time. Lima managed Rosana at São Jose and also as manager of the Brazilian national team. For this reason, Lima knew Rosana's attributes and knew the player had the adaptability necessary to play as a centre-forward rather than a second forward. The trust between the two meant that Rosana was prepared to try, at 36 years old, to play as a back to goal striker rather than front to goal. This type of in-depth knowledge of women footballers appears thin on the ground at a lot of women's clubs. In the absence of appointed scouting teams and mass televised games, much of the process of searching for players can be hit and miss. Like many of the Santos players Rosana acknowledges that the conditions at the club are favourable relative to most other clubs in Brazil. She mentions that, having a *carteira assinada* (a formal contract offering social security benefits), the support of the club and the benefits of the structure which the club offers are all beneficial. Many players across the age-range concur about the benefits Santos offers, ranging from senior players reaching the end of their careers like Thais Picarte and Maurine, to the new generation coming through such as Angelina Costantino, Karla Alves and Nicole Ramos. Santos has certainly been quicker off the mark in starting to professionalise women's football in Brazil, hence her remark about officially recognised contracts. It is certainly encouraging that players like Rosana are looking towards moving into coaching or further roles in football. In the immediate term, however, there are other battles that need to be fought. I quickly realised that Thais Picarte was the figurehead trying to offer collective representation to an often fragmented group of players.

Conclusion

This chapter has considered how the rootedness of male hegemony affects everyday practice within one of Brazil's prestige clubs, Santos FC. It has argued that the omnipresence of banal patriarchy within the club has meant that the incorporation of women's football has always felt like – in the words of Emily Lima – 'something extra grafted onto the male tradition' of the club. The strength of male hegemony – largely personified by the King Pelé – means that even a women's team that has achieved significant honours and is a pioneer at a national and continental level is barely incorporated into the club's mythology. The strength of the 'tradition' that Santos FC has invented is such that using women players to hand out prizes to watch men's games goes relatively unnoticed on account of its perceived banality rather than being seen as just the type of action that creates a hierarchy of importance – an action that is overtly discriminatory and demeaning towards the women players. Similarly, reserving the best training facilities for the men's team and sending the women's team to train with children has also long been a normalised occurrence rather than plainly prejudicial. Moreover, the women's team are habitually given more than an 'equal opportunity' when it comes to promoting Santos in the community. Indeed, duties involving children seem to be disproportionately allotted to the Sereias. On the other hand, players are acutely aware of these aspects and do use their agency to draw attention to them.

Clearly, the players' athletic performance inherently destabilises the matrix of male hegemony. By being involved in a sphere still seen as eminently male, they inherently weaken certain limits of an activity seen as exclusively male and they also break with the idealised image of femininity that the club attempts to present with its Sereias branding. Secondly, by continuing to campaign for further recognition through activism they challenge the assumptions of institutional figures. Players are achieving representation at federation level, within clubs and on the coaching side of their respective clubs. The previous couple of decades have seen women gain a toehold within Brazil's clubs, through the policy of *obrigatoriedade* and through societal pressure and the players' own efforts. For this to become further consolidated clubs will need to proactively incorporate women players into their discursive mythology. One of the clubs where this is most feasible is Santos, which has in some sense been more proactive than other clubs in the recent past. Nonetheless, their significant role in providing players to the Brazilian national team that reached Olympic and World Cup finals is significantly underplayed. Instead of being emphasised as outstanding achievements of a generation that achieved so much with so little, women players are ignored at the expense of the hegemonic, masculinised tradition.

When I spoke to Angelina Costantino, an 18-year-old prodigy who is already a first-team regular for Santos and a fixture in Brazil's under-21 setup, she inverted the habitual pessimism about the potential of women's football, asking me to imagine how much Sereias had achieved in spite of all the barriers, and wondered just how much further they could go with the right conditions. Revealing of both the barriers that remain and of the potential of the women's game, Angelina asked rhetorically 'imagine how

Figure 4.4   Ketlen Wiggers during her career with Santos FC

popular we could be if we were treated equally?' Tellingly, the provocation had a conditional structure that suggested it was not on the cards in the foreseeable future; however, it did seem symptomatic of a newly emboldened type of player, benefiting from the struggles of the previous generation.

This chapter has argued that there is a need to commemorate a growing tradition of women's football at a club like Santos FC. Having invested in women's football two to three decades earlier than many of their rivals, it seems a missed opportunity not to celebrate more widely the achievements of Sereias da Vila. A clear example of a milestone moment for consolidating the growing tradition of Santos FC Women in the officialised era was the moment Ketlen Wiggers became the first player to score 100 goals for the Sereias. Rather than reaching the milestone during a period of continuous service like Pelé, Ketlen achieved it in spite of a fragmented Santos career, which is symptomatic of the wavering support for women's football during that period. For example, she was left without a club when the Santos FC women's team was discontinued in 2012.

In fact, after I returned from the 2018 Christmas break, I noticed one of the most familiar faces in the squad was missing. Ketlen had decided not to re-sign with the club and was spending a period of time with family in the United States. I knew she was far and away the club's all-time leading goal-scorer and had expected her to continue with the team in the following season. Ketlen became one of the two youngest scorers ever in Santos' history when she scored for the first team at the age of 15. She was chosen to play for the club from 800 girls who attended trials. Having moved from Santa Catarina at such a young age, she lived at the family home of then team manager Rene Simões in order to help her adaptation.

After my departure from Santos FC, Ketlen did re-sign for the club for at least the third time and continued figuring in the first team. At the onset of the coronavirus crisis she had scored 97 goals for Santos. In a stadium with no supporters present Ketlen scored the 100th goal, which was celebrated by Santos and also in the Brazilian media. I wonder how many other women players reached 100 goals but never had it commemorated because of the lack of records? I also wondered how the club would celebrate this achievement. At the next training session Ketlen broke into tears, after receiving a Santos shirt signed by the most emblematic icon of Santos FC and of Brazilian football – the king Pelé.

On 5 December 2020 Santos FC announced the inauguration of a new, dedicated training facility for Sereias da Vila named Campo Sereias da Vila at the Rei Pelé facility, together with the foundation of a Santos Social Responsibility Institute. Three days later Santos paid homage to Ketlen, placing her image on the wall of the Rei Pelé (see Figure 4.4) alongside other idols from the club's history.

This chapter is representative of the struggles that women's football faces in occupying a truly equal space where male national identity has become so deeply embedded over the past century. As with many large clubs across the globe, the possibility of being joint and equal tenants of the club's main stadium appears distant. The next chapter will consider an alternative, if fleeting, moment in the recent history of women's football. The unexpected rise of Iranduba of Manaus pointed to another possible model for the growth of women's football.

CHAPTER FIVE

The Team from the
Heart of the Amazon

Introduction

At first glance, the choice to carry out an ethnographic study with Esporte Clube Iranduba may appear counterintuitive. The development model for South American women's club football in recent years has been character- ised by the priority given to the integration of women into the traditionally male-dominated clubs. This paradigm shift is inextricably linked to the South American confederation CONMEBOL's flagship policy requiring the larger traditional clubs to open a women's division in order to keep their seat at the top table in the lucrative men's Copa Libertadores (Barreira et al., 2020; Goellner, 2021). This policy, as outlined in Chapters One and Two, is driven by the confederation wishing not to look out of step with global policy prescriptions. In turn, this has changed the landscape of women's football on the continent. It has undoubtedly multiplied the number of opportunities for women players across the continent to earn from the game. However, on many occasions, there has already been evidence that women's divisions within the traditional clubs have been treated merely as an (obligatory) addendum to the main part of the club (Mendonça, 2019a). In this way, male hegemony over the game has not only been left untouched but, arguably, has even been consolidated by the changes. In summary, while to some degree the women's game is markedly more visible than it was a decade ago (Rial, 2013b & 2013b), it is already clear that dislodging the banal patriarchy pervasive in many of the leading clubs will be a much greater undertaking.

For precisely this reason, this chapter draws upon an ethnographic visit to a club that is a clear outlier to the paradigm described above. Esporte Clube Iranduba differs significantly from many of its rivals in that its women's team is the main attraction and the principal concern of the club's owners. For example, the club president Amarildo Dutra told me that the women's team always occupies over two-thirds of the club's budget. Being from Manaus, a place as distant as possible from the 'country of football' social imaginary (Fontes & Buarque de Holanda, 2014; Goldblatt, 2014; Kittleson, 2014; Bocketti, 2016), the club and players are able to mobilise an antagonistic identity, pitting the local Amazonian team against the *clubes de camisa* (big-name clubs) of the perceived economic, sporting and political centre.

Despite many of the laudable achievements of the club, this chapter finds both ruptures and continuities of a gendered social order expressed through football. In ways different to the other clubs I visited, Iranduba also typifies the peculiar stage of semi-professionalisation at which the women's game currently finds itself (Garton, 2020; Garton et al., 2021). To even be at this stage marks significant progress as less than ten years ago it was only possible to earn a living, even semi-professionally, in 30 out of 123 FIFA-listed women's football countries (Agergaard & Tiesler, 2014, p. 3). On one hand, the surprise success of the club proffers a profound symbolic challenge and offers an alternative to the top-down mainstream develop-ment model. By the same token numerous instances evidence deep-rooted, unacknowledged assumptions about the social masculinity of football. The women players are presented as being strong characters with considerable control over their career paths. The reality on the ground is one of precarious contracts, the continued objectification of women and the persistence of male gatekeepers overseeing every step of the women's sporting lives. As Toffoletti (2016, p. 200) has it, 'the complexities of a postfeminist cultural landscape cast women as empowered agents and yet it fails to dislodge the persistent devaluing and marginalisation of female athletes and women's sporting pursuits more generally'. This chapter, then, considers the balance of these experiences, arguing that the particularities of Manaus, as a place outside the country's traditional (masculine) football imaginary, have allowed women's football to make significant ground over a short space of time in ways that would be difficult, if not impossible, elsewhere in the country.

I travelled to Manaus in October 2018 just as Iranduba were about to host the 2018 Women's Copa Libertadores. This event represented the culmination of a period of breakneck growth for the club. Unexpectedly, they challenged many of the *clubes de camisa* on a regular basis in women's competitions. In 2017 they reached the semi-finals of the Brazilian women's championship and in 2018 they had another run to the quarter-finals. Meanwhile the Iranduba men's team languish in the fourth division of Brazilian football, not even making a serious impact on the Amazonian state league.

At 7.45am the humidity in Manaus is already stifling. The cadences of cicadas, the chirping of crickets and the incessant noise of hundreds (or thousands) of white-winged parakeets perched on the trees along the Avenida Efigênio Salas all compete with the sounds and sights of urban sprawl. Owing to the climate of the Amazon region all Iranduba's training sessions begin at 8am or earlier to avoid the unbearable midday heat. The audible presence of nature juxtaposed with urbanity remind me that, in a context of unprec-edented climate change and environmental destruction, I am in a region inextricably linked to our survival as a species. Seeing the reality of Manaus, a humanitarian crisis of urban migration from Venezuela, crawling city traffic visibly churning out pollution and smoke billowing from industrial-zone factories brings home what a symbolic battleground for conflicting visions of the future of Brazil, and indeed the planet, this is. These particularities of Manaus, I will learn, explain in large part the club's appeal and success. I return to thinking about the purpose of my visit – to see one of the surprise success stories of Brazilian women's football – Iranduba – and wonder what it is about Manaus that has allowed women's football to take centre-stage in a country where football ordinarily carries such deeply gendered meanings. Is it possible that women's football will grow from the periphery of the country's social imaginary rather than from the centre? Manaus is an outpost in every regard: politically, economically and, far from coincidentally, in a sporting sense too. For this reason, it has been possible for a women's team to attract the spotlight in a country with a distinctly masculinised footballing identity. Manauarans are able to feel a loose sense of belonging to the country of football (Kittleson, 2014; Goldblatt, 2014; Bocketti, 2016) and at the same time feel estranged from it, creating a fierce centre–periphery antagonism on which the club feeds. Moreover, the approach of the club places women's football at the centre of its business model rather than making it merely a sub-division of a men's team. These factors have meant that the players have embraced their role at the club and built a meaningful relationship with the public.

On the way to my first training session with Iranduba our relatively short trip takes in dozens of precarious, informal settlements.[1] As the traffic grinds to a standstill once again, my final destination, the Barbosa Filho training ground, comes into view beyond the disturbingly normalised presence of the growing Venezuelan diaspora fleeing a humanitarian crisis. I ask my taxi driver if he knows anything about Iranduba: a surprise, local, success story of recent years. He replies that the municipality south of the Rio Negro is a point of local pride. Its rich biodiversity means it is frequented by foreign academics like me. This gives me some insight into the connotations the chosen club name Iranduba conjures in the local imaginary.[2] I reformulate my question to include 'women's football team'. He has heard of them too, but like many Manauarans he has always supported Rio giants Flamengo.[3] Iranduba have won the Amazonian women's championship six

---

1 A number of the *favelas* near the Free Trade Zone have names like Xerox, Panasonic and Sharp, acknowledging the various multinationals that at one time or another invested in the Manaus experiment (Brianezi, 2013, p. 83). Each is pronounced according to Brazilian phonetics. Due to catastrophic performance Sharp has abandoned the Americas everywhere except Brazil.

2 There is in fact another women's football team in the city, named 3B (or triple B) after owner Dom Bosco Brasil Bindá, which has also enjoyed relative success at national level.

3 In the pre-globalised era Clube de Regatas do Flamengo could have made a credible claim to be the club with the largest fanbase on the planet. The Rio club traditionally draws support from across the country.

consecutive times and have reached the semi-final of the Women's Brazilian Championship too. Whilst he has never seen them play he has heard and read about them filling the Arena da Amazônia – a stadium tipped to become a white elephant after the 2014 Brazil World Cup (Villoro, 2016, p. 248). We arrive at our destination. I am warned to put on much more insect repellent and sun cream as everyone knows there are a lot of mosquitoes carrying dengue fever in this area.

Upon getting out of the car I initially wonder if I have come to the right place. Having read every article and watched every videoclip I could find about Esporte Clube Iranduba prior to fieldwork I had credulously believed a team that performs in the glamour of a sparkling new World Cup stadium like the Arena da Amazônia would also be training in swanky facilities befitting often international-level women footballers.[4] I eventually see a ramshackle training ground in the distance that I later discover belongs to lowly, local, Serie D men's team Nacional FC.[5] At this point I glimpse the faces of three established Brazilian international players: Andressinha, Camilinha and Raquel.[6] Andressinha and Camilinha are both contracted to the United States NWSL,[7] while Raquel has just returned from playing in the Spanish women's league. The three have been borrowed at considerable expense by Iranduba, especially to compete in the Women's Copa Libertadores in December 2018. Their mid-November arrival coincides with mine. They appear jetlagged and justifiably a little spaced out but seem relatively unperturbed, or at least unsurprised, by being asked to turn up early the day after long flights to train immediately. It appears par for the course. Andressinha clearly knows many of the other players and is given a hero's welcome. She has a rapport with players from a previous loan spell. She competed in the Amazonian league for the club in 2018. Because the North American and Brazilian seasons do not coincide, and are both relatively short, this means that star players like Andressinha are in the privileged position (relative to other women players) of being able to play both the North and South American 'seasons', thus not falling out of practice for prolonged periods. I also see Djeni, Monalisa and Koki, three other well-known players and mainstays of the Iranduba project. My contact Lauro Tentardini, a

---

4 The Arena da Amazônia was one of a number of stadiums purpose-built at considerable expense for the 2014 Brazil World Cup.

5 Nacional FC are the oldest club in the state of Amazonas. In the 1970s and early 1980s they participated in Serie A but the highest level at which they finished the season was 16th.

6 There is a long tradition of referring to Brazilian players both by first name and by diminutives and nicknames, a custom which may be misread as rude or condescending by other cultures. For more on this see Piovezani (2011, 2012).

7 The National Women's Soccer League, the latest attempt (after several aborted efforts) to launch a commercially successful US women's soccer league, launched in 2012.

director of the club, greets me and introduces me to the team and all of the staff. The team are used to announced and unannounced media attention and so are not at all surprised at receiving yet another visitor. Tentardini announces that there is little time to lose and the training session begins.

Locating the fieldwork site

Figure 5.1   The Amazon city of Manaus by night

Modernity in the forest

Manaus is a sizeable city by any standards. It has the seventh-largest GDP and is also the seventh-largest city in Brazil with 2,182,763 inhabitants in 2019 (Instituto Brasileiro de Geografia e Estatística, 2019b). Amazonia's other large city, Belém, is of a similar size – meaning the great majority of the Amazon states' population is urban. Despite narratives suggesting otherwise, Manaus and the Amazon have been integrated within the systems of global trade for over half a millennium. The steady growth of Manaus has been punctuated by two paradigmatic and fleeting periods of boom capitalism – the *ciclo de borracha* (rubber boom) from 1879 to 1912 and the post-1967 development of a free-trade manufacturing economy that brought mass migration to the city (Brianezi, 2013; Despres, 1991; Seráfico & Seráfico, 2005). The free-trade zone has seen more than a tenfold increase in the population of Manaus from just 200,000 in 1960, a period over which, for the first time on record, Manaus has become home to around 60 per cent of the population of the

Amazonas state (CEPAL, 2007).[8] These boom phases saw the ruling class attempt to re-imagine Manaus as a modern cosmopolitan city (Chernela & Pereira, 2018). Coinciding with the *belle epoque* in Europe, at the peak of the rubber boom then-governor Eduardo Gonçalves Ribeiro (1892–96) embarked on a programme of ambitious developments aimed at turning the city into the 'Paris of the Jungle'. With electric lights, an ornate cathedral, paved roads, a British-designed floating wharf, architecturally advanced bridges and the Opera House as the jewel in its crown, the aesthetic makeover was complete (Despres, 1991; Brianezi, 2013; Zouein, 2016). A period of substantial international investment and the levying of steep export duties meant that Manaus enjoyed electricity before London, telephones before Rio de Janeiro and a network of electric trams at a time when New Yorkers were still riding in horse-drawn coaches (Burns, 1965; Zouein, 2016; Pinheiro, 2018). A desire for the rest of the world to acknowledge this rapid embrace of modernity is discernible in a study of late-nineteenth-century Manaus postcards that attempt to represent the advanced 'technometropolis' to the world (Oakdale & Watson, 2018; Zouein, 2016).

Nonetheless these discourses have been undermined in two crucial ways: firstly, by an inability to universalise progress. That is to say, its progress has been fleeting and built upon extreme inequality. Secondly, its discursive purchase has always been overpowered by the pervasive Eurocentric imaginary that continues to see the Amazon as a place of nature or an anachronistic and non-modern place (Killick, 2018).[9] The Amazon is persistently imagined as the antithesis of modernity (Nugent & Harris, 2004). Reformulated by Oakdale and Watson (2018, p. 1) 'whether green hell or the lungs of the planet or simply a land out of time, the Amazon region is consistently seen as a space of nature rather than culture'. For its own discursive ends, the Eurocentric imaginary of the centre needs a dichotomous point of comparison which it can portray as the antithesis of modernity. For example, *Orientalism* by Edward Said (1978) and *Imagining the Balkans* by Maria Todorova (2009) portray dyadic categories of analysis in which a necessarily nebulous geographical area is stigmatised by comparison to a central *locus* of modernity. The areas demarcate racial, political and social hierarchical

---

8 Amazonas state has a land area of 1,570,745.7km², which is roughly the size of metropolitan France, Germany, Italy, the United Kingdom and Greece combined. It would be the 16th-largest nation in the world.

9 When Manaus was announced as a host city for the 2014 Brazil World Cup, then-England manager Roy Hodgson instinctively named the city 'the one to avoid'. Predictably, Hodgson's diplomatic slip triggered a round of lazy, ignorant stereotyping from tabloid and broadsheet press alike (Coelho, 2013; Longman, 2014). Upon being criticised heavily, not least by Manaus mayor Arthur Virgilio in an interview with Sky Sports (2014), Hodgson backtracked significantly, suggesting 'it may actually be rather titillating to visit Manaus, a location where the famous Werner Herzog film *Fitzcarraldo* was partially filmed'.

orders and boundaries imposed by modernity. This is discernible in the Latin American context where value is attributed to whiteness, Europeanness and urbanity at the expense of blackness, indigeneity and nature (Quijano, 2000; Lugones, 2007; Mignolo, 2009, 2011). Whilst writers like Milton Hatoum (1990) rebut these arguments, portraying Manaus as a liquid, liminal space that resists these narratives, the city and the Amazon continue to be errone-ously conflated as is convenient, as will be shown in this chapter.

The position of Manaus in the Brazilian social imaginary is crucial to the growth of Esporte Clube Iranduba. Football is a game that offers multiple symbolic opportunities to contest and reproduce prevailing discourses. Furthermore, the game is inextricably linked to urban expansion and imaginaries of modernity – neither of which tend to be associated with the Amazon. This explains, in part, how a successful women's football team has caught the collective imagination of the Manaus public and beyond as a manifestation of modern sensibilities in a region still portrayed as pre-modern or even backward. Within its fanbase, I noted a fanatical passion which, thus far, has generally been reserved for male clubs with much longer histories.

Iranduba, Amazonas and Esporte Clube Iranduba

The club took its name from the municipality (shown in Figure 5.2) and, even before embarking on fieldwork, this caught my attention. Iranduba means 'the land of an abundance of honey or bees' in Tupi Guaraní. At the instigation of president Dutra, the club also has 'o clube do coração da floresta' [the team from the heart of the Amazon] emblazoned on its merchandise (see Figure 5.3).

Representing Iranduba/Amazonas

Whilst the directors have clearly encouraged certain narratives, the following sub-section sets out how over three months of ethnographic experience in Manaus, through a mix of participant observation and semi-structured interviews, I learned that the way in which Iranduba as a club has caught the imagination of the Manauaran and Brazilian public has much more to do with the agency of the players themselves and the way in which they have engaged with playing for the club and the public alike. I argue this is possible, firstly due to the determination and enthusiasm of the players, in spite of many obstacles, and secondly, because of a perfect storm of circumstances thrown up by being in Manaus.

Players from the south-east in the north-west

Only upon attending a number of training sessions did I realise that for the great majority of the club's players Manaus represents a home away from home. The club has uprooted a number of young aspiring players and brought them to the Amazon region. Owing to the lack of youth opportunities in the region (and many of the other states), the club pursued an accelerated route to getting a competitive women's team – they decided to recruit proven players from elsewhere in the country. Using the contacts of Lauro Tentardini (described later in this chapter), a significant number of players were brought to Manaus from Santa Catarina. This involved a challenging period of adaptation, almost akin to living abroad, for many players. Others joined from the north-east and on occasions the states of São Paulo and Minas Gerais. Perhaps the shared experience of each being far from home in Amazonas has been the main factor influencing the strong bond that has developed between the players. Since the beginning of the Iranduba project there have been mainstays who have almost come to personify the club in different ways. One of these is Djeni Becker, who is part of the Santa Catarina contingent. She has been one of the star players going on to represent Brazil

Figure 5.2   Iranduba, looking across the Rio Negro

Figure 5.3   The official Esporte Clube Iranduba logo

at youth and senior level. She moved to Manaus at the age of 20. At the beginning, she recalled immense difficulties in connecting with the public in Amazonas. She explained that at first bridging a perceived cultural gap was difficult as the players were initially pigeon-holed as outsiders to the region. It was perceived that, as they were not from Manaus, they were unlikely to represent the city and region with pride. When the team proved to be a runaway success these fears were quickly allayed. When interviewed Djeni concurred with Tentardini in believing the embrace of the club is, in large part, related to being successful and more than anything to the feeling of challenging and often beating the *clubes de camisa* – who to many Manauarans represent the country's political and social elites. This theme will be investigated in more detail later.

A number of the players from Santa Catarina commented on the deep sense of isolation they felt upon joining the club. It was impossible to go home during the season and even visiting other places was out of the question. Each day at training it is evident that the players have consciously turned this negative into a positive. They seem intent on enjoying every moment at the club, knowing that the relatively short contract lengths in women's football mean that a visit home will soon come around again. The players have the strength of friendship that can only be built when facing challenges collectively in an unfamiliar context. This is particularly evident in the cliques among players from the south-east, who make regular references to home whilst embracing the place that has given them an opportunity to shine on the national stage. On an academic level a huge *lacuna* in the literature is the state of mental health of women footballers – given the precarious contracts, living conditions and discriminatory treatment many face. Only in the context of COVID has the topic begun to be recognised (Clarkson et al., 2020). Nonetheless, at training it was evident that the players were determined to turn this negative into a positive or at least put a brave face on each day.

In this vein, Priscila Back, who is from the interior of Paraná, recalls making the move to Manaus. Crucially, she recalls unconditional support from her parents – a support that not all players have had and that is more likely to be present in places like the south-east where women's football has long been on a better footing. She began, as per most players, joining games with male players, but moved to a women's team as soon as the opportunity presented itself. In spite of this, Priscila is clear that prejudice against women players is omnipresent:

> Acredito que toda mulher que joga futebol já tenha sofrido algum tipo de preconceito. Sempre tem aquelas perguntas desnecessárias ... mas temos que ser educadas e responder. [I believe all women who play football have suffered some kind of prejudice. There are always the unnecessary questions ... but we just have to be polite and answer them.]

Such is the ferocity of these reactions, she admits she has even considered quitting on multiple occasions. She emphasises that '[j]á pensei e penso até hoje sobre parar de jogar futebol, principalmente por ter que ficar longe da minha família' [I have already thought about and still think about quitting, mainly because of having to be so far from home]. Priscila's career has taken her to Paraguay and even to Trinidad and Tobago, two countries where she struggled with the language as much as other adaptation issues. From numerous similar conversations over the course of this fieldwork it seems Priscila typifies the determination and sacrifices of women players, along with the soul-searching they do about whether it is all worth it. The continued presence of the players, at training each day, in the stadiums where they face discrimination, and their continued willingness to uproot to new cities and even countries, suggest that they ultimately believe it is worth it.

Laudably, Iranduba is a club that has tried to compete in youth tournaments in order to create a base for the senior squad and to develop future players. The lack of youth opportunities been a long-standing problem stunting the growth of women's football in Brazil – a problem many of the *clubes de camisa* have not done enough to address. In this context, Iranduba has given much-needed opportunities to developing players – though once again these are mostly recruited from states where women's football is on a better footing at youth level. Running a team of largely 15-, 16- or 17-year-old players from different parts of the country clearly comes with some duty of care, particularly when bringing them to a region from which they cannot easily return to family at weekends, or at all during the season. Players reach the club at a very early age and are expected to adapt to entirely new surroundings away from family, with minimal help. Clubs often house players together in large groups to save on expense. This is true of both major women's clubs in Manaus – both 3B and Iranduba. The excellent spirit within the group notwithstanding, the experience of adapting to communal living arrangements in Manaus must be extremely tough for young players. Monalisa Belém, from the interior of Tocantins, explained how she joined at just 16, before completing secondary education. More recently, one of the country's most promising young players, Júlia Beatriz, migrated to Manaus from Teresina, Piauí at just 17. The CBF introduced Under-18 and Under-16 women's tournaments for the first time in 2019. Iranduba reached the semi-final of the Under-18 tournament. Indeed, the 'senior' Iranduba squad, which reached the semi-finals of the senior women's Brasileirão in 2017, and the quarter-finals in 2018, was composed of a remarkably young squad with only occasional senior professionals who shoulder the burden of working as surrogate coaches and mentors. Mirroring a long-standing problem in men's football, the moral issues attached to separating players from parents and family at a young age are not given sufficient attention either by clubs or by the academic literature to date. Indeed, particularly at clubs like Iranduba, provision to deal with issues of welfare is wafer-thin. The mental health of women footballers, and indeed male footballers, is a delicate area where research is urgently required. Many clubs build squads of thirty or more players, meaning that at any given time more than half of them are not even playing games, leaving them with time on their hands to reflect or indeed to fall into depression and anxiety without the support of family or even friends from home. The following sub-section suggests that these circumstances provide fertile ground for fast-growing religious groups, particularly evangelical groups, where players often find solace while away from home.

Banal religiosity

I am immediately struck by the omnipresence of prayer and religion at each training session. Nobody kicks a ball until every player has gathered in a team huddle for the morning prayer. The person who leads this changes each day, but every day the prayer will last between two and three minutes and will take in a multitude of themes, from wanting hunger and poverty in Brazil to reduce, to simply wanting to win the next match. Beyond this, away from the training ground one of the most common meeting places for players is the church. Far from home this gives players a social outlet and a sense of routine that provides a coping mechanism in an unfamiliar place. Given that, added to this, many players have emerged from particularly troubled backgrounds in the first place, it is unsurprising that many turn to religion as an outlet. This has been termed 'banal religiosity' in reference to the fact that religious practices or gestures form an unacknowledged part of routine (Rial, 2012, 2013b). In interviews, the absence of communal prayer before a game is one of the first aspects that Brazilian women players first note when playing abroad. Beyond this, banal religiosity is also often present in goal celebrations, pre-match huddles, before and after penalties and during after-match celebrations. One player who is particularly devout is goalkeeper Rubi. She explains that

> antes de cada jogo, fico mais quieta conversando com Deus e pensando nas situações que podem ocorrer durante o jogo e como tenho que me portar diante de cada uma delas. Isso facilita na hora das tomadas de decisões que às vezes tem que ser tomadas em fração de segundos. [before each game, I like to be quiet, speaking with God and thinking about situations that could happen during the match and how I need to deal with them. This makes it easier to take the kind of decisions that need to be made in milliseconds.]

In the absence of parental or authority figures the players tend to look for surrogates. In addition, the deep political polarisation of Brazilian society and the accompanying recent surge of Pentecostalism mean that it is unsurprising that players look for a consistent moral cosmology with which to order their fragmented lives. Players seem attracted by the comforting presence of moral absolutes that help them to make sense of the situations in which they find themselves. Beyond this, it gives them a routine outside training sessions and an opportunity to meet others with similar interests. Other than Rial (2012), very few researchers to date have dealt with the confluence of football and religion. Further research as to how religious beliefs dialogue with the day-to-day struggles of women players would contribute greatly.

A flechada – evoking/appropriating the Amazons

Early on in my stay with Iranduba I became aware of a popular pre-match ritual in which the players mimic firing an arrow. It is a shtick often repeated when the club signs a new player.[10] My immediate instinct was to believe that this formed part of a wider strategic instrumentalisation of indigeneity emanating from the club's hierarchy (already responsible for *o clube do coraçao da Floresta*, the name Iranduba, the Amazon green kit). It would appear that whilst the club hierarchy has appropriated the gimmick, using it for official photoshoots, the gesture originated with the players themselves, referring to indigenous stereotypes of the Amazon that remain pervasive.[11] This manifestation of player agency was particularly interesting as a body of work testifies to the multifarious strategies women players draw from their own creativity to promote themselves in the absence of significant media or institutional support. The players engage in what Pooley (2010, p. 78) calls 'calculated authenticity'. In other words, consciously or otherwise, the players are 'constructing themselves as empowered, in-control and can-do subjects at the nexus of post-feminist discourses that celebrate women's self-production and the broadcasting of *authentic* female identities' (Toffoletti & Thorpe, 2018, p. 18).

One quiet morning at training, I broached the topic, sensing it to be of significance in terms of the players' integration here in Manaus. Various players were keen to talk about the *flechada* (arrow-motion) as they felt it represents the way in which they, as outsiders to the region, had both embraced being and been embraced as representatives of Amazonas.

The *flechada* became part of that feeling which clearly goes beyond football – mocking the racist stereotyping and the reductionist way the Amazon is imagined by the rest of the country. The consensus is that it began at an away match in Araraquara, São Paulo state, when a small but vocal group of Ferroviária supporters put their hands in front of their mouths and began making 'Indian noises' and shouting '*indias*' at the Iranduba players. Upon scoring, the Iranduba players spontaneously celebrated in front of the home fans with the *flechada*. The gesture has been repeated ever since, especially at home games where the Manaus public, acutely aware of how Amazonas is portrayed and imagined, has instinctively embraced this burlesque performance of ethnic identity. The players are clearly aware that it is delicate territory and, whilst they laugh about it, they are savvy in realising its symbolic significance. A number of players from the south admitted that

---

10 For example, when the club signed Yoreli Rincón from Atlético Huila in January 2019 (@yorelirincón, 2018c).

11 Stripped of its cultural context the *flechada*/arrow motion also appears to mimic the gesture popularised by Usain Bolt.

the Brazilian social imaginary tends to depict Manaus and the Amazon in backward terms. 'Ainda no 2018 os brasileiros acham que Manaus é um lugar culturalmente atrasado' [even now in 2018 Brazilian people see Manaus as a culturally backward place], one of the players added at training. Having experienced the reality of Manaus – composed largely of migrants from various regions of Brazil who came after the introduction of the 1967 Free Trade Zone – the players' spontaneous reaction to the racism of the crowd was not aggression or anger, but rather to mock it in an ironic way.

One of the more popular players with fans and within the club alike is Giselinha Teles. Whilst she is another of the players who followed director Lauro Tentardini from Kindermann, Giselinha and teammate and close friend Mayara Vaz actually hail from the Atlantic gateway to the Amazon: Belém do Pará.[12] Both players are of *mestiça* (mixed-race) appearance, which allows them, in a sense, to personify more convincingly the Esporte Clube Iranduba that has been constructed. Much of the discrimination players face justifies the need for an intersectional approach (Crenshaw, 1990), in particular one that takes into account the particularities and partial visibility of racism against indigenous peoples in the Brazilian context (Rocha, 2021). Moreover, there is a particular need for a nuanced approach in the case of football where recent research has discovered women players are often black and tend to come from poorer backgrounds (Martins et al., 2021).

Giselinha remembers another moment important in the consolidation of the *flechada* as part of the club. She dates it back to the club's run to the final of the 2016 women's Under-20 competition. There was an impressive attendance for a youth game – 8,413 for the visit of Vasco da Gama (one of the prestigious Rio clubs) to the Arena da Amazônia (Amazonas Governo, 2016). Giselinha recalled that the crowd was fairly divided with approximately two-thirds supporting Iranduba and the remaining third cheering for Vasco da Gama. After an extremely close penalty shoot-out Iranduba prevailed and went to celebrate with the local fans who had helped them to victory. At this point, in frustration one of the Vasco fans hurled a trainer from the second tier of the stand at the Iranduba players. Luckily it did not hit anyone. Spontaneously, the players celebrated with the shoe as a 'trophy' of victory and began making the *flechada* motion at the Vasco supporters to show that the prestigious *clube de camisa* had been picked off by the Amazonian team. In recounting the story, Giselinha recognises that it could be seen as a 'brincadeira de mau gosto' [a joke in bad taste] but feels strongly that most people would have understood that the players were parodying racist attitudes stigmatising the Amazon region. By both performing football, an activity inextricably linked with tropes of modernity, and simultaneously mocking the Amazon of the Eurocentric imagination, the players immediately gained the

---

12 The city was used to export the vast quantities of rubber emanating from the Amazon during the boom phase. It has a similar tropical rainforest climate to Manaus.

respect of a public who had previously regarded them as outsiders. Indeed, according to the players I spoke to during fieldwork, even the Manauarans who had come to support Vasco acknowledged that the expression of how their region is portrayed elsewhere was realistic and thus worthy of being parodied.

Regional pride at the Copa Libertadores 2018 Manaus

From the moment I first set foot on the training ground in Manaus, all the players talked about the hosting of the 2018 Women's Copa Libertadores. The club hierarchy was hell-bent not only on successfully hosting the largest continental club competition in women's football, but actually winning it to prove a point.[13] At one point the ambitious hierarchy of the club even made enquiries about loaning six-times-world-player-of-the-year Marta Vieira da Silva for the duration of the tournament (Dantas, 2018; Lima, 2018). This endeavour never got off the ground.

The 2018 Copa Libertadores tournament brings a number of hitherto unseen journalists to the Iranduba training sessions I attend. Club officials do not seem to know who many of them are. There is no-one to check their credentials. At some training sessions members of the public – mostly children – are allowed to watch so they can get photos with their favourite player when the session finishes. Each day seems to bring more members of the public and a larger huddle of eager journalists reporting on preparations for the tournament.

When the actual matches begin, the extent of the bond between players and fans becomes clear. Each team is allowed a squad of no more than 22 players for the tournament. This means a good dozen of Iranduba's players are left out of the tournament squad. Rather than sulk about this, the players mingle with the fans to watch the game, happily signing autographs and posing for photographs. This level of accessibility to players is unthinkable in men's football, where a well-known player would rarely be seen out in public and, if he was, would be flanked by bodyguards. This access allows a relationship to develop between players and fans that belongs to a bygone age in men's football. Speaking to fans is easy, so I can easily corroborate the strong desire to take on the traditional sides that the players cite as a main reason for the club's success. Indeed, many of the fans' anecdotes usually include a fierce battle with a team from São Paulo or Rio. They include an enmity with those cities and usually, for my benefit, it is clarified that Manauarans feel those places look down on them. Cliched social representations of the region have created a dyadic relationship between the perceived centre of the nation

---

13 To contextualise a little it is worth mentioning that, prior to my visit in 2018, teams from São Paulo state had won the women's Copa Libertadores seven out of nine times it had run since it began in 2009. The other two winners were Colo Colo of Chile and Sporting Limpeño of Paraguay.

(particularly São Paulo and Rio) and a supposedly barbaric and backwards periphery (ethnically Amazonas and in more racialised terms the north-east).

The engagement of players with the crowd is clearly sincere. Especially in Manaus the players are acutely aware that 'a gente que assiste paga nossos salários' [the public pay our salaries]. This thought is not a natural link to make at other clubs, in Brazil or Colombia for example, where women's football remains free. These elements are important in allowing a full professionalisation to happen, which means that women's football can offer genuine career opportunities. The game finds itself in a transitional period – but already there are signs that players from extremely underprivileged backgrounds are benefiting from the gradual growth of professionalism. The following section of this chapter considers two such cases.

Football and social mobility

Coming up tough: Brenda Woch

Whilst there is a lot of work to do with regard to player welfare, it is clear that football provides a much-needed distraction from the violent, unforgiving world of the Brazilian periphery, or even a lifeline for players who have grown up in it. Listening to tales of the urban periphery reminds me of another non-geographical centre/periphery divide in Brazil. The urban periphery of any sizeable city is as far removed from comfortable middle-class Brazil as São Paulo is from Manaus. My experience of the Brazilian periphery is non-existent or at best anecdotal. I could have visited the diluted versions of *favelas* that have been commodified for tourists but felt there would be little point. The players' recollections give me much-needed insight into the extent of social division in the country. One such player at Iranduba was Brenda Woch. Brenda, like many women players of this footballing generation in Brazil, began playing mixed gender football in the street at the age of 6 in her home town of Maceió, Alagoas. From an early age her talent was recognised and Brenda saw the game as a potential route out of the grinding poverty that characterised her youth. Through sheer insistence, at the age of 12 she found herself in a boy's team called Parma Brejal. Tragically, the same year her mother was murdered. Brenda recalls the day her life changed:

> Minha mãe vendia drogas para sustentar a família, somos oito filhos. Ela entrou no mundo do crime para nos dar de comer. Quando eu tinha doze anos, invadiram nossa casa e atiraram na minha mãe. Eu estava ao lado dela, presenciei tudo, vi eles tirarem a vida dela. Depois de um ano, meu irmão Diego, que era usuário de drogas, também foi assassinado. E no ano seguinte, mataram meu pai. [My mum sold drugs to pay for our upkeep, there are eight of us to support. She got involved in the world of crime in order to put food on the table. When I was 12 they broke into our house

and shot her. I was by her side, I saw everything. I saw them take her life
A year later, my brother Diego, who was a user, was also murdered. And
the following year they murdered my father.]

In the absence of the state, of any kind of formal therapy, Brenda took refuge
in football:

> não deixei me abalar, sempre segui meu sonho de ser jogadora de futebol.
> Minha fé em Jesus e a vontade de orgulhar minha mãe me deram forças..
> Passei muitos anos sem conseguir falar sobre o assassinato da minha mãe,
> que vi com meus próprios olhos, porque doía muito. Mas hoje quero
> contar, por saber que posso ajudar muitas meninas que necessitam e que
> me têm como espelho. [I didn't allow myself to give up. I always followed
> my dream of being a footballer. My faith in Jesus and wanting to make my
> mum proud gave me the strength. I spent years without being able to talk
> about the murder of my mum, the murder that I saw with my own eyes,
> because it hurt so much. But today, I want to tell the story, because I know
> I can help so many others that need it, and that see me as a role model.]

After these tragic events, Brenda led a nomadic existence, living with various
relatives for short periods. At 15 she joined another local neighbourhood
team, Craques do Futuro. Similar to many other women players Brenda was
first spotted by scouts when she was playing *futsal*. She was playing in an
indoor tournament organised by the Serviço Social da Indústria (SESI – a
not-for-profit providing social services to industrial workers) when she was
seen by San Francisco do Conde (a team from Salvador, Bahia). She moved
there at 17 but struggled to settle. For this reason she returned to Maceió
where she joined União Desportiva, competing in Serie A2 and in the *futsal*
league. Finally, Woch shone in this team and was called up for the Brazilian
Under-20 national team. From this moment forward she became a regular
in the Brazilian Under-20 team and was signed first by 3B and finally by
Iranduba. Brenda managed to adapt to Manaus and is a popular player within
the group.

While representing the Under-20 team she won the Copa America in
Ecuador. She recalls that 'para uma menina que perdeu tudo, foi muito
importante ser campeã' [for a girl who lost everything, it was so important
to be a champion]. Football's importance also goes way beyond the pitch.
Brenda explains that one of the most abiding memories in her young career
was visiting an orphanage for Ecuadorian children with the Brazilian national
side that year. She speaks passionately about it making her grateful for the
family memories she has and making her want to help disadvantaged children
after her career. Brenda adds that owning a house where all her family can
stay is among her greatest ambitions. The growth of women's football is such
that these ambitions, whilst not easy to fulfil, appear more possible each day.

Koki: between generations

The book *O negro no futebol Brasileiro* (1947) by journalist Mário Filho incorporated Afro-Brazilians into Brazilian identity, but at the same time was guilty of essentialising in ways that drew on nineteenth-century ideas of scientific racism. Moreover, the gendered title is testament to the exclusion of women within this national identity trope. Whilst the importance of links between sport and national identity were only acknowledged later, it could be argued *O negro no futebol Brasileiro* was every bit as influential as *Casa Grande e Senzala* (1933) by Gilberto Freyre in promoting the idea of Brazil as a racial democracy with unique sensuousness, physicality and individuality derived from its ethnic mix.

Renata Costa is another prominent Afro-Brazilian from an underprivileged background. Better known to teammates as Koki, Costa is clearly respected on the training ground owing to her multiple achievements wearing the famous yellow shirt of Brazil. She played in three World Cups and three Olympic tournaments for Brazil, partnering Aline Pellegrino, as well as winning the Copa America and Panamerican games. Despite all these achievements, Koki explains how she had represented Brazil at the World Cup in 2003 before receiving her first salary as a player in 2005. Before receiving a paid position, Koki played for Portuguesa Londrinense and Marília. Like many players she began playing *futsal* and street football, in the absence of other outlets for women players. Similar to Pellegrino, when asked whether women's football has advanced, the transition during her own career tells her it clearly has. Nonetheless Costa believes that much needs to be done at all levels to really establish women's football. Unlike many less experienced players Koki is quick to point out that the experience of women's football is not significantly different or better in many European countries. Koki's travels have taken her to Denmark, Sweden and Russia. She explains that she played in Denmark in 2008, Sweden in 2009 and finally Russia in 2014 and 2015. She points out that Denmark only had two strong teams but otherwise was characterised by amateur conditions and competitive imbalance. She is most complimentary about Sweden, pointing out that Marta remained there so long she is now a Swedish citizen and finally said that in Russia, though the pay is a lot better, the level is actually considerably lower than that of Brazil. This is an insightful comment, which warns against the danger of reductionist analysis that only takes economic factors into consideration. In the cases of the two Scandinavian countries she emphasises the manner in which the supporters and club hierarchies treat women's players seriously. She now criticises the fact that in Brazil most clubs do not charge spectators to get into women's matches (not the case with Iranduba). Similarly, she notes an almost banal gender differentiation in the way *clubes de camisa* hype *clássicos* (derbies) in the men's game but don't count the equivalent women's games as *clássicos*.

Koki insists that those small details make a huge difference. In this respect she believes the marketing of women's football within *clubes de camisa* must improve drastically. Despite her reservations about the current situation, Koki is confident that greater changes are coming. She concludes that the presence of women's football is going to become more normalised and that from there people will see women's football 'com outros olhos' [in another way]. Koki is at the back end of her career and like many senior women players fully intends to continue in football. A generation of women of Koki's experience in coaching roles would surely make a difference in the treatment of players. She is among the last of the players who can remember women's football being an unpaid activity, and thus is well placed to comment on the ruptures and continuities in the women's game. The years to come will be crucial for players like Koki who want to formalise their vast experience and, in her words, 'give something back' by coaching others. It is hard to imagine how these experienced figures, who already act as surrogate coaches, could do more. The question is whether the doors will be open for them when they apply for positions.

This leads to the next sub-section of this chapter, which considers the final barrier or glass ceiling that has yet to be broken – the incursion of women *en masse* into positions of authority within the game. There are a few pioneers, like Emily Lima who managed the national side, and Aline Pellegrino who now oversees women's football for the CBF. Will they become the rule rather than the exception?

Continuities of a gendered social order

Male coaches and mansplaining

One of the most notable aspects of Iranduba is the dominance of male figures in technical roles. The deficit of women coaches has been covered amply in the literature but usually in other countries and in other sports (Norman, 2008; Lavoi & Dutove, 2012; Norman, 2010; Norman & Rankin-Wright, 2018). The club has employed women to carry out media work on behalf of the team, and obviously women players. Beyond this there was no other female representation – this is an important factor as it surely affects self-perception and maybe even causes the players to undervalue themselves. For that reason pioneering women coaches like Emily Lima and Tatiele Silveira from Brazil and Vanessa Arauz from Ecuador are so important in breaking the cycle. While I was with Iranduba the team manager was Igor Cearense. He gained playing experience at the top level, most notably at Flamengo, Coritiba and Fortaleza, before winding down his career with Peñarol and Nacional.[14] After gaining some managerial experience with fourth-division, amateur, male teams in Manaus he was placed in charge of Iranduba. To date Iranduba Women have never appointed a female manager. This is clearly problematic for the aspirations of a player like Koki.

14 Two of Manaus' major clubs, Peñarol and Nacional are named after Uruguay's two largest clubs. Coritiba of Curitiba was named so by the German immigrants who formed the club; this was the old name of the state capital.

The career of Andressinha, one of the current stars of the national team, is located within the next generation. By the player's own assessment conditions are improving. Andressinha is the first to admit that there are more opportunities now and that she has had things easier than some of the more senior players. She is similarly quick, however, to cut short the notion that prejudice has somehow disappeared. Referring diplomatically to male gatekeepers Andressinha explains that 'talvez alguns possam ter esse receio de que a mulher não vá entender sobre o que está falando, mas na parte tática aí eu me garanto' [perhaps some of them have this fear that women are not going to understand what they are talking about, but talking about tactics I feel more than confident]. This chimes with experiences of watching players on the training ground. A tendency towards simply playing full-scale matches rather than focusing on tactical areas on a more micro level could be seen as merely a primitive or underdeveloped tactical understanding of the game. Nonetheless, there is a convincing case, backed up by a number of other players' remarks, that *machismo* or a sense of male sporting superiority is at the root of the reluctance to talk tactics with women players. There is a clear tendency for male gatekeepers to treat women's football entirely differently to the men's game (or as a deeply inferior sub-division of men's football) and not to engage in detail with tactical issues. There is an overly jovial atmosphere at times on the training ground, which detracts from the seriousness of the task in hand. When tactical matters are touched upon, it is generally in a superficial way, in a tone that, subconsciously or otherwise, suggests that the female player receiving the explanation is likely to understand only part of what is being explained. Andressinha clearly recognises a certain tendency towards mansplaining in the current coaching team–player relations, which at Iranduba are always male–female and in many cases hierarchical in tone and language. This appears to constitute one of the principal barriers that the new generation faces. Male coaching staff and managers appear to be a final bastion of male hegemony in football. Until a critical mass of former women professionals are involved on the coaching side, there is a fair chance that, consciously or otherwise, there will not be sufficient technical development for players, or that the players will feel talked down to. The problems do not stop at mansplaining. The following issue is perhaps exacerbated by the media – but can also arise on the training ground.

Foregrounding whiteness

During my stay another persistent factor was the objectification of certain players. This is a long-standing problem in Brazil – to the point where a tournament took place in which only players considered beautiful were encouraged to join teams (Knijnik & Horton, 2013). Little appears to have changed in this regard. There is a strong sense on the training ground of an idealised type of player. The two players who receive by far the greatest attention are Djeni Becker and Andressinha Machry – both now part of the senior international squad. It may be coincidence, as the pair are without doubt two of the best midfielders in Brazilian women's football, but there seems to be a strong bias towards players of European appearance as well as name. The players who have played abroad also garner greater prestige, though they do not always happen to have a European appearance. The training ground today makes me think of Brazil's bid to host the 2023 Women's World Cup. From the early stages, the bid made nominal mention of Manaus as the capital of women's football without giving any sense of how or why this was. Moreover, the bid chose an Iranduba player for the front cover (FIFA, 2020b).

Rather than using the image of any of the best-known, experienced, senior players who had taken Brazil Women to World Cup and Olympic finals – for example, Marta, Formiga, Cristiane, Maurine and Érika – the cover page foregrounds Djeni Becker playing at the Women's World Cup Under-20 tournament in 2014. The foregrounding of Djeni appears symptomatic of framing players within a heterosexual male gaze and detracting from their athletic performance (Wood, 2018, p. 576). A similar tendency occurs in US women's football where Alex Morgan (also an extremely accomplished player) receives similarly sustained media attention as an idealised type of American femininity. A regional documentary about Iranduba consistently foregrounds Djeni Becker (*Iranduba da Amazônia: A história*, 2016) and, in addition, the club hierarchy consistently choose her to give media interviews and to advertise the club, to the point where the player often spends prolonged periods of training tending to media work.

Even bearing in mind that Djeni Becker is the captain of the team, the frequency with which she is foregrounded in interviews, documentaries and promotional material provides a telling counterpoint to the appropriations of indigeneity harnessed to garner support for the team. The club carefully cultivates and invokes an oppositional ethnic identity, against the perceived centre and Europeanness of the south, in order to galvanise local support. However, within the club, and the local and national media and football institutions, there are clear manifestations of the very Eurocentric imaginary Iranduba uses as an oppositional force to garner support. As international team mate Andressinha explains,

> o que mais me incomoda, é quando focam mais na beleza do que no que está fazendo, como está jogando, o que está desenvolvendo dentro de campo. Falam mais da ropri do que sua ropria vida, que é o esporte. [what makes me most uncomfortable is when they focus more on beauty than on what we are doing, how we are playing, what is happening on the pitch. They talk more about beauty than about your life, which is the sport.]

In this statement she emphasises the extent to which players are reduced to appearance, to the point where the very activity to which they have dedicated their entire life is placed as secondary. The players' views are often politically savvy and show an awareness of the issues at hand that can only come from experience. Beyond this, it is notable that across nine months in the field I could not discern any divisive consequences of the privileging of certain players

– players seem to accept things 'how they are' and do not dwell on the issue. It is testament to the maturity of the players that they largely recognise the fundamental problems as being the result of wider institutional and structural discrimination rather than allowing this treatment to divide them. Nonetheless, whilst I did not bear witness to any such animosity, it would be naïve on my part to believe that players openly express all their feelings about such matters or that I, as a male researcher, would be likely to hear anything of such tensions.

In a similar vein, the players recalled another moment when Iranduba found themselves under the media spotlight. When they had a surprise run to the semi-finals of the women's Brasileirão in 2017, the sports programme 'Globo Esporte Espetacular' carried a long feature on the secrets of the team's success (Globo Esporte Espetacular, 2017). The players recalled the frivolous, fun nature of the feature. My personal interpretation was that the frivolous tone would never have been used in a feature on men's football and ultimately sought to diminish the importance of women's football. The feature began with Djeni telling the now mythologised story of how the Iranduba *flechada* came into being, followed by an explanation of the club's popularity in Manaus. With the help of figures from the club hierarchy, the film then narrated the match day atmosphere: 'O vestiário com som, ambiente é o salão de beleza do Iranduba. A capitã Djenifer só joga cheirosa – passa perfume, desodorante, creme. Ela e todas' [The boisterous Iranduba dressing room is like a beauty salon. The captain Djenifer always smells good when she plays – she puts perfume, deodorant and cream on. Herself and all the team]. The final line betrays the way Djeni is made to personify the team as a sexualised figure. The treatment of her owes as much to media coverage and is even mirrored by institutional representations – as the CBF World Cup bid showed. However, on numerous occasions the club reduces the player to body and appearance (Langton, 2009), instrumentalising her to generate the image they consider necessary to increase the club's popularity.

Instrumentalising the players

The feature touches upon another specificity of being a player at Iranduba. Players are expected to 'chip in' with extra-football duties aimed at promoting and helping the club. For example, for players who are not playing, the film states 'enquanto isso a artilheira Gláucia, que está lesionada, vende picolé nas arquibancadas' [while this goes on Gláucia, the striker, who is injured, sells lollies in the stand]. Gláucia then adds 'temos que ajudar o Iranduba vender picolé' [we need to help Iranduba sell lollies] with restrained enthusiasm. She is asked to perform more than the usual contractual obligations of a professional footballer.[15] It is almost inconceivable that a male player would be asked to do the same. In some sense, being a 'small, recent start-up' gives the club

---

15 In 2019 Gláucia, playing for Santos, finished the season as the leading scorer in the Brazilian women's championship.

a pretext to ask players to carry out extra duties. Nonetheless, I'm not aware of the male team being asked to do these things. The club's willingness to use women players to sell lollies, tickets, shirts and merchandise shows a sense of the club's perception that it owns the players, a willingness to instrumentalise them and a denial or lack of concern for their feelings. This usage of players beyond simply playing football, was explained by the director of marketing for Iranduba Adriano Pereira. He outlined how the club goes about promoting its matches, pointing out how the club 'became aware' of the popularity of 'certain players', and said that they were approached to help sell tickets for the club's matches on their social media account. Pereira explains:

> queremos o público perto do clube, temos aberto as portas para o torcedor enxergar o time como um clube que representa o Estado do Amazonas e fazendo que o povo se sinta orgulhoso [we want the public to feel close to the club, we have tried to let the supporters see that the club represents Amazonas state and for people to feel proud of it].

Giselinha explains how she used to help the club by selling match tickets to fans in person:

> Pego a imagem do ingresso, com local, horário e coloco no meu Face. Eles passam o telefone e marco um lugar para entregar os ingressos. Pedem para tirar fotos, dar autógrafos, conversar. [I post pictures of the tickets with the place and the time on Facebook. They pass me their phone numbers and I arrange a place to meet them. They ask for photos, autographs and to chat a little.]

As Bauer argues (2011, p. 128), women will always have reasons to succumb to the temptation to objectify themselves. In the case of players, there are multiple opportunities to make much-needed extra income, advertising products for example. Nonetheless, it is worth noting players are often vulnerable to this kind of objectification as they are alone in a new environment, away from their parents, as young as 16, as the following sub-section explains.

Ruptures with a gendered social order – Manaus: a perfect storm?

Home-match culture/public interest
At all the Iranduba games I attend, it is quite clear that fans identify strongly with, and recognise individual players in a way that is extremely rare in women's football. This is not matched by tannoy announcers who consistently get the names of players, goal scorers and substitutes wrong, to the point of it seeming intentional. With Iranduba as the central attraction at the Arena, the fans naturally go out of their way to get to know the players' names and to become familiar with their playing style. This stability is a given for men's teams, but many women's teams play at more than one venue, sometimes behind closed doors; and also games can be moved at short notice. Attending games, it is clear that Iranduba has a 'home-match' culture and familiarity,

Figure 5.4   Iranduba training at the Barbosa Filho training ground

which is an example that must be repeated for women's club football to really establish itself in Brazil and indeed globally. Fans shout players' names and are familiar with players' styles, strengths and weaknesses, temperaments, favoured foot and everything else that goes with genuine interest. The fact that this is relatively rare in women's football speaks to the lack of social capital the women's game has accrued within many established male clubs.

Speaking with Iranduba players there is little doubt that they feel something unique about playing football in the city of Manaus. Indeed, such is the strength of this feeling that, whilst carrying out another part of the fieldwork in Santos (see Chapter Four), Tayla, a Brazilian international who has played football in a variety of settings, recalled fondly a short three-month spell with Iranduba. Despite suffering an unfortunate injury that curtailed her stay, her recollections were overwhelmingly of how positive the stadium atmosphere was and how valued she felt as an athlete there.

Among the numerous factors that have made the club so welcoming to players is the permanent home at the Arena da Amazônia and the position of being the premier sporting attraction in the city. Santos Women play games at numerous venues, including the club's own training centre and the home stadium of another local club, Portuguesa Santista. Similarly, rather than using the Arena Corinthians, in the past Corinthians Women have played numerous games in the industrial area of Osasco. The stability enjoyed by Iranduba players imbues them with a sense of importance that is denied women players who are shifted from stadium to stadium, and allows a routine to develop among fans, who know where games will be played and when games will be afforded importance (visits of *clubes de camisa*). Similarly, whilst the CBF has the habit of scheduling games for 11am, while most people are at work, Iranduba has repeatedly requested to play its games in the evening, making it possible for spectators to attend. The identification of the fans with the stadium has begun a process that must continue if women's club football is to become an established part of everyday life in the country and beyond. Several players reported being stopped in the street, or approached at games, for autographs, and of all the teams I visited during fieldwork Iranduba was the only one at which (even male) supporters regularly wore shirts with the names of players from the women's team printed on the back.

Players consistently gave me the impression that their level of engagement and their sense of belonging corresponds to an unplanned, coincidental set of circumstances. When the club perceived interest in Iranduba women they started promoting women's football with vigour. Whilst the springing up of a club like Iranduba is not actively encouraged by the institutional model of keeping women's football in check by placing it in a relationship of dependency to men's teams, it is certainly revealing of the potential of women's football, were it not straitjacketed in every way possible. Players regularly attested to feeling 'something different' about the atmosphere in Manaus. It does appear in keeping with the notion that the extreme popularity of the men's game in certain areas makes this kind of perfect storm more difficult to achieve in areas or countries where men's football is deep-rooted (Saavedra, 2003). The sense that Manaus provides a special atmosphere is typified and felt deeply by defender Monalisa Belém, who explained that playing for Iranduba she often felt compelled to run the length of the field to celebrate goals energetically with teammates and fans. Monalisa explains: 'no futebol tem que ter união e a gente é uma família. Independente de quem faça gol a gente tem que sair de onde estiver e comemorar, até as meninas no banco' [you need a togetherness in football and we are like a family. Regardless of who scores, we all have to come from wherever we are and celebrate, even the girls on the bench]. She leaves a slight doubt as to whether the players are 'obligated' to celebrate like this or do it of their own volition. Naturally, the moments that generate the most exuberant reactions are those perceived to be of higher importance to supporters and players alike. This exuberance in Manaus is generated by a number of factors that cannot be artificially engineered: the sporting and economic sense of centre–periphery antagonism; the importance that this confers upon players representing Iranduba; and the particularities of Amazonas and the way it is imagined among others. All of these factors create an atmosphere of fierce pride which the players clearly feed upon.

The gradual establishment of rivalries in men's football, to an extent, hinged on similarly contingent factors. Whilst nowadays such rivalries are taken for granted, exploited and commodified, the conditions in which they were created were often accidental. It could be argued that many of these rivalries were subsequently embellished or even to an extent invented, aided by the social capital men's football accrued over time. The experience of Iranduba shows the potential and indeed the contingent factors upon which rivalries depend.

Investment in women's football: Iranduba

One of the defining features of Iranduba is that players perceive an attempt to place women's football within the same market logic as the men's game. This consolidation depends firstly upon the amount of effort made by club directorates, federations and the media to promote the women's game and secondly upon the pre-existing social and economic conditions and inter-relationships between places within a given country. The entire coaching staff of Iranduba are male, as are all the decision makers at the Amazonian Football Federation and the great majority at national level. Mayara Vaz, another native of Belém do Pará who has migrated to Manaus for the opportunity to earn a living from the game, sees the consolidation of the women's game as hinging upon the demography of institutions – namely more female representation. She notes the lack of multiple competitions (customary in men's football). Mayara is keen to point out a positive aspect of life with Iranduba – to some degree the club breaks the vicious circle between a lack of marketing and serious investment and the lack of public interest. The interest generated by Iranduba has disproven the prevailing assumption (or pretext for inaction) at institutional level that the public are not interested – one that is also disproven by a billion people watching the Women's World Cup.

The best of both worlds?

During the Libertadores tournament in particular, it strikes me that, in a sense, Iranduba benefits from the best of both worlds. The meeting of teams from different countries brings to the fore the national importance the Brazilian crowd attach to football. For a fleeting period the Manauarans who struggle to identify with other regions of Brazil become more Brazilian. On one hand, Iranduba are not encumbered by having to compete with large, established, male clubs that have a large Manauaran fanbase. This means the club has the (almost) undivided attention of the Manaus sporting public. On the other hand, the club does benefit from the established nature of football in Brazil because it is from the social capital of the Rio and São Paulo clubs that the will to defeat the centre is derived. In this way, Iranduba benefits from being from a non-footballing city in the country of football. This cultural capital places the club's potential on a different level to clubs in the USA, for example. In the USA the club game always faces the central, fundamental problem of lacking history.

Nonetheless, Duda Pavão, a Brazilian player who has spent a number of years both studying and working in the United States, most notably for NWSL team Orlando Pride in the communications and marketing department, is keen to emphasise what she sees as the clear relationship between the efforts made by Iranduba and the attendances which they have achieved. Having experienced the marketing of women's football in the United States she is well placed to comment on the level of interest that Iranduba generates in its local community. Asked about differences between the experiences in the two countries, Duda emphasises how well developed communications, the marketing department and the training facilities were in Orlando, but maintains that there is 'something about the environment here (in Manaus)' that is impossible to imitate or recreate in Orlando. Pavão is unable to describe exactly what she means. The growth of North American club football (both male and female) has met with the obvious barrier of a lack of social capital and prestige within clubs that largely were only founded recently. Without historical football antagonisms or points of reference it has been difficult to forge rivalries and thus to grow a sizeable fanbase. Despite the runaway success of the US women's national team, its clubs' lack of social capital means that most Americans would be at a loss to name where its star players perform – and perhaps more importantly, the club league has not been a runaway success by any means. Indeed, it has been aborted and re-launched on occasions. The social capital tied up in football, which is lacking in the United States, is abundant in Brazil and Latin America – though the hidden history of women's football within clubs remains an area requiring urgent attention. As Pavão points out, women's football is the same game as men's football – what is different are the cultural meanings attached to it.

Conclusion

The Iranduba players have been able to provoke a particularly passionate response from the local people. This appears to be due to a perfect storm of circumstances that allows women's football to grow beneath the radar of the country's footballing centre. The club has been successful in positioning itself to leverage ethnic identity and invoke regional pride. The centre–periphery dichotomy that the club mobilises (via its appeals to an Amazonian ethnic identity) parallels the power imbalance between the men's and women's games – which the club is also contesting. In this way, the club has also been a vehicle for the promotion of a more dominant mode of thinking that wants to promote a 'celebration of athleticism and female empowerment' (FIFA, 2020b, p. 5).

There are few (if any) other sites in the world where the women's team command far and away the most media attention and whose highest attendance of the season is nine times that of male teams. The case of Iranduba cannot be understood in a unidimensional way as the club generates multiple meanings for different actors. The *flechada* has been commodified as part of the club brand and its attempts to sell itself internationally as a success story, but it also represents the players' bond with the Manaus public and their enjoyment of representing the city of Manaus against the *clubes de camisa*.

These players have proved over a long period to be among the most consistent players in the country, and when Iranduba fans wear players' names on the back of their shirts, they recognise those players' undoubted footballing ability. The story of the Team from the Heart of the Amazon speaks to the position women's football occupies in Brazil in the second decade of the twenty-first century – a position where progress is as clearly discernible as the multiple and stubborn obstacles that remain. Furthermore, it hints at the possibilities for women's football in cases where it is uncoupled from its dependence on male football. Iranduba displays problematic aspects, such as the objectification of players, but it also allows women's football to grow independently in the kind of unpredictable way football institutions are not prepared to countenance.

In order for a serious reconfiguration of the country's footballing hierarchy to take place in women's football it would be necessary for 10 or 15 well-funded and vigorously promoted Irandubas to emerge. This does not seem to be the model being promoted, however. *Obrigatoriedade* centres around making the large (men's) clubs comply and will perhaps consolidate the sub-categorisation of women's football.

The level of support and interest Iranduba has generated since the club began in 2011 suggests that another way of imagining a future for women's football, both in Brazil and more globally, is possible. Stripped of the structural imbalances that ensure an unequal playing field in other regions, the case of Iranduba shows that women's football can and will be commercially viable. It suggests that with relatively modest public and private investment, relative to the sums of money bandied about in men's football, a model of growth that is not tied into a relationship of dependence on an already illustrious male club could also be viable, at the very least, alongside the mainstream model of integrating women's football into larger more established clubs. The final chapter of this book considers the balance of the experiences of players from across the continent. Chapters Three, Four and Five are rich in detail, but deal with some of the areas where women's football has had the most success and/or generated the most public interest in recent times. As is to be expected in a continent having the size and diversity of South America, this progress has not occurred across the board. Chapter Six brings together the experiences of players from Bolivia, Peru, Ecuador and Chile and brings them into dialogue with the perspectives of their Brazilian and Colombian counterparts.

Surveying the Field from the Players' Perspective

Introduction

An estimated television audience of more than a billion for the 2018 Women's World Cup evidenced the continuing, breakneck growth of global interest in women's football. Of all the continents, South American coverage reached the highest percentage of viewers, registering an astonishing 560 per cent increase from the previous World Cup (FIFA, 2019; Globoesporte.com, 2019) with Brazil enjoying the largest audience for the final despite not even being involved (Veja, 2019). However, whilst this quadrennial spike in visibility clearly indicates an enormous growth of interest in women's football, institutional inertia unchecked by a complicit media polity mean this public interest has not yet translated into a well-developed club game or, by extension, to high-profile club players. Indeed, particularly in South America, a continent where football has long been inextricably linked to tropes of national identity (Alabarces, 2002; Kittleson, 2014; Bocketti, 2016). Through an analysis of football, this work explores how stereotypes such as tropicalism and Europeanism are used to construct narratives of national identity in Argentina and Brazil. These stereotypes, which are the consequence of colonial perspectives that seek to reduce heterogeneity in order to gain symbolic power, appear to be effective when we consider their prominence in a range of media. This study argues that these stereotypes need to be deconstructed using methodologies based in the social sciences, while also considering the role of humour in their production and dissemination, women's club football remains barely visible. Moreover, when it is visible, it tends to be selective and episodic – coverage of extreme outbursts suggesting women should not even be playing the game, for example (ABC Fútbol, 2018; Gazeta Press, 2021) drown out more serious and substantive debate about how best to turn public interest in the Women's World Cup into a more sustained interest in the club game. Whilst tournaments like the World Cup and the Olympics require only the most fleeting passing interest, arguably the deeper, quasi-religious ties are often attached to the day-to-day progress of club football. These links are not present for South American women players, whose opportunities to make a living from club football remain scarce and transitory. For this reason, patterns of short-term, transnational migration are common, albeit on a far weaker footing than their male counterparts (Agergaard et al., 2014; Rial, 2014; Tiesler, 2016).

The ascent of men's football in recent decades tends to be conceived of primarily in terms of hypercommodification (Giulianotti & Robertson, 2009; Kuper, 2014) and secondarily in terms of cultural omnipresence. In the latter vein, Arthur Hopcraft's seminal work *The Football Man* articulates the unacknowledged assumption that the game is 'an everyday matter; built into the urban psyche, as much a common experience to our children as are uncles and school' (Hopcraft, 1968, p. 9). In this vein, this chapter, shaped by the concerns of players themselves, argues that in order to approach the quotidian ubiquity of men's football, the key struggle from here onwards for the women's game is establishing the game at youth and grass-roots level – at schools and universities, in youth divisions within clubs and informally. The role of schools, colleges and universities in countries where the game is deep-rooted, like the United States, must not be ignored (Markovits & Hellerman, 2003). Finally, the issue at hand in this book: that creating a women's football culture at club level is identified by players as fundamental. A closer approximation to each of these spaces is necessary.

I prepared a survey designed to identify a wide-ranging agenda of issues to explore in detail throughout the ethnographic chapters that provide the backbone to this work (Chapters Three, Four and Five). In this way I sought to ensure that the direction was driven by the participants/players' own concerns. It is split into quantitative and qualitative sections. The survey was carried out anonymously, meaning participants were allowed to express their opinions freely. Moreover, I felt an anonymous survey made it more likely players would be candid about delicate areas that they consider particularly problematic (Hammersley & Atkinson, 2007, p. 8). The first section gives an indicative gauge of satisfaction with football institutions, clubs and the media before proceeding to a qualitative discussion around how things can be improved, which was developed from a carefully chosen selection of representative comments from players based in Bolivia, Brazil, Chile, Colombia, Ecuador and Peru. It sought to consider the varying nuances across national settings using this data. The material collected fed into the richer ethnographic insight in Chapters Three, Four and Five.

This chapter, by design, aims to highlight the vastly differing panoramas in the countries surveyed. The survey questions reflected my hypothesis that the academic literature on contemporary women's football has focused disproportionately on the role of the media. Prior to carrying out the survey, I felt it was likely that players would highlight institutional shortcomings as a major barrier to the growth of the women's game. More specifically, a lack of women within football institutions means that clubs and federations, at regional, national and continental level have tended to pay lip service to the notional gender equality set out in FIFA statutes (FIFA, 2016) rather than attempt to enact it.

Beyond the media representations paradigm

Much of the scholarly work on women's football to date has tended towards analysing the shifting discourses used to represent women's football across print and broadcast media. Given the dearth of coverage of women's club football until recent times, this has usually meant that national teams have provided the central focus (Conde & Rodríguez, 2002; Ferretti et al., 2011; Mina & Goellner, 2015b; Pfister, 2015; Ravel & Gareau, 2016; Black & Fielding-Lloyd, 2019; Krasnoff, 2019). This has had the unintended effect of deflecting attention from neglect at institutional level, placing disproportionate emphasis on the media. The introduction to this book sets out how scholars have demonstrated that women's football is often mis-represented, wilfully or otherwise. Nevertheless, the day-to-day struggle of players to professionalise the women's game and ultimately be able to make a full-time living from it have not featured.

This has been complemented by recent literature noting a growth of alternative media with groups like Dibradoras in Brazil, Fémina Fútbol in Colombia and Burn It All Down in the United States. Indeed, in Brazil these counternarratives have already garnered academic attention (Vieira, 2018; Firmino, 2019). Similarly, socially engaged academic work continues to address the under-representation of women's football and forward pragmatic proposals for change (Rial, 2013a; Goellner & Kessler, 2018; Goellner, 2021). Building upon these bodies of scholarship, this book addresses inaccurate or disingenuous representations by attempting to strip away the mediation of broadcasters and commentators, foregrounding the perspectives of women footballers themselves.

Historical work has hinted at the omissions in the media-heavy analysis to date. For example, Elsey and Nadel (2019, p. 18) identify three ideological camps they consider have historically shaped the politics of sports. They suggest the state, civic associations (religious and charity) and sports clubs to be significant actors. A fourth, highly ideological addition to these, in the case of football, is surely the regional, national, continental and global federations responsible for the governance of the game. Mirroring the development of critical studies of men's football on the South American continent, the pioneering works focusing on women players have emanated from Brazil, and to a lesser extent Argentina. Historians have shown the pernicious and lasting legacy of the deliberate erasure of women from tropes of national identity (Goellner, 2005b, 2012; Knijnik, 2014; Elsey & Nadel, 2019; Bonfim, 2019). This has fed into more contemporary work, some of which is more critical of institutions responsible for running the game (Knijnik & Horton, 2013), the role of clubs in promoting the women's game (Rial, 2013a), work focusing on the oral history of women players (Joras, 2015; Ardila Biela, 2022, 2023; Biram, 2022), and even ethnographic work juxtaposing the lived experience of a player with the critical tools of sociology (Garton & Hijós, 2017; Garton, 2019, 2023). Thus far, however, there have been no attempts to record the perspective of women players in survey form. Similarly, there has been no work that compares similarities and differences across national settings. This chapter therefore contributes a broad span of quantitative data to complement the qualitative research that has hitherto been a staple of the field.

Survey methodology

Taking advantage of teams from each country congregating in one city for the CONMEBOL Women's Copa Libertadores 2018 event held in Manaus, Brazil in November and December 2018, I used convenience sampling to collect data from a diverse range of players based in different settings. Convenience sampling essentially involves drawing sample data from a target group who are close at hand at a given time (De Vaus, 2013; Fowler Jr, 2013). The tournament comprised 12 teams in total: 10 national league champions (1 from each member of CONMEBOL), the host team (Esporte Clube Iranduba) and the defending continental champions, Audax Osasco (formerly Corinthians-Audax, from São Paulo).[1] It is worth noting that the logistical advantage of having several teams in the same place to carry out the survey also comes with a potential disadvantage. This is that each team involved in the study represents the highest achieving teams (and often the best conditions available) in each country, and thus the best-case scenario of player conditions is presented rather than a more representative, middle-of-the-table team.

All surveys were self-administered via group administration: the rest of the club delegation left me for half an hour to first explain the survey to players and then allowed them time to answer the survey questions. Group administration normally results in a higher rate of response (Fowler Jr, 2013, p. 65) though it was made clear to players that participation was entirely voluntary and accordingly numerous players chose not to take part.

The questions used simple short words in order to ensure a consistent meaning to all respondents and to minimise any possibilities for ambiguity (Fowler Jr, 2013; Sapsford, 2006). Ethical approval was granted and piloting was carried out in Bristol prior to fieldwork, and questions were adapted according to feedback and suggestions offered by native speakers of Spanish and Portuguese respectively. Once again, it is fair to note that those piloting were academics who were unaware of the lived realities of women footballers, particularly in the countries where the sport is least established, and thus

---

1 Corinthians-Audax was an agreement between two clubs – Corinthians and Audax Osasco – that allowed Corinthians to fulfil the requirement to have a women's team for the purpose of the Copa Libertadores and Audax to compete at national level in the top division.

due dispensation for how the questions would be read by those players is also problematic. This became apparent during fieldwork when it became clear that answers to certain questions were skewed by the wording in subtle ways. For example, there is a significant difference between asking whether the gender of a team manager is important and asking whether players would prefer a female manager. To the first question players naturally replied that competence was the more important factor, whereas to the second they often did reply that they preferred a female manager. These possibilities for the survey to mis-represent views justifies the decision to carry out larger-scale ethnographic research, that allowed these subtle nuances to be identified more easily.

The survey largely respects the conventions of survey research insofar as the majority of questions were of a closed nature, in order to guarantee the comparability of data from which to draw meaningful conclusions (Fowler Jr, 2013, p. 93). Considering the dearth of information available on the subject matter, I added five open questions, the responses to which I would pursue during the ethnographic part of my research (here covered in Chapters Three, Four and Five). The results section below juxtaposes quantitative results to questions scaled from 0 to 10 as described with the open answers to supplementary questions and the theoretical framework as set out below.

In recent years there has been considerable tension between players and their respective national federations, and the period when the survey was conducted was no exception. In Brazil, a number of players resigned from national team duty when Emily Lima was dismissed from the team coaching job in 2017 on grounds they believed spurious (Pires, 2017). In Colombia, multiple allegations of sexual harassment have been reported (Alvarado, 2019; Pinochet, 2017). In Chile and Argentina players have formed a union to represent their interests after their respective federations left the women's national teams inactive for prolonged periods. This is highly significant and influenced my decision to use self-administered procedures for this part of the research. It is well documented that this method can be preferable to carrying out direct face-to-face interviews on socially delicate topics, as participants do not have to talk about traumatic experiences with a stranger or to admit directly to socially undesirable or negatively valued characteristics or behaviour. Conversely, data has consistently indicated that sensitive but significant information is more frequently offered in self-administered modes than when the interviewer directly asks the question. (Fowler Jr, 2013, p. 63). In this sense the survey methodology complemented the ethnographic material by eliciting more candid answers, which allowed me to hone lines of questioning used later in more detailed interviews.

A total of 103 players from the 7 teams (2 Brazilian and 1 each from Bolivia, Chile, Colombia, Ecuador and Peru) responded to this part of the research. Prior to being handed the surveys players were asked to fill in the survey alone, and to discuss any feelings or thoughts thrown up by questions after handing their survey in. With a mixture of jest and thoughtfulness the players debated particular questions with greater intensity – for example the suggestion of mixed gender football. These players came from a potential pool of 154 players (22 in each squad) who were at the tournament in question. At the time of carrying out the surveys, the squads from Bolivia, Ecuador and Peru contained only players from those countries, whereas those from Brazil, Colombia and Chile contained a number of foreign players, most notably, though not exclusively, from Argentina and Venezuela. The multinational presence in some teams is significant insofar as it means the realities of their respective home nations inevitably contribute to some of the open questions. Of the 154 players targeted, 32 declined to participate and 19 were not available at the time my visits were carried out. Owing to availability and the tight schedules of players at the tournament, it was only possible to carry out the survey with players from 8 of the 12 teams. Nonetheless, the completion rate of the survey was around 66 per cent of the players at the tournament, constituting a significant representative sample. Players were informed that findings would be made available to them upon request once this book was completed.

Quantitative survey results

For the quantitative section of the survey players were asked to answer a range of questions, either by picking an option from a list or rating their satisfaction on a scale from 1 (unsatisfied) to 10 (fully satisfied). The results are shown in Figures 6.1 to 6.8 respectively and analysed below.

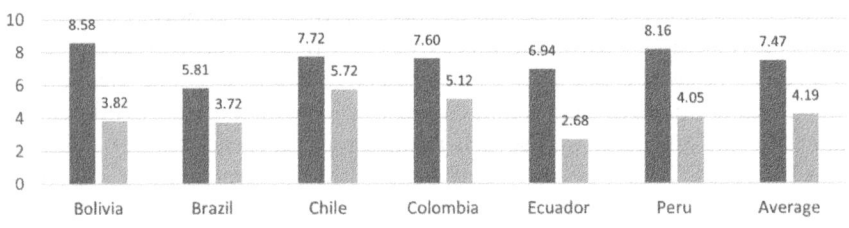

■ 1 How well organised was the Copa Libertadores 2018?

■ 2 How well organised were events in your respective national league in 2018?

Figure 6.1   How satisfied are you with the organisation of national and continental women's club competitions?

As Figure 6.1 shows, without exception players from every country were always more satisfied with the shorter Copa Libertadores tournament than with their national leagues. Whilst fleeting in duration, in the continental tournament players are able to play in large stadiums like the Arena da Amazônia and are accommodated in good-quality hotels, with training facilities and travel all covered by CONMEBOL. The Brazilian players registered the lowest level of satisfaction with the tournament as perhaps their expectations are higher since, in the Brazilian league, they had experienced playing games in large stadiums like the Pacaembu in São Paulo. Conversely in Bolivia, Ecuador and Peru, two countries where women remain unable to earn a salary from football, the gap between satisfaction with the national leagues and with the Copa Libertadores shows itself to be far greater. The second question considers the organisation of competitions by the respective national federations over the previous five years, a period chosen to take into account the likelihood of positive changes in reaction to global growth and *obrigatoriedade* (discussed in detail in Chapter Two).

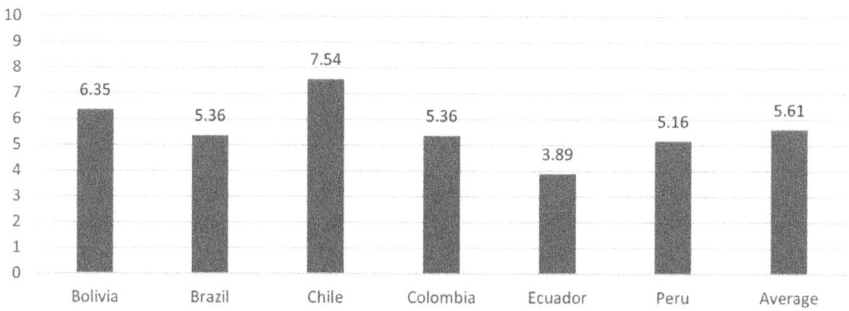

Figure 6.2   How much has organisation of national club competition improved in last five years?

As shown in Figure 6.2, the average satisfaction exceeded 5 in every country except Ecuador (3.89) but was never higher than 7.54. The scores suggest a complex and mixed panorama. The notion that organisation had improved is not rejected outright; however the middling results suggest players believe much more can be done, and much better. Clearly, the question deals with generalities and there are some particular insights that follow later, when we examine indicative remarks made by players in the qualitative section.

Figure 6.3 shows perceptions of whether media coverage of women's football is skewed towards club football, national football or neither. Here, participants were asked simply to choose one of these three options, and the graph shows the number who chose each one. The question emerged from the academic literature, which tends to pay more attention to national team football. I wanted to see whether my hypotheses that this bias is mirrored in the media and that overall the day-to-day business of club football is often forgotten about in debates about the growth of women's football, are views the players hold. The results suggested that most did, particularly Brazilian and Peruvian participants who felt international women's football eclipsed the importance of the club game in their country, but that Bolivian and

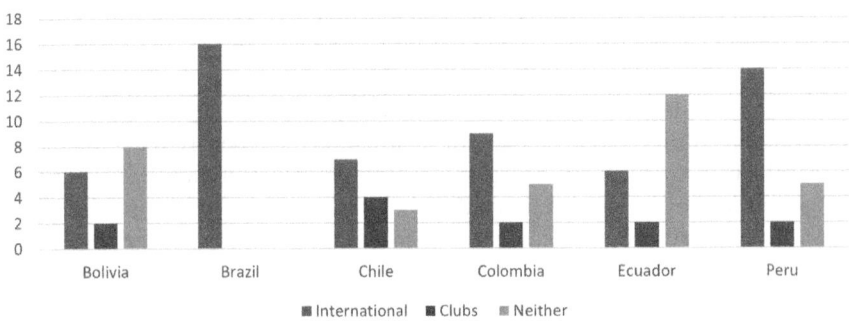

Figure 6.3   Does club or national team football get more attention in your country?

(particularly) Ecuadorean players felt the media balance is not skewed in their countries.

Figure 6.4, then, registers that satisfaction with the coverage of women's football is higher for coverage of national teams. However, it remains far from satisfactory. Moreover, many of the differences are marginal, indicating most likely that neither club football nor national football is covered adequately.

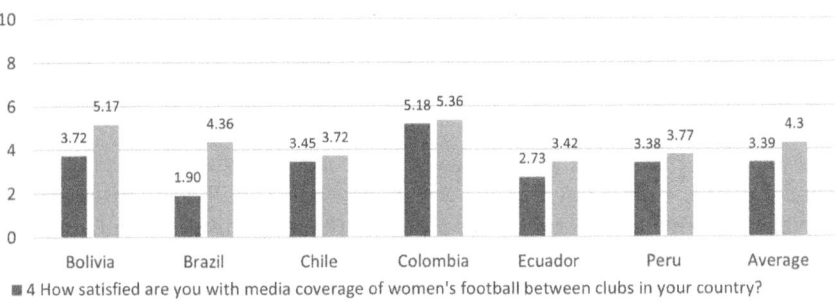

Figure 6.4   Satisfaction with media coverage of women's club and national team football

For Figures 6.5 and 6.6 I asked hypothetical questions about policy recommendations that could be made to encourage the growth of women's football. Participants were asked, firstly, whether they would like to play back-to-back games with the male team in front of larger crowds, and secondly whether press conferences promoting men's and women's football at the same time would be a positive step. The graphs show how many participants answered Yes or No; in both cases the results were resoundingly in favour.

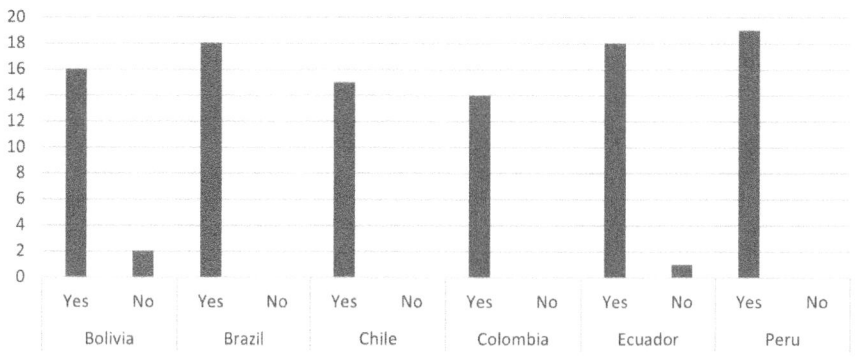

Figure 6.5   Would it be a good idea to play double bill (male/female) matches?

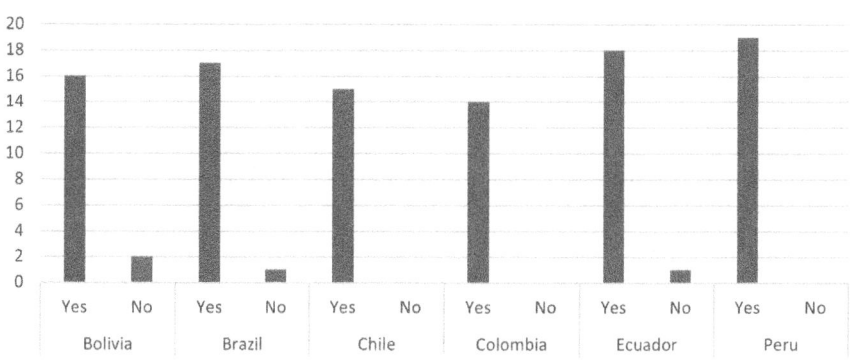

Figure 6.6   Should the clubs promote women's football together with men's football (at press conferences and public events)?

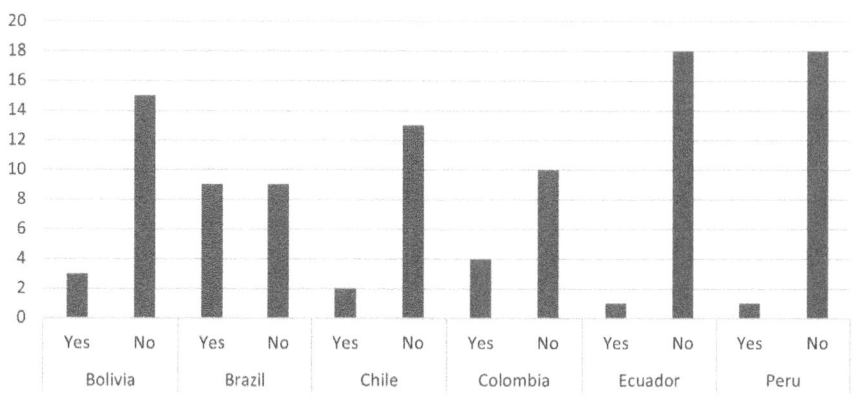

Figure 6.7   Is it important if your manager is male or female?

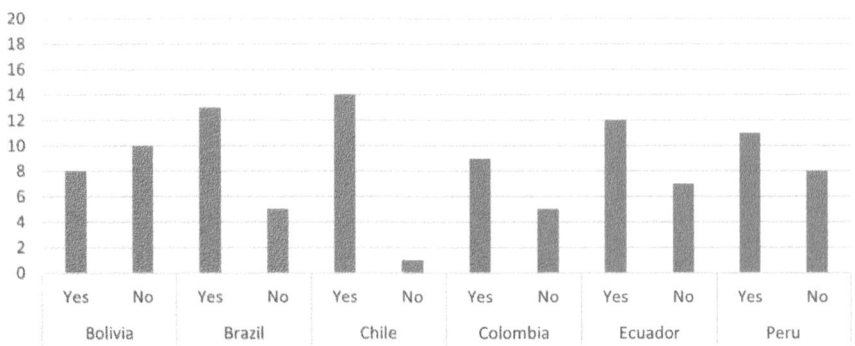

Figure 6.8   Do you think it would be a good idea to play tournaments with mixed teams?

Along similar lines, in Figure 6.7 players were asked whether the gender of their manager is important. When I later engaged players in far more detail during the ethnographic studies discussed in Chapters Three, Four and Five, it became clear to me that wording this particular question differently might have yielded different results. For example, if it had asked 'would you prefer to have a female manager?' results might have been different. However, with the question worded as it was, very few players were prepared to answer in the affirmative: the great majority of players answered no to the question.

A further hypothetical policy question (as set out in Figure 6.8) concerned mixed gender football. Even in non-physical competitions such as chess, gender division is deep-rooted and rarely questioned in sports – with occasional historical anomalies like mixed doubles in tennis (Lake, 2016; Wilson, 2021). For this reason, a number of players were taken aback by the question. Whilst some participants found it divisive, a majority of players from all countries except Bolivia were in favour of the proposal.

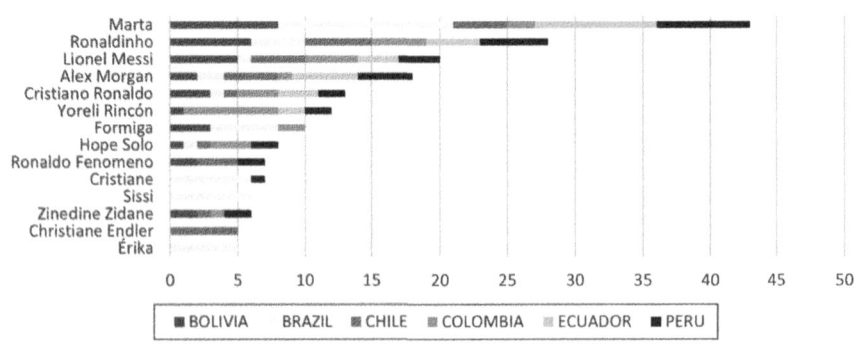

Figure 6.9   Who are your reference points in world football?

Finally Figure 6.9 shows the responses players gave when asked to list players they regard as footballing reference points. The question was deliberately worded in a gender-neutral way, to see how players would interpret it. The answers reflected a bias towards South American players and also an admiration for US women's football as the pre-eminent force of the modern era. The question was planted intentionally to catch the players off-guard, as a seemingly throwaway question about personal preference. The intention was to see whether the players' footballing idols were in fact male or female players from the past. In both the Spanish and Portuguese versions of the questionnaire this meant avoiding the masculine or feminine words for players (*jogador/a* or *jugador/a* respectively). For this reason the wording I adopted was the neutral *referente* (reference point, in the sense of role model/hero in Spanish and Portuguese). Whilst national omissions from the survey (the Argentinean and Venezuelan women players did not participate) have no doubt impacted upon results, it is still worthwhile to reflect upon the choices made by players.[2] From the 103 players surveyed, 7 chose to name no player, either writing 'none' or in two cases 'uno mismo' [myself], hinting at positive self-esteem. A total of 54 players were named, 17 female and 32 male. Selections were largely South American (39 different players), with only 6 North Americans (all women) and 9 European players mentioned. The preponderance of South American players reflects the players' knowledge but more likely the extent to which football is linked to national pride and identity. Predictably, these choices were often along national lines with Sissi or Érika only chosen by Brazilians, Christiane Endler only chosen by Chileans and so on. Of all the players named there were only two whose playing days pre-dated the date of birth of most of the players surveyed (Pelé and Teófilo Cubillas respectively). It seems relevant that these two players were trailblazers in their time, contributing to a re-imagining and consolidation of narratives around Afro-Brazilian and Afro-Peruvian players respectively. Whilst choices were often along national lines, the players most mentioned are clearly known continent-wide or worldwide. Encouragingly for the growth of the women's game, six of the ten most chosen players were women. Of those, Marta was named by respondents from all of the participating countries.[3] Perhaps symptomatic of the commercial growth of the women's

---

2 It is merely my speculation that further participation from Venezuelan players (some Venezuelans based at clubs in Chile and Colombia took part) would have skewed the final results towards choosing a female player (Deyna Castellanos) and that Argentinean participation might well have had the opposite effect (Diego Maradona, Lionel Messi, etc).

3 Peculiarly, Marta's name was often spelt wrongly (12 times out of 42, including Brazilian participants), as Martha, while none of the male players' names (including linguistically less familiar names) in the entire survey had any spelling mistakes whatsoever.

national game in the period since I carried out my survey, a player Marta herself recognises as a true pioneer of the women's game, Sissi, was only named by six Brazilian respondents.[4] The much-vaunted player, along with Pretinha and Maravilha from the same early Brazil women's teams, played before the mediatisation of World Cups, whereas Marta's generation, it would appear, has become the lightning rod that has truly opened debates about the game. The reach of Marta, together with her phenomenal and surely unparalleled achievements, are both discernible in the answers to this question. The fact that she was named one-and-a-half times as often as any male player is symptomatic of the growing self-confidence of the Marta generation.

Qualitative discussion

In addition to the quantitative questions described above, players were given the opportunity to explain their choices in further detail and to highlight areas they feel to be particularly pertinent and worthy of comment. The following discussion is led by players' observations and perspectives and feeds into the agenda of the rest of the book.

On club competitions

Players' responses reflected two major issues that dominate the panorama of women's club football in South America: the issue of *obrigatoriedade* and the varying states of professionalisation in each country. Both are discussed in this section. Beyond this, players showed an acute awareness of the need for youth divisions to be set up and also for women's football to be established as a staple at school level. They also pointed to a lack of marketing and promotion of the women's game and differential treatment within their clubs.

Obrigatoriedade, the CONMEBOL policy requiring clubs to have a women's team and youth division in order to be able to enter men's teams in the Copa Libertadores and Copa Sudamericana, generated lively debate among players. An Ecuadorian participant suggested: 'hay que obligar a la gente tener equipo femenino, sino (*sic*) nunca va a pasar' [we must oblige clubs to have a women's team, if not, it's never going to happen]. In a context in which, at the time of carrying out the survey, none of the larger Ecuadorian clubs had a women's team, meaning an unpaid amateur league was the only option for players, this attitude seems logical. Indeed, since I carried out the survey, the policy of *obrigatoriedade* has seen action, with a number of larger clubs like Barcelona and Emelec opening women's teams.

Another perspective, not necessarily at odds with the one just presented, comes from Brazil, emphasising the longer struggle. In Brazil all the major

4 Sisleide do Amor Lima (Sissi) was Brazil's Number 10 before Marta, representing the country with distinction at the World Cup and Olympics. In 2019 she was inaugurated into the FIFA Hall of Fame (Cardoso, 2019b).

clubs now have a women's team; however the next stage is expressed in the following response: 'Temos que criar um interesse genuíno e não ter que obrigar a gente ter futebol feminino. Questão de educação mais geral na sociedade' [We have to create genuine interest and not to have to force people to have women's football. It's a broader educational problem in society]. Players recognise that the disinterest or outright rejection of women playing football comes from culture. That is to say that 'women being included or excluded from certain spaces or from belonging to a particular identity' (Louro, 1997, p. 84) is a generational question of education. It is not so much that some players oppose *obrigatoriedade*, so much as they realise it is insufficient and that the problems are deeper-rooted. They recognise sport as a key site where these identity markers are constructed and policed (Goellner, 2005b, 2012; Müller, 2016).

Whilst opinion seemed divided about the policy, seen either way, it is certainly encouraging that a number of players either reject or are sceptical about solutions being imposed from above and are aware that for women's club football to thrive a genuine interest must be generated. In this respect, when comparing, it is important to factor in the extent to which answers are linked to the expectations that have been generated over a period of time. Brazilian women players, for example, have long enjoyed a far more extensive club calendar (which gives them an enormous advantage at tournaments like the Libertadores), are more accustomed to playing in larger municipal stadiums like the Pacaembu, albeit occasionally, and more accustomed to staying in decent-quality accommodation and travelling in advance for away matches.

In Colombia, the women's league is nominally professional, but players' responses reflected a scepticism about the gap between the federation's claims and the lived experience on the ground. Similarly, in Brazil certain larger clubs offer players year-round contracts and a level of stability that allows them to dedicate themselves to football. These are not indicative cases, however, as players who were lucky enough to benefit from those conditions were keen to express in the survey. As one player wrote '[e]n casí todos los otros clubes no hay contratos anuales por nosotras' [at almost all the other clubs there are no annual contracts for women players]. Moreover, in many other countries, at the time of carrying out the survey, professionalisation was only an abstract notion that players understood to exist in other places. In all these cases, definitions of what constitutes professionalism remain nebulous, often spun to the discursive convenience of institutions or media. A body of work on men's football has often taken in debates on this topic (Taylor, 2001, 2005, 2013; Frydenberg, 2005, 2011) with concepts like *marronismo* falling between amateurism and professionalism (Garton, 2019).

Later comments from participants are perceptive in terms of linking the lack of adequate youth divisions to player development. A Chilean participant comments

con un sistema serio de categorias de base, ya sería mucho más competitivo nuestro fútbol, atrayendo más interés de los medios y de la gente – por ahora falta mucho el nivel de nuestro fútbol. Deberíamos jugar más joven en colegios también, estilo EEUU. [with a serious youth system our level would be more competitive, and that would attract more interest from the media and the people. We should play earlier at schools too, like in the USA.]

There is some scope for improvement at clubs in this regard as CONMEBOL's policy of establishing female teams within male clubs includes the prerequisite that they also have at least one youth division within the female club (CONMEBOL, 2018, p. 41).

Brazilian players largely concurred with the need for young women's divisions, to allow players to develop, adding another element that is outside CONMEBOL control and difficult to enforce in any case. Numerous participants mentioned the need for a focus on marketing and publicising the women's game, both at club and regional/national federation level: 'A gente sempre acha e fala que futebol feminino não dê retorno mas nunca tentou de verdade fazer um bom marketing, etc. [People say that there is no return on investment but they've never tried really]. The players showed in these responses that they are acutely aware of the commercial side of football, as the women's game has emerged at an entirely different conjuncture to the men's. Women's football is often presented as a counterhegemonic initiative railing against modern football in its hypercommercialised form (Goldblatt, 2019, p. 28). In reality, its emergence could easily be complexified as forming part of the march of modern football or as part of a neoliberal feminist agenda. Indeed, it has been argued that the pressure on players to market themselves has already resulted in the 'femming up' and whitening of national teams (Elsey & Nadel, 2019, p. 145). Women's football is certainly already deeply embedded within the divisive logic of the market – the best players enjoy the most stability and the longest contracts within clubs. Nonetheless, the players best paid for playing football are not necessarily those who benefit the most from lucrative spin-offs – the best profile for marketing purposes is usually linked to the heterosexual male gaze (Connell, 2005). As mentioned in several chapters, the women's season is usually much shorter than the men's. The inaugural season of the newly launched Colombian 'professional' league lasted just four months with the latest season (2019) being inexplicably shortened to just two-and-a-half months despite initial plans to extend it. The notion that such a short season should be labelled 'professional' by DIMAYOR, with the majority of players on short, precarious contracts, subject to dismissal should they get injured, is clearly dubious. Frequently during fieldwork Colombian players would note the disjuncture between professionalism and their lived experiences. As they juggled playing with working or studying they would frequently question the notion of DIMAYOR offering a professional league.

Indeed, in Chapter One I discussed Yoreli Rincón's symbolic struggle for professional recognition of Atlético Huila's triumph in the 2018 Copa Libertadores. Other players present instantly connect with the points

Rincón was trying to make about the true state of the professionalisation of women's football, and backed her publicly. Liana Salazar, for example, ended the press conference that followed the Copa Libertadores by saying that all the players back Rincón (Yoreli Rincón, WIN Sports, 2018). It would, in fact, be impossible to attach such a preposterously inaccurate label to a men's league in which players often only train twice or three times a week; such a league would correctly be called amateur or semi-professional. In Colombia's 'professional' women's league, the professional designation is used by the mass media, club directors, managers (almost all male) and even by players themselves (perhaps understandably, as players naturally seek recognition). Out of self-interest, a wide range of actors want the league to be seen as professional, and thus rarely question the meaning of the term. Whilst the discourse of professionalism is strong, players appear dissatisfied with the lived experience of it. A Colombian participant explained:

> los torneos de liga y libertadores deberían ser mucho más largas. Podría mejorar mucho poniendo divisiones menores también. Es importante también el apoyo de las empresas privadas. [Both the league and the Libertadores should be much longer. And they could improve a lot by adding youth divisions too. There's also an important role for private investors.]

Mention of the importance of private capital is significant. In Colombia particularly, whilst the larger clubs are happy to satisfy institutional requirements by having a women's team, they are often unwilling to fund it from what they continue to perceive as 'the men's team's budget'. The occasional success stories thus far have been propped up by outside investors like Diego Perdomo. This has created the illusion of commitment from Colombia's leading clubs, that until now has not really materialised.

At the other end of the scale, the Brazilian calendar, at least, is more likely to satisfy players. It runs for almost six months and is supplemented by (often strong) state leagues that can offer a further three to four months' football each year. Almost inevitably these end up running concurrently, but nonetheless the specificities of Brazil as a larger country with regional tournaments mean that Brazilian players benefit from far more competitive matches (although admittedly competitive imbalance is common in state championships, which often pit big clubs against tiny ones). This is reflected in the Brazilian answers, which prioritise 'mais marketing e divulgação' [more marketing and publicity]. The Paulista Federation (São Paulo state) is bound by its historical amateurism, meaning it does not allow charging for entrance tickets to women's games, but it has shown a very proactive approach to publicising the women's game online and at a number of events, organised by ex-Brazilian national team captain, Aline Pellegrino.

On media coverage

Following the focus on national teams in academic literature, it was my hypothesis that the majority of media coverage is most likely dedicated to national teams at major tournaments. For that reason, I asked players whether the women's national team or women's club football received more coverage. My rationale for this was that, once again, the infrequent nature of national team football often means that it is possible to pay lip service to the notion of supporting the growth of women's football, without having to dedicate resources to it on a sustained basis. Both the continental national championship (Copa America) and the World Cup are quadrennial, meaning that media coverage of national teams only really need take place every two years to maintain a façade of genuine interest. As has been noted, friendly games between South America's women's national teams are so rare, they have even been removed from the FIFA rankings (Elsey & Nadel, 2019, p. 246).

One Peruvian participant touched upon an important area, noting 'ha mejorado bastante con la transmisión en vivo por facebook y en otras redes sociales' [it has improved a lot with live streams on Facebook and other social media]. The existence of multiple platforms online has meant that those interested in women's football can now often find it outside traditional television options. This is important for keen fans who will look for the games anywhere they are shown. However, other players felt that, whilst acknowledging the incremental gains made, coverage was still deficient in many aspects.

For example, a Brazilian participant noted that 'a frequencia e a qualidade são diferentes – as vezes nem põem comentarista para jogos do feminino' [the frequency and the quality are different – sometimes they don't even supply commentary with the women's matches].[5] This brings into question the role of affect in constructing the hegemony of men's football. The often hyperbolic performance of the football commentator is remembered by the public as part of the most recalled moments the games produce.[6] At a level of interest where 'os comentaristas não se emocionam como nos jogos do masculino' [commentators don't get excited like they do for men's matches] and/or 'os comentaristas nao sabem nossos nomes' [commentators don't even know our names] it is difficult for these layers of melodrama to emerge. This was certainly true in my experience at the Copa Libertadores 2018 in Manaus where, with embarrassing frequency, goal scorers, substitutions and even team names were confused on the stadium tannoy. During televisual broadcasts namechecking of players tends to be much less frequent, replaced by generic terms like 'the defender' or 'the attacker'. Players are acutely aware

---

5 This is a common global practice for women's matches (the BBC are among many others in this regard) – particularly in the case of online live streams or on secondary channels.

6 Think 'they think it's all over – it is now' from England's World Cup Final victory in 1966, for example; or the 'barrilete cósmico' commentary of Victor Hugo Morales in 1986 – for more on this see Biram (2013).

of this and note it when they watch women's games. This chimes with the observations of Conde (2008), who argues that men refuse to relinquish their position of being the only ones who feel the true passion in football. Conversely, they note the increased level of interest from former women players now working as commentators/pundits. Whilst commentators may be able to moderate their language to suit shifting societal expectations, it is more difficult to feign being genuinely moved (or otherwise) by games.

Furthermore, there is opposition to the notion that some coverage is better than none. Another participant from Colombia voiced a common notion that in fact coverage was deliberately poor in order to prevent growth of the women's game:

> que se puede decir? Es de muy baja calidad, muy mal hecho, aburrido entre otras cosas. Lo hacen mal intencionalmente para evitar el crecimiento. [What can you say? It's very poor quality, really badly done, boring more than anything. They do it badly on purpose to stop women's football growing.]

This analysis is in keeping with a body of academic work discussed in further detail in Chapter One (Cooky et al., 2013; Musto et al., 2017; Van Dijk, 1995).

On the role of clubs

CONMEBOL's move to debar those without a women's team from the male Copa Libertadores has meant most of South America's prominent clubs have now opened a women's team. Smaller clubs with less probability of reaching the financially lucrative Libertadores appear less concerned. A pertinent issue, with or without this radical change, is the role of South American clubs as potentially independent political actors, who can challenge the status quo in society. Indeed, the most celebrated example is that of Corinthians of São Paulo and their two-year experiment with self-managed democratic practices between 1982 and 1984 (Florenzano, 2010). Whilst those democratic practices responded to a particular historical conjuncture and place, Brazil under dictatorship, it hints at the possibilities clubs offer, particularly social membership clubs that were formed with an entirely different ethos to the private membership model dominant in the UK, for example. Recent scholarship, however, signals an increasing shift towards the marketisation of clubs on the continent, most notably in Argentina (Hijós, 2013, 2014; Moreira & Hijós, 2013) and Chile (Vergara, 2019). In this context, sexism has taken refuge in the logic of the market, as in the case of Santos in 2012 when the women's division was temporarily closed, ostensibly to retain Neymar at the club for the hosting of the Brazil 2014 World Cup but in reality a spiteful cut to what amounted to less than 0.5 per cent of the club's budget.

Prior to carrying out research I was aware that questions around the integration of women into traditional clubs would appear more familiar to some participants than others. By that I mean that the integration of the female arms of Santos, Colo Colo, Cerro Porteño, Peñarol and Atlético Huila is an issue to which players can easily relate. Indeed, in the very season in which the research took place Santos announced the signing of David Braz to the men's team in a joint press conference with a female player (Mendonça, 2018c). Similarly, initiatives in Chile and Colombia have seen double-bill matches, albeit widely unreported and with the women's game billed as a 'preliminary' to the main action on both occasions (Prensafútbol, 2019; Futbolred, 2019). On the other hand, to participants from other countries, where the larger clubs remain closed to the paid participation of women's players, the mere concept of a double-bill game seemed far-fetched or outlandish, though possibly something they may in theory embrace.

The integration of women into press conferences was almost universally accepted with many players feeling that occupying the same physical space in the same stadium as the high-profile male players from their country would be beneficial on a number of levels. From a pragmatic perspective it was felt that the occasion would allow them to draw upon the significant support base of the male teams. Beyond this, participants felt that fans have an emotional attachment to the teams' home stadiums, and hence if they are moved to play 'professional' female matches at a training ground or smaller amateur facility then the authenticity of representing Santos, for example, is lost. This was borne out during my fieldwork when a full Vila Belmiro (the traditional home of Santos FC) saw Santos Women narrowly beat Corinthians Women. Entering the stadium, the murals of previous great matches involving Pelé and Coutinho and more recently Marta and Cristiane gave a sense of the history attached to the space. In more academic terms, there is a body of work from social geography attesting to the affective dimensions of sports grounds (Bale, 1991, 1994; Giulianotti, 1999). Similarly, the Maracanã, intentionally designed as the world's most impressive stadium of its era, symbolises Brazil's arrival as a footballing force in the world and thus occupies a particular space in the Brazilian and indeed international social imaginary (Lacerda Abrahão & Soares, 2009, p. 17). A feature of women's football that is partly attributable to federations and partly to clubs (who have the right to request changes to fixture times and locations as they wish) is the tendency to play women's games at times and places clearly inconvenient for the public during weekdays (at 9am on a Monday, for instance). Women footballers are acutely aware of their exclusion from these spaces and of the effects that this has upon the development of their teams.

In line with CONMEBOL's policy of excluding any club without a female division from the male Copa Libertadores, major clubs either have already opened up to women's football or are in the process of doing so. This means an opportunity to begin in a spirit of integration, taking advantage of such opportunities. As with the questions last considered, there was a mixed response according to the current state of development in each country. In Brazil, participants noted that this had already been trialled successfully – 'sim, no Brasil ja fizeram isso, no Santos e Corinthians. Foi uma grande iniciativa' [Yes, in Brazil they've already done this, at Santos and Corinthians. It was a really great initiative]. Conversely, in Bolivia and Peru participants noted that, at the time of carrying out the surveys, major clubs in their countries had not opened women's divisions; a participant wrote 'si seria bueno pero primero hay que abrir futbol femenino en los clubes masculinos' [yes, it would be great but first they need to open women's football within the male clubs]. Participants from those two countries were from amateur clubs. Accordingly, they saw the question hypothetically.

Almost all participants approved of the idea. It is worth noting however, that some participants did qualify the idea of double-bill matches with the following type of statement – 'la mejor idea que las mujeres sean los preliminares - eso ayudaria a fomentar el fútbol femenino' [the best way to do it would be for the women to be the support/opening event]. This type of comment echoed the media rhetoric sub-categorising the women's game. The degree to which players have internalised patriarchal media and institutional tropes, and at the same time the degree to which a wave of feminist consciousness across the continent has imbued them with a greater sense of self-confidence, is discussed in the following sub-section.

On the social attitudes of players

This final sub-section probes the social attitudes of the sample group of women footballers I spoke to. One of the pioneering sociological works opening up a conversation on the relationship between football in society suggests the game can be understood as a dramatisation of social life (Da Matta, 1982). In trying to understand the mass appeal of football, Da Matta considered the various roles within the game as a window through which to explore social identities within popular culture. These meanings are necessarily mutable – they change across time and place, are influenced heavily by discourse and by the social environment in which events occur. In Brazil, for example, the role of goalkeeper took on an extra dimension of symbolic importance in debates around race relations after a split-second error from Brazil's black goalkeeper Barbosa saw him widely vilified for defeat in the 1950 World Cup Final by Uruguay (Buarque de Hollanda, 2014).

A response to the growth of women's football and its perceived threat to the hegemonic male sporting identity is a charged ideological battle in women's football over the authority conferred upon the manager – historically characterised as el/o Mister in the Spanish and Portuguese-speaking worlds. The kudos attached to the position described as 'the Svengali of football' (Hopcraft, 1968, p. 95) has certainly evolved over time – with an important step in the ascension of the manager's authority being the introduction of the possibility of making substitutions. This change, it has been argued, resulted in the manager being discursively portrayed as a quasi-omniscient authority figure (Wisnik, 2013, p. 130). In this vein, then, it could be viewed that the role of manager, in many cases, remains the last bastion of male hegemony within the game. Further examination of the symbolic meaning of this could contribute to undoing or at least further unveiling the complex web of gender hierarchies (Louro, 1997, p. 24).

There are a few notable (and successful) exceptions such as Emily Lima (appointed the first female coach of the Brazilian national team in 2016) and Tatiele Silveira (the first woman to coach a team winning the Brazilian Women's Championship in 2019), Vanessa Arauz (in Ecuador) and Macarena Deichler (a Chilean based in Brazil). From longer, semi-structured interviews carried out in Brazil and Colombia I gleaned from players a strong preference for more female involvement in coaching and management. Players often expressed feeling more empathy from female ex-players. The current crop of female managers were perceived, from lived experience, to understand the precarity and lack of stability of players employed for short periods.

The narrow scope of the question most likely fed into the logical meritocratic answer to the question – 'no tengo preferencia porque el desempeño no depende de género' [I don't mind as performance is not related to gender]. Nonetheless, a number of players did qualify their initial answer in the comments box with a simple but revealing remark that frequently came through quite strongly during my fieldwork – 'prefiro treinadora pessoalmente. Mas obviamente pode ser qualquer pessoa competente' [I prefer a female manager personally, but obviously it could be anyone as long as they're competent].

Supporting my sense that Brazil is an outlier rather than a typical case, both regionally and more globally, Brazil was the only country where the number of players answering that the gender of the team manager is and is not significant was equal. It is worth adding that, of the eight teams surveyed, only Santos FC had a female coach at the time of carrying out the research. Beyond this, the Brazilian teams had more players with experience playing in other countries (particularly in Europe and North America) where female coaches have already won major honours (USA, Germany, Sweden, etc). The preference was by no means unique to the Brazilian players, in any case. For example, a Chilean participant added the following:

> una entrenadora nos entendería mejor – una ex-jugadora preferiblemente – aspiro a hacer eso cuando termine. Los hombres entienden poco nuestra realidad. [a female manager would understand us best, an ex-player ideally – which is what I plan to do when I finish. Men don't really understand our reality.]

These comments from the survey fed into my line of questioning when I went on to carry out detailed ethnographic research with three specific teams. Numerous players expressed a desire to continue with coaching roles after they retire from playing.

If the previous questions could be said to have divided the continent's players in terms of whether they were understood hypothetically or otherwise, the final quantitative question in this survey, about mixed gender games, was unambiguously hypothetical. It is worth pointing out at this point, for the sake of problematising the oft-cited biological arguments, that it is a common practice for women's teams to train against young adult male teams, and/or male teams of a lower standard (players who do not earn a living playing the game) and that there is no evidence to suggest that women are placed in danger or get injured as a result of the practice. At training sessions in both Brazil and Colombia I saw both Iranduba and Atlético Huila Women defeat male sides said to be under-17 and under-18, though no age confirmation was provided and some of the male players appeared older to me. This question, of all the questions in the survey, caused the most debate between players.

Whilst competitive inter-gender sport has occurred for some time in non-contact sports such as tennis, there is an overriding sense, expressed by some players, that women would be physically unable to compete with male players and might even be at risk of injury. Indeed, whilst carrying out in-depth interviews with players in Brazil and Colombia the disturbing notion that male players might intentionally try to injure women players was mentioned more than once. Nonetheless, results from the survey show that around two-thirds of players (67 to 36) would be in favour of mixed matches. Players were allowed to comment in further detail upon their answers. A number of strands of thought emerged. Amongst those who rejected the proposition out of hand, there was a sense echoing the historical investigation that it would be like a circus and beyond that an assumption that physical injury would inevitably ensue for the female players: 'no – seria un absurdo, como un circo, no deberíamos mezclarnos nunca – sería peligroso para nosotras' [no, it would be absurd – like a circus. We shouldn't mix ever, it would be dangerous for us.] The choice of the word circus is interesting as during prohibition in Brazil one of the ways women found to participate was as part of circuses (Bonfim, 2019, p. 72). Underlining the pervasiveness of socially constructed notions of gender (Goellner, 2003, p. 33) one partici-pant suggested the following: 'no sería tan parejo ya que los hombres por naturaleza son más físicos bien más agresivos' [it wouldn't be very equal as men are naturally more physical and more aggressive].

As the results suggest, however, the great majority of responses suggested enthusiasm for mixed games, adding a number of positive effects this would hypothetically have and seeing no major obstacles to impede it from happening. For example, one participant suggested 'sería buenísimo, nos ayudaría muchos a nosotras a superarnos y subir nuestro nivel. Ojalá fuera varios partidos con hombres al mes' [it would be great, it would help us set goals and improve our level. If only we could play a few games with men each month]. This comment implies that the male level is currently much higher and that it could provide a learning opportunity for female players. It could well be, however, that the belief in male players having a more developed level is not so much connected to naturalistic beliefs of male superiority, so much as a more practical view based on the infrastructural differences that male and female players have faced during their formative years as footballers. These structural advantages should clearly be factored in, and indeed were quite prominent during interview material with women players that I presented in Chapters Three, Four and Five. Along with the potential learning opportunity, players also saw the idea of mixed games as a chance to lay to rest tired cliches and stereotypes about the women's game. For example, one participant noted 'uma oportunidade para mostrar que jogamos muito também. Enfrentar os estereótipos de que o futebol feminino é chato' [it would be an opportunity to show that we play the game too. To face those stereotypes that women's football is boring/rubbish]. Players who were more aware of the commercial potential of the women's game felt that a mixed game would be a great opportunity to amplify the media growth of women's football and to announce the presence of women's football within the traditional clubs of the country. For example:

> sim, claro. Seria bom para melhorar o nível de divulgação, especialmente agora que os clubes grandes tem futebol feminino aquí. Vai repercutir bem nos clubes, na federação e para nós. [Yes, sure. It would be good for improving the level of promotion we get, especially now the big clubs have women's football. It would have positive effects for clubs, for the federation and for us.]

Conclusion

The responses to the survey presented in this chapter suggest the need for holistic approaches that take into account the discursive, economic and political power of football clubs and institutions and the way those interact with the power of the mass media. It follows logically that the very same actors responsible for the historical marginalisation of women's football have a significant role in making it visible and effecting a shift in public attitudes. Across participants' answers, whether experienced first-hand or derived from an awareness of developments elsewhere, there is a sense of the ever-more prominent profile of the women's game and the potential for significant change in the coming years.

Nonetheless, a number of players are also wary of depending on a top-down approach where political will to effect change cannot be taken for granted. The policy of *obrigatoriedade* is a case in point. The potential financial implications of missing the male Copa Libertadores coerces larger clubs towards opening women's teams but as a stand-alone policy it does little to address deeply ingrained attitudes about women's football. In theory clubs are a step down from federations hierarchically. Nonetheless, individually and collectively they are an extremely powerful group with autonomy to act in or against the interests of women's football if they so wish. The accumulated cultural capital of clubs is a factor that until now has clearly been underestimated. They have enormous reach and wield significant influence with the public of each country. Moreover, the power of fans as a collective (Bundio, 2013) could be harnessed to push women's football forward. Closer relations with fan groups might be advantageous. Whilst it is true (and more in keeping with the tone of academic work to date) to note that Santos FC closed its female team for three years between 2012 and 2015, the club has also had one of the only female managers on the continent and in recent times has presented several joint press conferences with male and female players together. This is to say, there is a significant internal struggle within each club around these issues. In Colombia, both Atlético Nacional of Medellín and Santa Fe of Bogotá have already organised double-bill games, exposing the women's team to a mass audience for the first time. Corinthians, a club with a progressive history, has run a number of campaigns urging respect for women's football (Mendonça, 2018a). Players' responses reflect the extent to which they are aware of the possibilities for growth that clubs offer.

The survey results suggest that players are acutely aware of clubs that only pay lip service to institutional discourse. Until regulation is tightened up, there is a possibility of carrying out the bare minimum to meet CONMEBOL requirements without making any serious commitments. Players overwhelmingly back integration into the continent's larger clubs. Many of South America's clubs have active women's and anti-fascist fan groups. Closer relations with these groups may be advantageous.

The agency of players themselves in these changes has been neglected thus far. In 2015, Spanish international Verónica Boquete, through an online petition, managed to get women's players included in the EA Sports FIFA video game series (Goldblatt, 2019, p. 22). There are players actively involved in both the media and federations. Alline Calandrini has begun a career in journalism and ex-Brazil captain Aline Pellegrino was prominent in the Paulista Federation and now coordinates women's football for the CBF in Brazil. Mediatic tropes about women's football continue to be highly gendered with clearly differential treatment of women's football. Nonetheless, this area of male domination is also slowly being eroded. Indeed, particularly in Brazil, podcasts and webpages initially aimed at a niche media are slowly seeping into the most read and most viewed media. The influential podcast Dibradoras is among the best known. Similarly, Globo now has dedicated women's football journalists like Cintia Barlem, albeit even the name 'Donas de Campinho' (owners of the little pitch) – the section of the Globo website dedicated to women's football – hints at the continued sub-categorisation and/ or sense that women are invading the territory of the real owners of the campo.

Overall, results from the survey are inevitably uneven given the large group and variety of contexts from which they are drawn. In countries like Brazil, Colombia and Chile levels of satisfaction with national leagues are closer to those expressed for the Copa Libertadores. In Peru, Bolivia and Ecuador it would appear the level of investment in the Copa Libertadores far outweighs what players see at national league level. It is clear from the survey that these clubs each have different dynamics according to their history, location, size of following and economic means, among other factors. The following section draws together thoughts from this chapter with the conclusions to Chapters One to Five, to provide a series of policy recommendations for women's football in South America.

Overall Conclusions and
Policy Recommendations

This book has broadened the existing literature on women's football by foregrounding the experiences of players and bringing those into dialogue with vibrant and varied academic debates. Players are acutely aware of a lack of female representation and the implications of this. Policy both nationally and continentally has tended to pay lip service to the global growth of women's football and the continental prominence of feminist movements, rather than deliberate thoughtfully about what these two developments mean for the future. The trickle down from the continental federation CONMEBOL to national federations and leagues and finally to clubs is symptomatic of prevailing vertical relations between men's and women's football at institutional level.

The ethnographic chapters (Chapters Three, Four and Five) reflect the tensions between pressure to grow women's football and the persistence of male hegemony within football's institutions. Moreover, they expose a gulf between institutional representations seeking to portray progress and conformity with global growth and the stubborn reality for women players at a local level. The day-to-day existence of women footballers is much harsher than many would imagine, and the sacrifices players must make to pursue a career as a footballer much greater. In the introduction to *Futbolera,* Elsey & Nadel ask (2019, p. 1) 'why would they keep playing?' And yet so many do – a stoic determination to do what they love impels them to carry on in spite of the considerable obstacles and discrimination they face. Further ethnographic work on the motivations of players, the mental health issues some suffer, the identities they develop and how those come into tension with institutional representations would all build upon the work this book has begun.

In the closing chapter, 'Surveying the Field from the Players' Perspective', the concerns of players themselves reveal their acute awareness of insidious but often blatant exclusions that shape how the women's teams are incorporated into their clubs and into the institutions of football and the sport's wider culture more generally. Moreover, players were aware of their own agency along with the attendant power imbalances that snub their attempts to highlight inequalities at every turn. As actors, they play a significant part in making their role visible and effecting a shift in public attitudes. Across participants' answers there is a sense of the ever-more prominent profile of the women's game and the potential for significant change in the coming years, whether experienced first-hand or derived from an awareness of developments elsewhere.

The opening chapter built upon the media representations paradigm in research on women's football by considering the agency of players and how this is counteracted by mass media in an environment of deeply uneven power relations. Citing a particular instance at the 2018 Women's Copa Libertadores the chapter considered how Atlético Huila's Yoreli Rincón became a lightning rod, both for those looking to gain more exposure for the plight of women's football and for more retrograde and patriarchal strains of thought, which attack the player for highlighting significant gender inequalities in travel arrangements, prize money (and how/whether it is shared) and how far the women's teams have been incorporated within clubs in Colombia and beyond. The vitriolic and defensive response to Rincón's justified pleas is instructive insofar as it fed into ongoing debates about the divergent visions of what the sport means to Colombians. In this chapter, mass media output showed little concern for accurately portraying the issues Rincón wished to highlight. Their attempts to deflect attention from Rincón's agenda appear to have been partially successful. Nonetheless, the player achieved some media recognition for her teammates and also a financial agreement under which the players were rewarded for winning the tournament. Both Rincón and her fellow players felt that media representations of women's football were disingenuous at best and that, despite improvements in the form of sympathetic alternative media outlets covering the game, overall the media portrays a misleading picture of the women's game that not only does not help its growth but actually goes a few steps further and actively attempts to trivialise and disrespect the game at every turn.

The second chapter paid particular attention to a single policy that is revealing of how the continental federation envision women's football. It concluded that nowhere in the *obrigatoriedade* policy are there any mechanisms to ensure, or even encourage, the professionalisation of the women's game. Moreover, by wording the policy in a way that allows outsourcing, the practice immediate became common as clubs merely observed the letter of the policy rather than engaging with the spirit of it. Once again, players' responses to the survey I conducted (discussed in more detail in Chapter Six) were savvy and showed an acute awareness of these factors. Tellingly, despite their reservations with the policy, the overwhelming majority of players supported *obrigatoriedade* on the grounds that they felt it might trigger a domino effect leading to the betterment of conditions as large clubs who have recently opened women's teams try to compete with the isolated examples who have already committed significant resources in order to ensure they reach the women's Copa Libertadores year on year and compete to win it.

Nonetheless, there was an overwhelming sensation among players that the achievements of women's clubs have come not because of the federations and their policy, but rather, in spite of them. For that reason, the period of nine months that I spent in Manaus, Santos and Neiva on ethnographic fieldwork brought the most telling insights with regard to the everyday experiences of women footballers in Brazil and Colombia. Summarised in Chapters Three, Four and Five, they hinted at the different experiences players have according to the status of the club that they represent.

At Santos it is argued that a banal patriarchy surrounding the club means that, even when there is a will to incorporate women, and even a significant history of women's football at the club, it is still possible for renowned coach Emily Lima to feel that the women's team was only 'something extra grafted onto the male tradition' of the club. This is balanced against the significant economic and social capital that the club holds, meaning that they are able to amass a squad of 35 women players and to compete consistently on a continental level.

Conversely, the experience at Iranduba presents the opposite challenges. Players felt especially appreciated playing in a city where there is no men's team of note with whom to compete. The setup of the club has long favoured the women's team as there is 'less distance to travel to reach the top' in the words of the club's president. Consistently playing home games at a large stadium and attracting large crowds hints at the levels of popularity women's football could reach if it were properly legislated for at institutional level. The story of Iranduba is as relevant as the stories of any of the *clubes de camisa* insofar as it speaks to the wider panorama in which progress is discernible but at the same time is straitjacketed by a neoliberal logic that favours the larger, more established clubs. This, to some degree, negates the possibility of an organic 'home-match' fan culture, akin to that described by Selmer (2021), developing for women's football. As explained, fans of Iranduba have built up a familiarity with individual players that is the direct result of the players being the star attraction rather than an addendum to the men's team. Moreover, the identification with the stadium itself speaks to the need for permanent venues and consistent time slots that allow fans to engage properly. The club has leveraged and even commodified ethnic identity in order to invoke regional pride. Moreover, by not being an offshoot of an existing male club, the centre–periphery dichotomy that the club has mobilised so successfully (via its appeals to an Amazonian ethnic identity) runs parallel to the power imbalance between the men's and women's games – which the club is also contesting.

The case of Atlético Huila sits somewhere between the two polar opposites described above. The club has nowhere near the cultural capital of Santos, but yet systematically prioritises its men's team until the logical conclusion of finally disbanding the women's team altogether as a short-term means to address a financial crisis. The experience at Huila revealed the considerable gulf between the professionalisation of women's football claimed by the Colombian federation DIMAYOR and the lived reality on the ground for

Colombian women players, even ones who had won the national and Copa Libertadores championships. The players themselves engage with the public and create a façade of professionalism, but the level of institutional support is threadbare at best. Indeed, shortly after my stay, the club cut all ties with the donor who had met all the expenses of the women's team and, having lost this funding, decided that the women's team was an expense they could do without. The wording of CONMEBOL's policy 'the solicitant must have a women's first team or be associated to someone that has' (if their male team is to be eligible to compete in the Copa Libertadores) is far from inconsequential to what happened at Huila. Effectively, the upkeep of the women's team was outsourced to a willing donor rather than taken on by the club.

As noted within Chapters Three, Four and Five, one of the three teams I visited is struggling to survive (Iranduba) whilst another has stepped away from women's football (Atlético Huila). With the new financial challenges brought about by the onset of COVID, it is imperative that football institutions act to safeguard the future of women footballers in the medium to long term.

Neither within academia nor from a journalistic or institutional perspective has a body of ethnographic research of this length been produced about women's football in South America. For this reason, this research is well placed to make a raft of well-informed policy recommendations. The following section lists some practical recommendations.

Chapter Two observed how *obrigatoriedade* has been the central plank of institutional policy on the continent in recent years. Whilst representing progress of sorts, it is abundantly clear that meaningful affirmative action is needed. Until now, without significant female representation at board/director level at each club, there has been a tendency to fulfil the requirement of having a women's team without apportioning significant chunks of the club's budgets to it. As a minimum, proactive policy to ensure that at least 15 per cent (increasing each year) of club's budgets be spent on women's football is needed in the short to medium term. Moreover, this ought to be complemented by policy requiring 15 per cent women or gender non-binary representation at board/director level. Again, with time this ought to be reviewed and increased. These requirements could be replicated at regional, national and continental federation level to help ensure women's football has a calendar of the same length as men's in each country, to accompany full professionalisation.

Moreover, many independent women's clubs existed long before the arrival of the *clubes de camisa* so, to protect their expertise and endeavour I also recommend formal recognition of these. This could come from national federations, which have received significant funds from programmes like FIFA Forward, as a drive towards full institutional transparency. For example, independent clubs with a proven track record for developing women players should be included among a number of centres of excellence for the development of women players. These should be distributed strategically across each country, taking note of areas where insufficient infrastructure currently means that players are forced to relocate at extremely young ages. Given that many of the players interviewed suggested to me that they had learned to play football on the streets after reaching 10 years old, these centres of excellence should cater for a range of ages, always prioritising girls' football for under-10s. In a similar vein, greater coordination between national sporting institutions and federal/national government should be encouraged. It is no coincidence that girls' football begins at a very young age in primary and secondary schools in many of the most successful countries in women's football. In order to build for the future, regional and national federations should be actively involved in visiting schools to encourage the playing of women's football. Furthermore, legislation to make football a part of national curricula for girls should be enacted to ensure that girls have the same opportunities as boys from an early age. With the adoption of these measures women's football would assert itself as a vital component part of national identity in keeping with the speed of change in other areas of society. Football is clearly a key symbolic arena – gradual changes to a deeply gendered polity should be monitored more closely and more regularly in order to reflect the speed of change in wider society.

Recommendations for further research

Clearly there is much work to be done in exposing and addressing the extent to which *machismo* and sexism are institutionalised in South American sporting institutions. The precarious structure and ambiguous semi-professionalisation of the players' status found in this book are testament to this. This research consistently shows that women players are not only politically savvy *vis-à-vis* their position, but also are willing to tackle head on some of the hostility they face (as did Yoreli Rincón). In other cases, however, they may harbour serious grievances that they are unable to voice publicly without risking significant damage to their career trajectories. For this reason, particularly in the cases of LGBTQ+ and racial discrimination, I advocate that research interviews should be conducted anonymously and only after significant trust is built up with participants. There is much to be gained from centring the perspectives of ex-players and contemporary players, as in this book, in order to nourish dialogues with scholars of media representation and historians seeking to uncover the hidden history of women's football.

References

@10yorelirincon (2018a) *Disfrutemos que nos atrevimos soñar – somos campeonas continentales.* [Online]. No longer available (accessed 3 December 2018).

@10yorelirincon (2018b) *Ese premio nunca va a llegar a nosotras.* [Online]. No Longer Available (accessed 4 December 2018).

@10yorelirincon (2018c) *Presidente Camargo respete!* [Online]. Available from: https://twitter.com/10yorelirincon/status/1075812460966408197 (accessed 14 May 2020).

@10yorelirincon (2018d) *Seré el Nuevo refuerzo de EC Iranduba de Brasil.* [Online]. Available from: https://www.instagram.com/p/BsDkyK4hwQT/ (accessed 22 June 2020).

ABC Fútbol (2018) *La Liga femenina es un caldo de cultivo de lesbianismo.* [Online]. Available from: https://www.abc.es/deportes/futbol/abci-liga-femenina-caldo-cultivo-lesbianismo-201812211351_noticia.html (accessed 12 May 2020).

ACOLFUTPRO (2019) *Informe Fútbol Profesional Femenino en Colombia 2019.* [Online]. Available from: https://acolfutpro.org/informe-liga-profesional-femenina-2019/ (accessed 8 July 2020).

ACOLFUTPRO (2020) *Informe ACOLFUTPRO Situación de las futbolistas de la liga femenina 2020.*

Agergaard, S. (2019) 'Nationalising minority ethnic athletes: Danish media representations of Nadia Nadim around the UEFA Women's Euro 2017', *Sport in History*, 39(2), pp. 130–46.

Agergaard, S. & Tiesler, N.C. (2014) *Women, Soccer and Transnational Migration.* London: Routledge.

Agergaard, S., Botelho, V.L. & Tiesler, N.C. (2014) 'The typology of athletic migrants revisited', in Agergaard, S. & Tiesler, N.C. (eds), *Women, Soccer and Transnational Migration*, pp. 191–211.

Aguiar, L., Ramos, S. dos S., Joras, P.S. & Goellner, S.V. (2018) 'Guerreiras Project: futebol e empoderamento de mulheres', *Revista Estudos Feministas*, 26(1).

Aiyegbayo, O. (2015) *Did Pelé cause a ceasefire during the Biafran War?* [Online]. Available from: https://africasacountry.com/2015/10/did-pele-by-playing-a-match-in-nigeria-cause-a-ceasefire-during-the-biafran-war (accessed 17 November 2020).

Alabarces, P. (2002) *Fútbol y patria: el fútbol y las narrativas de la nación en la Argentina*. Buenos Aires: Prometeo Libros Editorial.

Alvarado, S. (2019) 'Las futbolistas encabezan la lucha contra el acoso sexual en Colombia', *The New York Times*, 8 March.

Amazonas Governo (2016) *Iranduba vence Vasco diante de 8.413 torcedores e encara Adeco-SP, na final da 1a Liga Feminina de Futebol Sub-20.* [Online]. Available from: http://www.amazonas.am.gov.br/2016/06/iranduba-vence-vasco-diante-de-8-413-torcedores-e-encara-adeco-sp-na-final-da-1a-liga-feminina-de-futebol-sub-20/ (accessed 22 June 2020).

Antunovic, D. & Hardin, M. (2012) 'Activism in women's sports blogs: fandom and feminist potential', *International Journal of Sport Communication*, 5(3), pp. 305–22.

Antunovic, D. & Hardin, M. (2013) 'Women bloggers: identity and the conceptualization of sports', *New Media & Society*, 15(8), pp. 1374–92.

Antunovic, D. & Hardin, M. (2015) 'Women and the blogosphere: exploring feminist approaches to sport', *International Review for the Sociology of Sport*, 50(6), pp. 661–77.

Archetti, E.P. (1998) 'Masculinidades múltiples. El mundo del tango y del futbol en la Argentina', in Balderston, D. & Guy, D.J. (eds), *Sexo y sexualidades en América Latina*. Buenos Aires: Paidós, pp. 291–313.

Archetti, E.P. (1999) *Masculinities: Football, Polo and the Tango in Argentina*. Oxford: Berg Publishers.

Ardila Biela, G. (2022) 'An oral history of women's football in Colombia: building tools for collective action', in Knijnik, J. & Garton, G. (eds), *Women's Football in Latin America: Social Challenges and Historical Perspectives*, Vol. 2, *Hispanic Countries*. London: Palgrave Macmillan, pp. 247–67.

Ardila Biela, G. (2023) *A las patadas. Historias del fútbol practicado por mujeres en Colombia desde 1949 | comprar en libreriasiglo.com*. Bogotá: Editorial Javieriana.

AS.com (2017) *Final Femenina: Santa Fe campeón y récord de asistencia – AS Colombia*. [Online]. Available from: https://colombia.as.com/colombia/2017/06/26/futbol/1498428926_426737.html (accessed 29 June 2020).

Bale, J. (1991) 'Playing at home: British football and a sense of place', in Williams, J. & Wagg, S. (eds), *British Football and Social Change: Getting into Europe*. Leicester: Leicester University Press, pp. 130–44.

Bale, J. (1994) *Landscapes of Modern Sport*. Leicester: Leicester University Press.

Barreira, J., Mazzei, L.C., Castro, F.D. & Galatti, L.R. (2020) 'O futebol de mulheres: uma análise das estratégias de desenvolvimento (in) existentes na América do Sul', in Zuaneti Martins, M. & Wenetz, I. (eds), *Futebol de mulheres no Brasil: desafios para as políticas públicas*. Curitiba: CRV, pp. 29–44.

Barreto Januário, S. (2017) 'Marta em notícia: a (in) visibilidade do futebol feminino no Brasil', *FuLiA/UFMG*, 2(1), pp. 28–43.

Barreto Januário, S., Rodrigues Lima, C.A. & Leal, D. (2022) 'Changing values: media coverage of the 2019 Women's World Cup on Brazilian sports news sites', in Knijnik, J. & Costa, A. (eds), *Women's Football in Latin America: Social Challenges and Historical Perspectives*, Vol. 1, *Brazil*. London: Palgrave Macmillan, pp. 123–41.

Bauer, N. (2011) 'Beauvoir on the allure of self-objectification', in Witt, C. (ed.), *Feminist Metaphysics*. [Online]. London: Springer, pp. 117–29.

BBC Mundo (2018) '"Caldo de cultivo del lesbianismo", el ataque del presidente de un club al fútbol femenino que causa indignación en Colombia', *BBC News Mundo*, 21 December.

BBC Sport (2017) 'Women's FA Cup final: Birmingham City 1–4 Manchester City', *BBC Sport*, 13 May.

BBC Sport (2019) 'Raheem Sterling has set standard on combating racism, says Andre Gray', *BBC Sport*, 17 May.

Belas Trindade, J. (2023) 'Linda Caicedo: "Ever since I was a little girl I have dreamed of playing abroad"', *The Guardian*, 18 January.

Bermúdez, J.A. (2019) *Caso de éxito en Fútbol Femenino: El Modelo del Huila Campeon de la Copa Libertadores*. Madrid: Libro Fútbol.

Billig, M. (1995) *Banal Nationalism*. London: Sage.

Biram, M. (2013) *Barrilete cósmico: Malvinas, Maradona, Argentina and England*. [Online]. Available from: http://inbedwithmaradona.com/journal/2013/10/29/barrilete-csmico-malvinas-maradona-argentina-and-england (accessed 2 February 2021).

Biram, M. (2022) 'Invisible champions: an ethnography of Peruvian women's football', in Knijnik, J. & Garton, G. (eds), *Women's Football in Latin America: Social Challenges and Historical Perspectives*, Vol. 2, *Hispanic Countries*. [Online]. London: Palgrave Macmillan, pp. 147–63.

Biram, M.D. & Goellner, S.V. (2020) 'A pretext for regression? The gendered institutional response to COVID-19 in the country of football', *Bulletin of Latin American Research*, 39, pp. 112–16.

Biram, M.D. & Mina, C.Y. (2021) 'Football in the time of COVID-19: reflections on the implications for the Women's Professional League in Colombia', *Soccer & Society*, 22(1–2), pp. 35–42.

Black, J. & Fielding-Lloyd, B. (2019) 'Re-establishing the "outsiders": English press coverage of the 2015 FIFA Women's World Cup', *International Review for the Sociology of Sport*, 54(3), pp. 282–301.

Bocketti, G. (2016) *The Invention of the Beautiful Game: Football and the Making of Modern Brazil*. Gainsville: University Press of Florida.

Bonfim, A.F. (2019) *Football Feminino entre festas esportivas, circos e campos suburbanos: uma história social do futebol praticado por mulheres da introdução à proibição (1915–1941)*. São Paulo: FGV.

Borba, R. (2021) 'Disgusting politics: circuits of affects and the making of Bolsonaro', *Social Semiotics*, 31(5), pp. 677–94.

Bourdieu, P. (1990) *In Other Words: Essays towards a Reflexive Sociology*. Palo Alto, CA: Stanford University Press.

Bowes, A. & Culvin, A. (2021) *The Professionalisation of Women's Sport: Issues and Debates*. London: Emerald Group Publishing.

Bradshaw, S. & Howard, P.N. (2018) 'Challenging truth and trust: a global inventory of organized social media manipulation', *The Computational Propaganda Project*, 1. [Online]. Available from: https://demtech.oii.ox.ac.uk/wp-content/uploads/sites/12/2018/07/ct2018.pdf (accessed 12 March 2010).

Branz, J. (2012) 'Fútbol, mujeres y espacio público', in Cachorro, G. (ed.), *Ciudad y prácticas corporales*, Universidad Nacional de La Plata, Facultad de Humanidades y Ciencias de la Educación, pp. 339–52.

Brewster, C. & Brewster, K. (2019) '"A lesson in football wisdom"? Coverage of the unofficial women's world cup of 1971 in the Mexican press', *Sport in History*, 39(2), pp. 147–65.

Brianezi, T. (2013) *O deslocamento do discurso sobre a Zona Franca de Manaus: do progresso à modernização ecológica*. PhD thesis, São Paulo: USP.

Buarque de Holanda, B.B. (2009) 'Torcidas organizadas no Brasil e na França: considerações preliminares para uma comparação', *Razón y palabra*, 14(69).

Buarque de Hollanda, B.B. (2014) 'Echoes of the tragedy: the sport memoir and the representation of the 1950 World Cup', *The International Journal of the History of Sport*, 31(10), pp. 1287–302.

Buitrago, R. (2020) 'Atlético Huila en la historia de la Liga Femenina', *Fémina Fútbol*. [Online]. Available from: https://feminafutbol.com/ligas/atletico-huila-en-la-historia-de-la-liga-femenina-28028/ (accessed 5 June 2020).

Burch, L.M., Billings, A.C. & Zimmerman, M.H. (2018) 'Comparing American soccer dialogues: social media commentary surrounding the 2014 US Men's and 2015 US Women's World Cup teams', *Sport in Society*, 21(7), pp. 1047–62.

Burns, E.B. (1965) 'Manaus, 1910: portrait of a boom town', *Journal of Inter-American Studies*, 7(3), pp. 400–21.

Butler, J. (1990) *Gender Trouble: Feminism and the Subversion of Identity*. New York: Routledge.

de Campos, F. & de Toledo, L.H. (2013) 'O Brasil na arquibancada: notas sobre a sociabilidade torcedora', *Revista USP*, 99, pp. 123–38.

Campos, P.A.F. (2010) 'Mulheres torcedoras do Cruzeiro Esporte Clube presentes no Mineirão', *LICERE–Revista do Programa de Pós–graduação Interdisciplinar em Estudos do Lazer*, 13(2).

Caracol Radio (2018) *Yoreli Rincón: 'Logramos llegar a un acuerdo. Es un premio merecido' | Deportes | Caracol Radio*. [Online]. Available from: https://caracol.com.co/radio/2018/12/05/deportes/1543971266_553042.html (accessed 14 May 2020).

@CaracolDeportes (2018) *Logramos llegar a un acuerdo*. [Online]. Available fr om: https://twitter.com/caracoldeportes/status/1070095266097872897 (acces sed 14 May 2020).

Cardoso, R.N. (2019a) *Por que as Sereias da Vila não estão jogando na Vila Belmiro em 2019?* [Online]. Available from: https://dibradoras.blogosfera.uol.com.br/2019/05/23/por-que-as-sereias-da-vila-nao-estao-jogando-na-vila-belmiro-em-2019/ (accessed 29 October 2020).

Cardoso, R.N. (2019b) *Sissi recebe homenagem fora do Brasil, mas é 'esquecida' pela CBF*. [Online]. Available from: https://dibradoras.blogosfera.uol.com.br/2019/12/06/sissi-recebe-homenagem-fora-do-brasil-mas-e-esquecida-pela-cbf/ (accessed 3 February 2021).

Cardoso, V. (2019) *Iranduba faz seletiva em busca de jovens amazonenses para o Brasileiro Sub-18 | Esportes*. [Online]. Available from: https://www.acritica.com/channels/esportes/news/iranduba-faz-seletiva-e-busca-jovens-jogadoras-amazonenses-para-brasileiro-sub-18 (accessed 4 July 2020).

Carey, K.M. (2007) 'The aesthetics of immediacy and hypermediation: the dumb shows in Webster's *The White Devil*', *New Theatre Quarterly*, 23(1), pp. 73–80.

Carlón, M. & Scolari, C. (2014) *El fin de los medios masivos: El debate continúa.* Buenos Aires: La Crujía.

Casal, C.A., Losada, J.L., Maneiro, R. & Ardá, A. (2020) Gender differences in technical-tactical behaviour of La Liga Spanish football teams', *Journal of Human Sport and Exercise*, 16(1), pp. 37–52.

Cashman, H.R. & Raymond, C.W. (2014) 'Making gender relevant in Spanish-language sports broadcast discourse', *Gender & Language*, 8(3).

Castro, R. (1995) *Estrela solitária.* São Paulo: Companhia das Letras.

Caudwell, J. (2002) 'Women's experiences of sexuality within football contexts: a particular and located footballing epistemology', *Football Studies*, 5(1), pp. 24–45.

CEPAL (2007) *Análise ambiental e de sustentabilidade do Estado do Amazonas,* [Online]. Available from: https://repositorio.cepal.org/handle/11362/3572 (accessed 12 March 2010).

Chernela, J. & Pereira, E. (2018) 'An end to difference: imagining Amazonian modernity at the dawn of the twentieth century', *Journal of Anthropological Research*, 74(1), pp. 10–31.

Chomsky, N. (1998) *The Common Good.* London: Pluto.

Christenson, M. & Kelso, P. (2004) 'Soccer chief's plan to boost women's game? Hotpants', *The Guardian*, 16 January.

Christopherson, N., Janning, M. & McConnell, E.D. (2002) 'Two kicks forward, one kick back: a content analysis of media discourses on the 1999 Women's World Cup soccer championship', *Sociology of Sport Journal*, 19(2), pp. 170–88.

Clarkson, B.G., Culvin, A., Pope, S. & Parry, K.D. (2020) 'Covid-19: Reflections on threat and uncertainty for the future of elite women's football in England', *Managing Sport and Leisure*, 27(1–2), pp. 50–61.

Clifford, J. (1983) 'On ethnographic authority', *Representations*, (2), pp. 118–46.

Coche, R. (2016) 'Promoting women's soccer through social media: how the US Federation used Twitter for the 2011 World Cup', *Soccer & Society*, 17(1), pp. 90–108.

Coelho, J. (2013) *Match Made in Hell. The Sun*, 8 December [Online]. Available from: https://www.thesun.co.uk/archives/news/406014/match-made-in-hell/ (accessed 17 June 2020).

Conde, M. (2008) 'El poder de la razón: las mujeres en el fútbol', *Nueva Sociedad*, 218, pp. 122–30.

Conde, M. & Rodríguez, M.G. (2002) 'Mujeres en el fútbol argentino: sobre prácticas y representaciones', *Alteridades*, 12(23), pp. 93–106.

CONMEBOL (2018) *CONMEBOL Reglamento de licencia de clubes.* [Online]. Available from: https://www.conmebol.com/sites/default/files/reglamento-de-licencia-de-clubes-portugues.pdf (accessed 24 March 2020).

CONMEBOL (2019) *CONMEBOL destina 217,5 millones de dólares en premios para las competiciones de clubes 2020 | CONMEBOL.* [Online]. Available from: http://www.conmebol.com/es/conmebol-destina-2175-millones-de-dolares-en-premios-para-las-competiciones-de-clubes-2020 (accessed 18 June 2020).

CONMEBOL (2020) *Estatuto Confederación Sudamericana De Fútbol 2020*. [Onlin e]. Available from:https://www.conmebol.com/sites/default/files/docs2020/ Estatutos-Conmebol-2020-esp.pdf (accessed 27 March 2020).

Conn, D. (1997) *The Football Business: Fair Game in the '90s?* Edinburgh: Mainstream Publishing Co.

Connell, R.W. (2002) *Gender*. Cambridge: Polity.

Connell, R.W. (2005) *Masculinities*. Cambridge: Polity.

Cooky, C., Messner, M.A. & Hextrum, R.H. (2013) 'Women play sport, but not on TV: a longitudinal study of televised news media', *Communication & Sport*, 1(3), pp. 203–30.

Cooky, C., Wachs, F.L., Messner, M. & Dworkin, S.L. (2010) 'It's not about the game: Don Imus, race, class, gender and sexuality in contemporary media', *Sociology of Sport Journal*, 27(2), pp. 139–59.

da Costa, L.M. (2007) 'O que é uma torcedora? Notas sobre a representação e auto-representação do público feminino de futebol', *Esporte e sociedade*, 2(4), pp. 1–31.

Crenshaw, K. (1990) 'Mapping the margins: intersectionality, identity politics, and violence against women of color', *Stanford Law Review*, 43(6), pp. 1241–99.

Culvin, A. (2019) *Football as Work: The New Realities of Professional Women Footballers in England*. PhD thesis. University of Central Lancashire.

Curi, M. (2011) 'Fútbol y globalización: sale Estado y entra Mercado. Una mirada desde Argentina', *Sociedad Hoy*, 21, pp. 129–38.

Curran, J. (2002) *Media and Power*. London: Psychology Press.

Curry, G. (2004) 'Playing for money: James J. Lang and emergent soccer professionalism in Sheffield', *Soccer & Society*, 5(3), pp. 336–55.

@cworswick (2018) *Atlético Huila star Yoreli Rincón claims*. [Online]. Availabl e from: https://twitter.com/cworswick/status/1070035132525015041 (accessed 14 May 2020).

Da Matta, R. (1982) *Universo do futebol: esporte e sociedade brasileira*. Rio de Janeiro: Edições Pinakotheke.

Dantas, M. (2018) *Sem Marta, Iranduba 'varre' o mercado e vence concorrência por selecionáveis para a Libertadores*. [Online]. Available from: https://globoesporte. globo.com/am/futebol/times/iranduba/noticia/sem-marta-iranduba-varre-o-mercado-e-vence-concorrencia-por-selecionaveis.ghtml (accessed 3 July 2020).

Das, A. (2020) *For USWNT and US soccer, equal pay ruling offers a way out*. *The New York Times*, 2 May [Online]. Available from: https://www.nytimes. com/2020/05/02/sports/soccer/uswnt-equal-pay-women-soccer.html (accessed 8 June 2020).

Davies, H. (1973) *The Glory Game*. London: Random House.

de Alencar, A.A., da Silva, A.S., da Silva Neto, E.J., Monteiro, M.S. & Gama, S.C. (2020) 'As seleções brasileiras de futebol feminino e empoderamento das mulheres', *Revista Ensino, Saúde e Biotecnologia da Amazônia*, 2(esp.), pp. 60–65.

de la Parra, M.A. (1989) 'El desencanto encantado. Monólogo de un publicitario ocasional en víspera del pospinochetismo', *Nueva Sociedad. Democracia y política en América Latina*, 100, pp. 78–89.

De La Torre, M.R.N. (2013) 'Bellas por naturaleza: mapping national identity on US Colombian beauty queens', *Latino Studies*, 11(3), pp. 293–312.

De Mello, G. (2007) 'A modernização de Santos no século XIX: mudanças espaciais e da sociabilidade urbana no centro velho', *Cadernos CERU*, 18, pp. 107–31.

De Mello, G. (2008) *Expansão e estrutura urbana de Santos (SP): aspectos da periferização, da deterioração, da intervenção urbana, da verticalização e da sociabilidade.* São Paulo: USP.

De Vaus, D. (2013) *Surveys in Social Research.* London: Routledge.

Delamont, S. (2004) 'Ethnography and participant observation', *Qualitative Research Practice*, 217, pp. 206–207.

Deportes RCN (2018) *Presidente del Atlético Huila aclara polémica de Yoreli Rincón por premios de la Copa Libertadores.* [Online]. Available from: https://www.youtube.com/watch?v=R-ztYFdsmi8 (accessed 12 May 2020).

Despres, L.A. (1991) *Manaus: Social Life and Work in Brazil's Free Trade Zone.* New York: SUNY Press.

Diario del Huila (2020) *Declaraciones Gerente del Huila sobre afirmaciones de Yoreli Rincón.* [Online]. Available from: https://diariodelhuila.com/declaraciones-gerente-del-huila-sobre-afirmaciones-de-yoreli-rincon (accessed 12 May 2020).

Díaz, F. (2020) *Atlético Huila no formará parte de la Liga Femenina 2020.* [Online]. Available from: https://feminafutbol.com/noticias/atletico-huila-no-formara-parte-de-la-liga-femenina-2020-28024/ (accessed 16 May 2021).

Dibradoras (2020) *Aline Pellegrino e Duda Luizelli coordenarão futebol feminino na CBF.* [Online]. Available from: https://dibradoras.com.br/2020/09/02/aline-pellegrino-e-duda-luizelli-coordenarao-futebol-feminino-na-cbf/ (accessed 12 March 2010).

DiMaggio, P.J. & Powell, W.W. (1983) 'The iron cage revisited: institutional isomorphism and collective rationality in organizational fields', *American Sociological Review*, 48(2), pp. 147–60.

Dos Santos, D.S. & Medeiros, A.G.A. (2011) 'O futebol feminino no discurso televisivo', *Revista Brasileira de Ciências do Esporte*, 34(1), pp. 185–96.

Dos Santos, G. (n.d.) *Ao lado de Sereias, David Braz alerta para força do Cruzeiro: 'Brigará pelo título'.* [Online]. Available from: https://globoesporte.globo.com/sp/santos-e-regiao/futebol/times/santos/noticia/ao-lado-das-sereias-david-braz-alerta-para-forca-do-cruzeiro-brigara-pelo-titulo.ghtml (accessed 23 August 2020).

Dos Santos, G. (2018) *Com a Vila Belmiro lotada, Santos vence o Corinthians no primeiro jogo da final do Paulista Feminino.* [Online]. Available from: https://globoesporte.globo.com/sp/santos-e-regiao/noticia/com-a-vila-belmiro-lotada-santos-vence-o-corinthians-no-primeiro-jogo-da-final-do-paulista-feminino.ghtml (accessed 23 August 2020).

Downie, A. (2017) *Doctor Socrates: Footballer, Philosopher, Legend.* London: Simon and Schuster.

Duarte, D. (2009) *Manaus: entre o Passado e o Presente.* São Paulo: Mídia Ponto.

Dubois, L. (2018) *The Language of the Game: How to Understand Soccer.* New York: Basic Books.

Dunn, C. (2016) 'The history of women's football', in Dunn, C., *Football and the Women's World Cup: Organisation, Media and Fandom*. Basingstoke: Palgrave Macmillan, pp. 5–15.

Dunn, C. & Welford, J. (2014) *Football and the FA Women's Super League: Structure, Governance and Impact*. New York: Springer.

Dunn, C. & Welford, J. (2016) 'Women's elite football', in Hughson, J., Moore, K., Spaaij, R. & Maguire, J. (eds), *Routledge Handbook of Football Studies*. Abingdon: Routledge, pp. 138–50.

Dunning, E. (1986) 'Sport as a male preserve: notes on the social sources of masculine identity and its transformations', *Theory, Culture & Society*, 3(1), pp. 79–90.

Dunning, E. (2000) 'Towards a sociological understanding of football hooliganism as a world phenomenon', *European Journal on Criminal Policy and Research*, 8(2), pp. 141–62.

Durkheim, E. (1964) *Rules of Sociological Method*. London: Simon and Schuster.

Dwyer, T. (2010) *Media Convergence*. London: McGraw-Hill.

Eberle, T.S. (2015) 'Exploring another's subjective life-world: a phenomenological approach', *Journal of Contemporary Ethnography*, 44(5), pp. 563–79.

Economist, The (2019) 'The Women's World Cup is drawing record audiences', *The Economist*, 7 May.

Efraim, A. (2020) *Maior artilheira da história do Santos, Ketlen será 1a a chegar a 100 gols – UOL Esporte*. [Online]. Available from: https://dibradoras.blogosfera. uol.com.br/2020/09/11/maior-artilheira-da-historia-do-santos-ketlen-sera-1a- a-chegar-a-100-gols/ (accessed 12 November 2020).

El Espectador (2018) *Yoreli Rincón critica al Huila: 'El premio que ganamos no es para nosotras'.* [Online]. Available from: https://www.elespectador.com/deportes/ futbol-colombiano/yoreli-rincon-critica-al-huila-el-premio-que-ganamos-no- es-para-nosotras-articulo-827331 (accessed 18 May 2020).

El País (2012) *Técnico de selección Colombia acusado por perseguir a Yoreli Rincón*. *El País*, 28 July. Available from: https://www.elpais.com.co/deportes/tecnico- de-seleccion-colombia-acusado-por-perseguir-a-yoreli-rincon.html (accessed 31 May 2020).

El País Cali (2014) *'El tema de mi apariencia es secundario': Nicole Regnier – YouTube*. [Online]. Available from: https://www.youtube.com/watch?v=sA- 6mlR4ThU (accessed 21 May 2020).

El Tiempo (2017) *Capturas sacuden a Neiva por escándalo en obras del estadio*. *El Tiempo*, 3 August. Available from: https://www.eltiempo.com/colombia/ otras-ciudades/capturas-por-irregularidades-en-renovacion-del-estadio-guill- ermo-plazas-alcid-de-neiva-116160 (accessed 2 December 2021).

El Tiempo (2018a) *Escándalo por declaraciones del dueño de Tolima sobre fútbol femenino*. *El Tiempo*, 20 December. Available from: https://www.eltiempo. com/deportes/futbol-colombiano/fuertes-declaraciones-de-gabriel-camargo- contra-el-futbol-femenino-307488 (accessed 12 May 2020).

El Tiempo (2018b) *Insólita queja de Yoreli Rincón tras ganar la Libertadores femenina*. *El Tiempo*, 4 December. Available from: https://www.eltiempo.com/deportes/ futbol-internacional/yoreli-rincon-se-queja-de-que-el-premio-por-ganar-la- copa-libertadores-no-llega-a-ellas-301414 (accessed 16 September 2019).

El Tiempo (2018c) *La historia completa de los premios del Huila femenino. El Tiempo*, 5 December. Available from: https://www.eltiempo.com/deportes/futbol-internacional/la-polemica-que-desato-el-premio-del-huila-femenino-por-la-copa-libertadores-301614 (accessed 16 September 2019).

El Tiempo (2019a) *Las pruebas de las jugadoras colombianas sobre vetos en la Selección. El Tiempo*, 7 March. Available from: https://www.eltiempo.com/deportes/futbol-internacional/pruebas-de-las-jugadores-de-la-seleccion-colombia-y-daniela-montoya-sobre-los-vetos-335292 (accessed 31 May 2020).

El Tiempo (2019b) *Yoreli Rincón insiste en que la Dimayor la tiene vetada para jugar con Colombia - Fútbol Colombiano - Deportes - ELTIEMPO. COM. El Tiempo*, 19 July. Available from: https://www.eltiempo.com/deportes/futbol-colombiano/yoreli-rincon-insiste-en-que-la-dimayor-la-tiene-vetada-para-jugar-con-colombia-390664 (accessed 31 May 2020).

Elsey, B. (2011) *Citizens and Sportsmen: Futbol and Politics in Twentieth-Century Chile*. Austin: University of Texas Press.

Elsey, B. (2018) 'Fútbol feminista: energized by the #NiUnaMenos movement, women's soccer teams take on the patriarchs of the beautiful game in Latin America', *NACLA Report on the Americas*, 50(4), pp. 423–29.

Elsey, B. & Nadel, J. (2019) *Futbolera: A History of Women and Sports in Latin America*. Austin: University of Texas Press.

Engh, M.H. (2010) 'The battle for centre stage: women's football in South Africa', *Agenda*, 24(85), pp. 11–20.

ESPNw (2018) *Campeã e craque do Atlético Huila, Yoreli Rincón revela que time feminino não receberá dinheiro do título da Libertadores*. [Online]. Available from: https://www.espn.com.br/espnw/artigo/_/id/5047971/libertadores-campea-e-craque-do-atletico-huila-yoreli-rincon-revela-que-time-feminino-nao-recebera-dinheiro-da-premiacao (accessed 14 May 2020).

Esporte Interativo (2020) *Botafogo e Cruzeiro lideram ranking de dívidas entre principais clubes da CBF*. [Online]. Available from: https://www.esporteinterativo.com.br/futebolbrasileiro/Botafogo-e-Cruzeiro-lideram-ranking-de-dividas-entre-principais-clubes-da-CBF-20200604-0008.html (accessed 10 August 2020).

Evans, A. (2019) 'FIFA Women's World Cup: five ways women's football beats men's', *BBC News*, 25 June.

Ezzell, M.B. (2009) '"Barbie dolls" on the pitch: identity work, defensive othering, and inequality in women's rugby', *Social Problems*, 56(1), pp. 111–31.

@FALCAO (2018) *Felicitaciones a todas las jugadoras del @AHuilaFemenino*. [Online]. Available from: https://twitter.com/FALCAO/status/1069569685853745152 (accessed 14 May 2020).

@farenet (2018) *What makes it even WORSE*. [Online]. Available from: https://twitter.com/farenet/status/1070635930346840064 (accessed 14 May 2020).

Feijoo, M. del C. & Gogna, M. (1990) *Women in the Transition to Democracy*. Geneva: Zed.

Ferretti, M.A. de C., Zuzzi, R.P., Viana, A.E. dos S. & Vilha Junior, F.M. (2011) 'O futebol feminino nos Jogos Olímpicos de Pequim', *Motriz: revista de educação física*, 17(1), pp. 117–27.

FIFA (2016) *FIFA Statutes April 2016*. [Online]. Available from: https://resources. fifa.com/image/upload/the-fifa-statutes-in-force-as-of-27-april-2016 (accessed 27 March 2020).

FIFA (2018) *FIFA Women's Football Strategy*. [Online]. Available from: https:// digitalhub.fifa.com/m/baafcb84f1b54a8/original/z7w21ghir8jb9tguvbcq-pdf. pdf (accessed 27 March 2020).

FIFA (2019) *FIFA Women's World Cup 2019 watched by more than 1 billion*. [Online]. Available from: https://www.fifa.com/womensworldcup/news/fifa-women-s-world-cup-2019tm-watched-by-more-than-1-billion (accessed 25 March 2020).

FIFA (2020a) *FIFA Forward 2.0 Vision*. [Online]. Available from: https:// resources.fifa.com/image/upload/fifa-forward-development-programme-regulations (accessed 27 March 2020).

FIFA (2020b) *FIFA takes steps for further development of women's football*. [Online]. Available from: https://www.fifa.com/womens-football/news/fifa-takes-steps-for-further-development-of-women-s-football?_branch_match_id= 676126454471938856 (accessed 27 March 2020).

Filho, M. (2003) *O negro no futebol brasileiro*. Rio de Janeiro: Mauad Editora Ltda.

Firmino, C. (2019) 'Empoderamento e relações de poder: a cobertura feminista da Copa do Mundo da Rússia pelo projeto "dibradoras"', *FuLiA/UFMG*, 4(1), pp. 23–38.

Florenzano, J.P. (1999) 'Corinthians: do time do povo ao futebol empresa', in Regina da Costa, M., Florenzano, J.P. & Quintilho, E. (eds), *Futebol: espetáculo do século*. São Paulo: Musa, pp. 97–111.

Florenzano, J.P. (2010) *A democracia corinthiana: práticas de liberdade no futebol brasileiro*. São Paulo: Educ/Fapesp.

@FonsiLoaiza (2018) *El Atlético Huila femenino ha hecho historia y se ha proclamado campeón de la Copa Libertadores. El premio de 50.000€ no irá destinado para las jugadoras sino para el equipo masculino. Vergonzoso*. [Online]. Available from: https://twitter.com/FonsiLoaiza/status/1070269006110736384 (accessed 14 May 2020).

Fontana, A. & Frey, J.H. (2005) 'The interview: from neutral stance to political-involvement', *The Social Science Journal*, 28(2), pp. 175–87.

Fontes, P. & Buarque de Holanda, B. (2014) *The Country of Football: Politics, Popular Culture, and the Beautiful Game in Brazil*. London: Hurst.

Fowler Jr, F.J. (2013) *Survey Research Methods*. London: Sage.

FOX Sports Brasil (2020) *Ranking das maiores dívidas dos clubes Brasileiros*. [Online]. Available from: https://www.youtube.com/watch?v=hYnXG5HfWaw (accessed 10 August 2020).

Franzini, F. (2005) 'Futebol é "coisa para macho"? Pequeno esboço para uma história das mulheres no país do futebol', *Revista Brasileira de História*, 25(50), pp. 315–28.

Fraser, N. (2013) *Fortunes of Feminism: From State-Managed Capitalism to Neoliberal Crisis*. New York: Verso Books.

Frydenberg, J.D. (2005) 'La profesionalización del fútbol Argentino: entre una huelga de jugadores y la reestructuración del espectáculo', *Entrepasados*, 14(27), pp. 73–94.

Frydenberg, J.D. (2011) *Historia social del fútbol: del amateurismo a la profesionalización*. Buenos Aires: Siglo XXI editores.

Futbolred (2017) *Por intoxicación de sus rivales, Santa Fe aplaza debut en Libertadores*. [Online]. Available from: https://www.futbolred.com/futbol-colombiano/futbol-femenino/jugadoras-de-la-copa-libertadores-femenina-2017-intoxicadas-53614 (accessed 30 March 2020).

Futbolred (2019) *Millonarios vs. Santa Fe: clásico femenino cuartos de final previo fecha hora y dónde ver 2019 | Futbol Colombiano | Fútbol Femenino | Futbolred*. [Online]. Available from: https://www.futbolred.com/futbol-colombiano/futbol-femenino/millonarios-vs-santa-fe-clasico-femenino-cuartos-de-final-previo-fecha-hora-y-donde-ver-2019-105517 (accessed 12 March 2020).

Futbolred (2019) *Pulla de Yoreli a la Federación de Fútbol por su ausencia en Selección*. [Online]. Available from: https://www.futbolred.com/futbol-colombiano/futbol-femenino/yoreli-rincon-denuncia-veto-en-la-seleccion-colombia-femenina-103442 (accessed 22 April 2021).

@futbolsinlimi (2018) *Muchas felicitaciones han recibido las chicas del Atlético Huila, pero lo triste es que este premio no será para ellas. Las declaraciones de #Nuestra10 @yorelirincon*. [Online]. Available from: https://twitter.com/futbolsinlimi/status/1069976521803292673 (accessed 14 May 2020).

G1 Amazonas (2018) *A distribuição de votos de Bolsonaro e Haddad no Amazonas*. [Online]. Available from: https://g1.globo.com/am/amazonas/eleicoes/2018/noticia/2018/10/29/veja-como-foi-a-distribuicao-de-votos-de-bolsonaro-e-haddad-no-amazonas.ghtml (accessed 4 August 2020).

Galeano, E. (1995) *El fútbol a sol y sombra*. Barcelona: Siglo XXI de España Editores.

Galindo, L.M. (2018) *La Liga Femenina de Fútbol de Colombia podría estar en peligro*. [Online]. Available from: https://www.vice.com/es_latam/article/vbaejb/liga-femenina-futbol-colombia-peligro-machismo-sueldos-equipos (accessed 14 May 2020).

Garriga Zucal, J. (2006) 'Acá es así. Hinchadas de fútbol, violencia y territorios', *Avá*, (9), pp. 93–107.

Garriga Zucal, J. (2007a) *'Haciendo amigos a las piñas': violencia y redes sociales de una hinchada del fútbol*. Buenos Aires: Prometeo Libros Editorial.

Garriga Zucal, J. (2007b) 'Entre "machos" y "putos": estilos masculinos y prácticas violentas de una hinchada de fútbol', *Esporte e Sociedade*, 2(4), pp. 1–28.

Garriga Zucal, J. (2009) 'Violencia e identidad: las hinchadas de fútbol en la Argentina', *URVIO: Revista Latinoamericana de Estudios de Seguridad*, (8), pp. 101–106.

Garton, G. (2019) *Guerreras: fútbol, mujeres y poder*. Buenos Aires: Capital Intelectual.

Garton, G.N. (2020) 'La profesionalización del fútbol femenino argentino: entre la resistencia y la manutención del orden', *Revista Ensambles*, (12), pp. 72–86.

Garton, G. (2023) 'Being "in" and "on the field": an auto-ethnographic reflection on elite women's football in Argentina', in Culvin, A. & Bowes, A. (eds), *Women's Football in a Global, Professional Era*. Online: Emerald Publishing Limited, pp. 145–57.

Garton, G. & Hijós, N. (2017) 'La mujer deportista en las redes sociales: un análisis de los consumos deportivos y sus producciones estéticas', *Hipertextos*, 5.

Garton, G. & Hijós, N. (2018) '"La deportista moderna": género, clase y consumo en el fútbol, running y hockey Argentinos', *Antípoda. Revista de Antropología y Arqueología*, 30, pp. 23–42.

Garton, G., Hijós, N. & Alabarces, P. (2021) 'Playing for change: (semi-) professionalization, social policy, and power struggles in Argentine women's football', *Soccer & Society*, 22(6), pp. 626–40.

Garton, G., Hijós, N. & Moreira, V. (2022) 'No nos callamos más: a turning point in women's football and women's rights in Argentina', in Knijnik, J. & Garton, G. (eds), *Women's Football in Latin America: Social Challenges and Historical Perspectives*, Vol. 2, *Hispanic Countries*. London: Palgrave Macmillan, pp. 11–34.

Gasparetto, T.M. (2013a) 'Internacionalização dos clubes de futebol do Brasil', *Revista Intercontinental de Gestão Desportiva*, 3(1), pp. 51–63.

Gasparetto, T.M. (2013b) 'O futebol como negócio: uma comparação financeira com outros segmentos', *Revista Brasileira de Ciências do Esporte*, 35(4).

Gasparetto, T.M. (2013c) 'Relação entre custo operacional e desempenho esportivo: análise do campeonato Brasileiro de futebol', *Revista Brasileira de Futebol (The Brazilian Journal of Soccer Science)*, 5(2), pp. 28–40.

Gazeta Press (2021) *Conselheiros do Santos cobram punição a sócio que chamou futebol feminino de lixo: "Mocinhas no campo são aquelas que a gente enche de porrada"*. [Online]. Available from: https://www.espn.com.br/futebol/artigo/_/id/8118605/conselheiros-do-santos-cobram-punicao-a-socio-que-chamou-futebol-feminino-de-lixo-mocinhas-no-campo-sao-aquelas-que-a-gente-enche-de-porrada (accessed 2 February 2021).

Geertz, C. (1973) *The Interpretation of Cultures*. Vol. 5019. London: Basic Books.

Geertz, C. (1988) *Works and Lives: The Anthropologist as Author*. Palo Alto, CA: Stanford University Press.

Gibbs, C. & Haynes, R. (2013) 'A phenomenological investigation into how Twitter has changed the nature of sport media relations', *International Journal of Sport Communication*, 6(4), pp. 394–408.

Giulianotti, R. (1996) 'Back to the future: an ethnography of Ireland's football fans at the 1994 World Cup finals in the USA', *International Review for the Sociology of Sport*, 31(3), pp. 323–44.

Giulianotti, R. (1999) *Football: A Sociology of the Global Game*. Cambridge: Polity.

Giulianotti, R. & Robertson, R. (2009) *Globalization and Football*. London: Sage.

Glass, A. (2020) *Brazil announces equal pay for women's and men's national teams*. Forbes, 2 September. Available from: https://www.forbes.com/sites/alanaglass/2020/09/02/brazil-announces-equal-pay-for-womens-and-mens-national-teams/ (accessed 13 December 2020).

Globo Esporte Espetacular (2017) *Hulk da Amazônia no Esporte Espetacular: 30/04/2017*. [Online]. Available from: https://www.youtube.com/watch?v=bm1JRoKHpVM&t=98s (accessed 2 July 2020).

Globoesporte.com (2019) *Com mais de 1 bilhão de pessoas, FIFA diz que Copa do Mundo Feminina foi a mais vista da história | copa do mundo feminina |*

Globoesporte. [Online]. Available from: https://globoesporte.globo.com/futebol/copa-do-mundo-feminina/noticia/fifa-divulga-audiencia-da-copa-do-mundo-feminina-e-diz-que-mais-de-1-bi-de-pessoas-assistiu-ao-torneio.ghtml (accessed 9 March 2020).

Globoesporte.com (2020) *Com vaquinha online, acúmulo de dívidas no Iranduba é de R$ 650 mil; doações superam os R$ 3 mil.* [Online]. Available from: https://globoesporte.globo.com/am/futebol/times/iranduba/noticia/com-vaquinha-online-acumulo-de-dividas-no-iranduba-e-de-r-650-mil-doacoes-superam-os-r-3-mil.ghtml (accessed 16 May 2021).

Goellner, S.V. (2003) 'A produção cultural do corpo', in Louro, G.L., Neckel, J.F. & Goellner, S.V. (eds), *Corpo, gênero e sexualidade: um debate contemporâneo na educação.* Petrópolis: Vozes, pp. 28–40.

Goellner, S.V. (2005a) 'Mulher e esporte no Brasil: entre incentivos e interdições elas fazem história', *Pensar e prática,* 8(1), pp. 85–100.

Goellner, S.V. (2005b) 'Mulheres e futebol no Brasil: entre sombras e visibilidades', *Revista Brasileira de Educação Física e Esporte,* 19(2), pp. 143–51.

Goellner, S.V. (2012) 'Mulheres e esporte: sobre conquistas e desafios', *Revista do Observatório Brasil da Igualdade de Gênero,* 2(4).

Goellner, S.V. (2021) 'Mulheres e futebol no Brasil: descontinuidades, resistências e resiliências', *Movimento (ESEFID/UFRGS),* 27, p. 21001.

Goellner, S.V. & Kessler, C.S. (2018) 'A sub-representação do futebol praticado por mulheres no Brasil: mudar o foco para visibilizar a modalidade', in Pinheiro, F. & Andrade de Melo, V. (eds), *Francisco Pinheiro; Victor Andrade de Melo. A Bola ao Ritmo de Fado e Samba.* Porto: Afrontamento, p. 100.

GOL Caracol (2018) *La amorosa celebración entre Yoreli Rincón y Jay Oliveros tras la obtención de la Copa Libertadores.* [Online]. Available from: https://gol.caracoltv.com/informacion-general/la-amorosa-celebracion-entre-yoreli-rincon-y-jay-oliveros-tras-la-obtencion-de-la-copa-libertadores-ie24043 (accessed 12 May 2020).

@GolCaracol (2018) *La amorosa celebración entre Yoreli Rincón y Jay Oliveros tras la obtención de la Copa Libertadores.* [Online]. Available from: https://twitter.com/GolCaracol/status/1069934342653272064 (accessed 14 May 2020).

Goldblatt, D. (2007) *The Ball Is Round: A Global History of Football.* London: Penguin UK.

Goldblatt, D. (2014) *Futebol Nation: A Footballing History of Brazil.* London: Penguin.

Goldblatt, D. (2016) *The Games: A Global History of the Olympics.* London: Pan Macmillan.

Goldblatt, D. (2019) *The Age of Football: The Global Game in the Twenty-First Century.* London: Macmillan.

Gomes, J.A. (2009) 'Futebol, nação e o homem brasileiro: o "complexo de vira-latas" de Nelson Rodrigues', *Organizações & Sociedade,* 16(48).

Gómez, J.E. (2022) *Ya hablan de cifras y de exámenes médicos de Linda Caicedo con el Barcelona, ¿es cierto? El Colombiano,* 27 October. Available from: https://www.elcolombiano.com/deportes/futbol/linda-caicedo-seria-nueva-jugadora-de-barcelona-asi-va-negociacion-GH18971403 (accessed 29 January 2023).

Gonçalves, J.C. de S. & Carvalho, C.A. (2006) 'A mercantilização do futebol brasileiro: instrumentos, avanços e resistências', *Cadernos EBAPE. BR*, 4(2), pp. 1–27.

González Otálora, G.A. (2003) *Mitos del Huila*. Bogotá: Ediciones Huertas.

Governo de São Paulo (2019) *LPIE – Lei Paulista de Incentivo ao Esporte*. [Online]. Available from: http://www.lpie.sp.gov.br/ConsultaPublicaImprimir/Create?IdProjeto=496&IdUsuario=360&IdConta=370&Protocolo=0914111752&CodigoEmpresa=359 (accessed 6 April 2020).

Grez, M. (2018) *'Unfortunately, that is women's football'*. [Online]. Available from: https://edition.cnn.com/2018/12/07/football/copa-libertadores-boca-juniors-river-plate-atletico-huila-spt-intl/index.html (accessed 27 May 2020).

Guedes, S.L. (1977) *O futebol brasileiro: instituição zero*. Rio de Janeiro: Universidade Federal de Fluminense.

Guedes, S.L. (1982) 'Subúrbio: celeiro de craques', in de Matta, R. (ed.), *Universo do futebol: esporte e sociedade brasileira*. Rio de Janeiro: Pinakotheke, pp. 59–74.

Guizardi, M., Valdebenito, F., López, E. & Nazal, E. (2019) *Des/venturas de la frontera: Una etnografía sobre las mujeres peruanas entre Chile y Perú*. Santiago: Ediciones Universidad Alberto Hurtado.

Gutiérrez Sánchez, M.C. (2015) *Representación de la mujer ecuatoriana en el ámbito deportivo mundial de fútbol femenino Canadá 2015*. B.S. thesis. Quito: USFQ, 2015.

Guttmann, A. (1991) *Women's Sports: A History*. New York: Columbia University Press.

Guzmán, L.C. (2010) 'Mitos y leyendas del Huila – los relatos de la sombra', *Revista Academia Huilense de Historia*, 13(58), pp. 113–22.

Haag Ribeiro, F. (2013) 'Futebol e o giro neoliberal: apontamentos e o caso Brasileiro', *PODIUM Sport, Leisure and Tourism Review*, 2(1), pp. 57–80.

Haag Ribeiro, F. (2018) '"O futebol pode não ter sido profissional comigo, mas eu fui com ele": trabalho e relações sociais de sexo no futebol feminino brasileiro', *Mosaico*, 9(14), pp. 142–60.

Hall, S. (1973) 'Encoding/decoding', *Media and Cultural Studies: Keyworks*, 2.

Hammersley, M. & Atkinson, P. (2007) *Ethnography: Principles in Practice*. London: Routledge.

Hatoum, M. (n.d.) *Relato de um Certo Oriente*. São Paulo: Companhia das Letras.

Hayes Sauder, M. & Blaszka, M. (2018) '23 players, 23 voices: an examination of the US women's national soccer team on Twitter during the 2015 World Cup', *Communication & Sport*, 6(2), pp. 175–202.

Helal, R. (1997) *Passes e impasses: futebol e cultura de massa no Brasil*. Rio de Janeiro: Vozes.

Helal, R., Soares, A.J.G. & Lovisolo, H.R. (2001) *A invenção do país do futebol: mídia, raça e idolatria*. Rio de Janeiro: Mauad Editora Ltda.

Hijós, M.N. (2014) 'El caso Boca Juniors: del juego y la práctica recreativa a la consolidación de una marca internacional', *Lúdicamente*, 3(6).

Hijós, M.N. & Ibarrola, D.S. (2018) 'El deporte como mercancía: un análisis comparativo entre los procesos de modernización en Boca Juniors y River Plate de Argentina', *Antropología y Ciencias Sociales*, 24.

Hijós, N. (2013) *El deporte como mercancía: un estudio sobre la dimensión económica y las múltiples lógicas en el Club Atlético Boca Juniors.* PhD thesis. Buenos Aires: Tesis de licenciatura inédita. Facultad de Filosofía y Letras, UBA.

Hirata, E. (2011) 'A mercantilização do futebol e os subterrâneos da legislação esportiva brasileira (1980–2010)', *Simpósio Nacional de História–ANPUH*, XXVI, pp. 1–13.

Hjelseth, A. & Hovden, J. (2014) 'Negotiating the status of women's football in Norway: an analysis of online supporter discourses', *European Journal for Sport and Society*, 11(3), pp. 253–77.

Hobsbawm, E. (2007) *Interesting Times: A Twentieth-Century Life.* London: Pantheon.

Hobsbawm, E. (2012) 'Introduction: the invention of tradition', in Hobsbawm, E., *The Invention of Tradition.* Cambridge: Cambridge University Press, pp. 1–16.

Hopcraft, A. (1968) *The Football Man: People & Passions in Soccer.* London: Aurum Press.

@HuilaSport (2018) *Así recibe Neiva a las campeonas de la Copa Libertadores Femenina de Fútbol. Atlético Huila.* [Online]. Available from: https://twitter.com/HuilaSport/status/1070319837728174080 (accessed 4 June 2020).

Instituto Brasileiro de Geografia e Estatística (2010) *Censo Demográfico 2010.* [Online]. Available from: https://www.ibge.gov.br/estatisticas/sociais/educacao/9662-censo-demografico-2010.html?t=destaques (accessed 16 July 2020).

Instituto Brasileiro de Geografia e Estatística (2018) *Diagnóstico Nacional do Esporte.* [Online]. Available from: http://arquivo.esporte.gov.br/diesporte/2.html (accessed 9 August 2020).

Instituto Brasileiro de Geografia e Estatística (2019a) *IBGE | Cidades@ | Amazonas | Iranduba.* [Online]. Available from: https://cidades.ibge.gov.br/brasil/am/iranduba/panorama (accessed 18 June 2020).

Instituto Brasileiro de Geografia e Estatística (2019b) *IBGE divulga as estimativas da população dos municípios para 2019.* [Online]. Available from: https://agenciadenoticias.ibge.gov.br/agencia-sala-de-imprensa/2013-agencia-de-noticias/releases/25278-ibge-divulga-as-estimativas-da-populacao-dos-municipios-para-2019 (accessed 17 June 2020).

Jones, R., Murrell, A.J. & Jackson, J. (1999) 'Pretty versus powerful in the sports pages: print media coverage of US women's Olympic gold medal winning teams', *Journal of Sport and Social Issues*, 23(2), pp. 183–92.

Joras, P.S. (2015) *Futebol e mulheres no Brasil: a história de vida de Aline Pellegrino.* Porto Alegre: UFRGS.

Kamarck, E.C. & Gabriele, A. (2015) *The News Today: 7 Trends in Old and New Media.* Washington: Brookings.

Killick, E. (2018) 'Rubber, *terra preta*, and soy: a study of visible and invisible Amazonian modernities', *Journal of Anthropological Research*, 74(1), pp. 32–53.

King, A. (1997) 'The lads: masculinity and the new consumption of football', *Sociology*, 31(2), pp. 329–46.

Kittleson, R. (2014) *The Country of Football: Soccer and the Making of Modern Brazil.* Vol. 2. Berkeley: University of California Press.

Klein, M.-L. (2018) 'Women's football leagues in Europe: organizational and economic perspectives', in Pfister, G. & Pope, S. (eds), *Female Football Players and Fans*. London: Palgrave Macmillan, pp. 77–101.

Knijnik, J. (2014) 'Gendered barriers to Brazilian female football: twentieth century legacies', in Hargreaves, J. & Anderson, E. (eds), *Routledge Handbook of Sport, Gender and Sexuality*. Abingdon: Routledge, pp. 141–8.

Knijnik, J. (2015) 'Femininities and masculinities in Brazilian women's football: resistance and compliance', *Journal of International Women's Studies*, 16(3), pp. 54–70.

Knijnik, J. & Horton, P. (2013) 'Only beautiful women need apply: human rights and gender in Brazilian football', *Journal of International Women's Studies*, 6, pp. 60–70.

Knijnik, J.D. (2018) *The World Cup Chronicles: 31 Days that Rocked Brazil*. Sydney: Fair Play.

Krasnoff, L.S. (2019) 'The up-front legacies of France 2019: changing the face of "le foot féminin"', *Sport in History*, 39(4), pp. 462–83.

Kuhn, T.S. (1962) *The Structure of Scientific Revolutions*. Chicago: University of Chicago Press.

Kuper, S. & Szymanski, S. (2014) *Soccernomics: Why England Loses, Why Spain, Germany, and Brazil Win, and Why the US, Japan, Australia – and Even Iraq – Are Destined to Become the Kings of the World's Most Popular Sport*. London: Nation Books.

La Piragua (2018) *Video de futbolistas colombianas besándose se hace viral*. [Online]. Available from: https://www.lapiragua.co/video-de-futbolistas-colombianas-besandose-se-hace-viral/actualidad/ (accessed 19 May 2020).

Lacerda Abrahão, B.O. & Soares, A.J. (2009) 'O que o brasileiro não esquece nem a tiro é o chamado frango de Barbosa: questões sobre o racismo no futebol brasileiro', *Movimento*, 15(2), pp. 13–31.

Lake, R.J. (2016) '"Guys don't whale away at the women": etiquette and gender relations in contemporary mixed-doubles tennis', *Sport in Society*, 19(8–9), pp. 1214–33.

Langton, R. (2009) *Sexual Solipsism: Philosophical Essays on Pornography and Objectification*. Oxford: Oxford University Press.

Lavoi, N.M. & Calhoun, A.S. (2014) 'Digital media and women's sport: an old view on "new" media?', in Billings, A. & Hardin, M. (eds), *Routledge Handbook of Sport and New Media*. Abingdon: Routledge, pp. 338–48.

Lavoi, N.M. & Dutove, J.K. (2012) 'Barriers and supports for female coaches: an ecological model', *Sports Coaching Review*, 1(1), pp. 17–37.

Lima, S. (2017) *Públicos recordes e jogadoras de seleção: Manaus vira 'capital' do futebol feminino | futebol | Globoesporte*. [Online]. Available from: https://globoesporte.globo.com/am/futebol/noticia/publicos-recordes-e-jogadoras-de-selecao-manaus-vira-capital-do-futebol-feminino.ghtml (accessed 17 June 2020).

Lima, S. (2018) *Iranduba inicia conversa e sabe o preço para contar com Marta na Libertadores*. [Online]. Available from: https://globoesporte.globo.com/am/futebol/times/iranduba/noticia/iranduba-inicia-conversa-e-sabe-o-preco-para-contar-com-marta-na-libertadores.ghtml (accessed 3 July 2020).

Lisboa, W.T. (2015) *Santos, em duas viradas de século (do século 19 ao século 20 e do século 20 ao século 21): dinâmicas de configuração social do território de migrações internacionais.* Master's thesis. São Paulo: Universidade Estadual de Campinas.

Llanos, G.C. & Accorsi, S. (2002) 'Sujetos femeninos y masculinos', *Boletín americanista*, (52), pp. 248–51.

Longman, J. (2014) *The snakes may not bite but the humidity devours.* The New York Times, 14 June. Available from: https://www.nytimes.com/2014/06/14/sports/worldcup/world-cup-2014-england-and-italy-prepare-to-play-in-manaus.html (accessed 17 June 2020).

Louro, G.L. (1997) *Gênero, sexualidade e educação.* Petrópolis: Vozes.

Louro, G.L. (1999) 'Pedagogias da sexualidade', *O corpo educado: pedagogias da sexualidade*, 2, pp. 7–34.

Lowndes, V. (2010) *The Institutional Approach.* London: Macmillan.

Lowndes, V. & Roberts, M. (2013) *Why Institutions Matter: The New Institutionalism in Political Science.* London: Macmillan International Higher Education.

Lugones, M. (2007) 'Heterosexualism and the colonial/modern gender system', *Hypatia*, 22(1), pp. 186–219.

Lugones, M. (2011) 'Hacia un feminismo descolonial', *La manzana de la discordia*, 6(2), pp. 105–17.

Magalhães, S.L.F. (2008) 'Memória, futebol e mulher: anonimato, oficialização e seus reflexos na capital paraense (1980–2007)', *Recorde: Revista de História do Esporte*, 1(2).

Majestic Produçoes (2016) *Iranduba da Amazônia: A história.*

March, J.G. & Olsen, J.P. (1983) 'The new institutionalism: organizational factors in political life', *American Political Science Review*, 78(3), pp. 734–49.

March, J.G. & Olsen, J.P. (2010) *Rediscovering Institutions.* New York: Simon and Schuster.

Marcos, A. (2017) *Adidas elige a una modelo para lucir la camiseta de la selección colombiana y deja fuera a las jugadoras.* [Online]. Available from: https://verne.elpais.com/verne/2017/11/08/mexico/1510099505_610276.html (accessed 20 May 2020).

Maricato, E. (2014) 'Cidades no Brasil: neodesenvolvimentismo ou crescimento periférico predatório', *Revista da Defensoria Pública: Edição Especial de Habitação e Urbanismo, São Paulo*, pp. 8–30.

Markovits, A.S. & Hellerman, S.L. (2003) 'Women's soccer in the United States: yet another American "exceptionalism"', *Soccer & Society*, 4(2–3), pp. 14–29.

Martín-Barbero, J. (1983) *De los medios a las mediaciones: comunicación, cultura y hegemonía.* Bogotá: Convenio Andrés Bello.

Martins, M.Z. (2017) 'Mulheres torcedoras de futebol: questionando as masculinidades circulantes nas arquibancadas', in XX Congresso Brasileiro de Ciências do Esporte e VII Congresso Internacional de Ciências do Esporte. [Online]. Available from: http://congressos.cbce.org.br/index.php/conbrace2017/7conice/paper/viewFile/9664/5121 (accessed 27 March 2020).

Martins, M.Z., Silva, K.R.S. & Vasquez, V. (2021) 'As Mulheres E O País Do Futebol: Intersecções De Gênero, Classe E Raça No Brasil', *Movimento*, 27.

Marwick, A. & Lewis, R. (2017) 'Media manipulation and disinformation online'. [Online]. Available from: https://www.datasociety.net/pubs/oh/DataAndSociety_MediaManipulationAndDisinformationOnline.pdf (accessed 27 March 2020).

Massey, D. (2013) *Space, Place and Gender*. London: John Wiley & Sons.

McDowell, J. & Schaffner, S. (2011) 'Football, it's a man's game: insult and gendered discourse in the gender bowl', *Discourse & Society*, 22(5), pp. 547–64.

McLintock, A. (1995) *Imperial Leather: Race, Gender and Sexuality in the Colonial Context*. New York: Routledge.

Mehta, J. (2010) 'The varied roles of ideas in politics', in Béland, D. & Cox, R.H. (eds), *Ideas and Politics in Social Science Research*. Oxford: Oxford University Press, pp. 23–46.

Mejía Quintana, O. & Jiménez, C. (2005) 'Nuevas teorías de la democracia de la democracia formal a la democracia deliberativa', *Colombia internacional*, (62), pp. 12–31.

Melo, J.G. (2013) 'Dimensões do Urbano: O que as narrativas indígenas revelam sobre a cidade? Considerações dos Baré sobre Manaus, AM', *Teoria e Cultura*, 8(1).

Mendonça, R. (2018a) *Corinthians, o 'respeito às minas' precisa ir além do clubismo.* [Online]. Available from: https://dibradoras.blogosfera.uol.com.br/2018/05/14/corinthians-o-respeito-as-minas-precisa-ir-alem-do-clubismo/ (accessed 30 March 2020).

Mendonça, R. (2018b) *'Futebol feminino é terra do lesbianismo', diz presidente do Tolima. Sério?* [Online]. Available from: https://dibradoras.blogosfera.uol.com.br/2018/12/20/futebol-feminino-e-terra-do-lesbianismo-diz-presidente-do-tolima-serio/ (accessed 14 May 2020).

Mendonça, R. (2018c) *Marco Aurélio Cunha: Há quem transmita até golfe, mas não futebol feminino.* [Online]. Available from: https://dibradoras.blogosfera.uol.com.br/2018/05/04/marco-aurelio-cunha-ha-quem-transmita-ate-golfe-mas-nao-futebol-feminino/ (accessed 12 March 2020).

Mendonça, R. (2018d) *Problemas de organização, calor e golaços: começou a Libertadores feminina – UOL Esporte.* [Online]. Available from: https://dibradoras.blogosfera.uol.com.br/2018/11/19/problemas-de-organizacao-calor-e-golacos-comecou-a-libertadores-feminina/ (accessed 9 March 2020).

Mendonça, R. (2018e) *Quem é a mulher que está mudando a realidade do futebol feminino no Brasil.* [Online]. Available from: https://dibradoras.blogosfera.uol.com.br/2018/12/19/quem-e-a-mulher-que-esta-mudando-a-realidade-do-futebol-feminino-no-brasil/ (accessed 9 May 2020).

Mendonça, R. (2019a) *Palmeiras sai atrás de rivais com feminino 'terceirizado' e pouca definição – UOL Esporte.* [Online]. Available from: https://dibradoras.blogosfera.uol.com.br/2019/02/13/palmeiras-sai-atras-de-rivais-com-feminino-terceirizado-e-pouca-definicao/ (accessed 27 May 2020).

Mendonça, R. (2019b) *Quem é Pia Sundhage, a nova técnica da seleção feminina de futebol – UOL Esporte.* [Online]. Available from: https://dibradoras.blogosfera.uol.com.br/2019/07/25/quem-e-pia-sundhage-a-nova-tecnica-da-selecao-feminina-de-futebol/ (accessed 8 November 2020).

Mendonça, R. (2020a) CBF não fiscaliza, e jogadoras ficam sem salário mesmo com ajuda aos clubes. [Online]. Available from: https://dibradoras. blogosfera.uol.com.br/2020/04/20/cbf-nao-fiscaliza-e-jogadoras-ficam-sem-salario-mesmo-com-ajuda-aos-clubes/ (accessed 25 May 2020).

Mendonça, R. (2020b) Mesmo com ajuda da CBF, clubes negam a jogadoras ajuda de custo de R$500 – UOL Esporte. [Online]. Available from: https:// dibradoras.blogosfera.uol.com.br/2020/04/27/mesmo-com-ajuda-da-cbf-clubes-negam-a-jogadoras-ajuda-de-custo-de-r500/ (accessed 25 May 2020).

Mendonça, R. & Torralba, K. (2019) 'A 1a menina a passar em peneira de categorias de base de um time masculino', *Justiça de Saia*. [Online]. Available from: https://www.justicadesaia.com.br/a-1a-menina-a-passar-em-peneira-de-categorias-de-base-de-um-time-masculino/ (accessed 6 March 2020).

Messner, M., Cooky, C. & Hextrum, R. (2010) 'Gender in televised sports', Center for Feminist Research, 39, pp. 437–53.

Messner, M.A. (1988) 'Sports and male domination: the female athlete as contested ideological terrain', *Sociology of Sport Journal*, 5(3), pp. 197–211.

Messner, M.A., Duncan, M.C. & Jensen, K. (1993) 'Separating the men from the girls: the gendered language of televised sports', *Gender & Society*, 7(1), pp. 121–137.

Messner, M.A. & Sabo, D.F. (1990) *Sport, Men, and the Gender Order: Critical Feminist Perspectives*. Vol. 10. Champaign, IL: Human Kinetics.

Michaelis (2020) *Michaelis Dicionário do Português Brasileiro*. [Online]. Available from: http://michaelis.uol.com.br/ (accessed 10 August 2020).

Mignolo, W. (2011) *The Darker Side of Western Modernity: Global Futures, Decolonial Options*. Durham, NC: Duke University Press.

Mignolo, W.D. (2009) *The Idea of Latin America*. London: John Wiley & Sons.

Milesi, R., Coury, P. & Rovery, J. (2018) 'Migração Venezuelana ao Brasil: discurso político e xenofobia no contexto atual', *Revista Aedos*, 10(22), pp. 53–70.

Mina, C.Y.M. & Goellner, S.V. (2015a) 'Estar allá, no es solo estar allá: narrativas de las dos únicas entrenadoras presentes en la Copa Libertadores Femenina 2015', *Labrys Estudos Feministas*, 28, pp. 49–66.

Mina, C.Y.M. & Goellner, S.V. (2015b) 'Representaciones sociales de la selección femenina de fútbol de Colombia en la copa américa 2014', *Educación Física y Deporte*, 34(1), pp. 39–72.

Mina, C.Y.M., Goellner, S. & Rodríguez, A.M.O. (2019) 'Fútbol y mujeres: el panorama de la liga profesional femenina de fútbol de Colombia', *Educación Física y Deporte*, 38(1).

Mina, C.Y.M., Martínez Mercado, C.M. & Roa Morantes, N. (2018) 'Fútbol y mujeres en Colombia: narrativas de las jugadoras profesionales de fútbol sobre su inicio en la práctica deportiva', in Navarro, J.R.S., Navarro, Y., Pérez, Y.S., Pirela, R.A.V., Pirela R. & Martinez, R.A. (eds), *La actividad física y sus ciencias aplicadas III*. Maracaibo: Fondo Editorial UNERMB, pp. 49–68.

Moehlecke, S. (2002) 'Ação afirmativa: história e debates no Brasil', *Cadernos de pesquisa*, 117, pp. 197–217.

Montoya, D. (2020) *Ver los partidos de las ligas top que han retomado en el fútbol masculino, ver tantos errores, tantas imprecisiones.* [Online]. Available from: https://twitter.com/06montoya/status/1272242456801742848 (accessed 29 June 2020).

Moraes, C.F. & Bonfim, A.F. (2017) 'Mulher no Futebol – no campo e nas arquibancadas', V Seminário Internacional Enlaçando Sexualidades. [Online]. Available from: https://ludopedio.org.br/arquibancada/mulher-no-futebol-no-campo-e-nas-arquibancadas/ (accessed on 12 March 2010).

Moreira, R.P. (2014) 'Marta past Messi: (re)definitions of gender and masculinity, patriarchal structures and female agency in international soccer', *Soccer & Society*, 15(4), pp. 503–16.

Moreira, V. & Garton, G. (2021) 'Fútbol, nación y mujeres en Argentina: redefiniendo el campo del poder', *Movimento*, 27.

Moreira, V. & Hijós, N. (2013) 'Clubes deportivos, fútbol y mercantilización: los casos de Boca Juniors e Independiente en la Argentina', *Question*, 1(37), pp. 149–62.

Morel, C.R.A. (2019) 'La discriminación de género en el deporte. El caso del futbol femenino', *Revista ScientiAmericana*, 6(2), pp. 81–90.

Mósca, H.M.B., da Silva, J.R.G. & Bastos, S.A.P. (2010) 'Fatores institucionais e organizacionais que afetam a gestão profissional de departamentos de futebol dos clubes: o caso dos clubes de futebol no Brasil', *Gestão & Planejamento – G&P*, 10(1).

Mourão, L. & Morel, M. (2008) 'As narrativas sobre o futebol feminino o discurso da mídia impressa em campo', *Revista brasileira de ciências do esporte*, 26(2).

Muelle, C.E. (2017) 'Cómo hacer necropolíticas en casa: Ideología de género y acuerdos de paz en Colombia', *Sexualidad, Salud y Sociedad (Rio de Janeiro)*, 27, pp. 172–98.

Müller, M. (2016) 'Constructing gender incommensurability in competitive sport: sex/gender testing and the new regulations on female hyperandrogenism', *Human Studies*, 39, pp. 405–31.

Musto, M., Cooky, C. & Messner, M.A. (2017) '"From fizzle to sizzle!" Televised sports news and the production of gender-bland sexism', *Gender & Society*, 31(5), pp. 573–96.

Nadel, J. (2015) 'The antinational game? An exploration of women's soccer in Latin America', in Fernández L'Hoeste, H., Irwin, R.M. & Poblete, J. (eds), *Sports and Nationalism in Latin/o America*. New York: Palgrave Macmillan, pp. 45–65.

Nauright, J. (2014) 'African women and sport: the state of play', *Sport in Society*, 17(4), pp. 563–74.

Norman, L. (2008) 'The UK coaching system is failing women coaches', *International Journal of Sports Science & Coaching*, 3(4), pp. 447–76.

Norman, L. (2010) 'Feeling second best: elite women coaches' experiences', *Sociology of Sport Journal*, 27(1), pp. 89–104.

Norman, L. & Rankin-Wright, A. (2018) 'Surviving rather than thriving: understanding the experiences of women coaches using a theory of gendered social well-being', *International Review for the Sociology of Sport*, 53(4), pp. 424–50.

Noronha, M.P. (2010) 'Futebol é coisa de mulher! Um estudo etnográfico sobre o "lugar" feminino no futebol clubístico', *Matrizes*, 2(1).

Noronha, M.P. (2012) *(Des) construindo identidades: ambiguidades, estereótipos e luta política nas relações mulher-futebol*. Master's thesis. Universidade Federal do Rio Grande do Sul.

Nugent, S. & Harris, M. (2004) *Some Other Amazonians: Perspectives on Modern Amazonians*. London: Institute for the Study of the Americas.

Núñez, S.I.B. (2020) *Colombia y Conmebol se quejaron ante FIFA por calificación recibida*. [Online]. Available from: https://www.vanguardia.com/deportes/futbol-internacional/colombia-y-conmebol-se-quejaron-ante-fifa-por-calificacion-recibida-HD2511191 (accessed 29 June 2020).

Oakdale, S. & Watson, M. (2018) 'The diversity of the modern in Amazonia', *Journal of Anthropological Research*, 74(1), pp. 1–9.

Orozco, G. & Miller, T. (2016) 'Television in Latin America is "everywhere": not dead, not dying, but converging and thriving', *Media and Communication*, 4(3), pp. 99–108.

Ortiz, C.F.S. (2012) 'Reseña histórica de Neiva', *Revista Academia Huilense de Historia*, 63, pp. 35–100.

Oxford, S. (2019) '"You look like a *machito*!": a decolonial analysis of the social in/exclusion of female participants in a Colombian Sport for Development and Peace organization', *Sport in Society*, 22(6), pp. 1025–42.

Oxford, S. & Spaaij, R. (2019) 'Gender relations and sport for development in Colombia: a decolonial feminist analysis', *Leisure Sciences*, 41(1–2), pp. 54–71.

Padin, G. (2017) 'Manaus, a capital do futebol feminino no Brasil', *El País Brasil*, 7 January.

Palmer, L. (2012) 'Cranked masculinity: hypermediation in digital action cinema', *Cinema Journal*, 51(4), pp. 1–25.

Park, A., Lee, K.J. & Casalegno, F. (2010) 'The three dimensions of book evolution in ubiquitous computing age: digitalization, augmentation, and hypermediation', in 2010 IEEE International Conference on Sensor Networks, Ubiquitous, and Trustworthy Computing, IEEE, pp. 374–78.

Pegoraro, A., Comeau, G.S. & Frederick, E.L. (2018) '#SheBelieves: the use of Instagram to frame the US women's soccer team during #FIFAWWC', *Sport in Society*, 21(7), pp. 1063–77.

Peinado, Q., Wyoming, E.G. & Espinosa, A.G. (2013) *Futbolistas de izquierdas*. Alcalá de Henares: Léeme Libros.

Pelé (2020) *Homenagem do Santos ao Rei*. [Online]. Available from: https://www.facebook.com/Pele/videos/726344928277847 (accessed 25 October 2020).

Pereira, E. (2018) *Con un tierno beso, Yoreli Rincón y su novia celebraron el título de Libertadores – Colombian*. [Online]. Available from: https://www.colombian.com.co/deportes/con-un-tierno-beso-yoreli-rincon-y-su-novia-celebraron-el-titulo-de-libertadores/ (accessed 12 May 2020).

Pereira, F. & Pinheiro, G. (2017) *Manaus, o lugar onde o futebol feminino é o verdadeiro esporte nacional*. [Online]. Available from: https://www.uol.com.br/esporte/futebol/ultimas-noticias/2017/07/08/manaus-o-lugar-onde-o-futebol-feminino-e-maior-que-o-masculino.htm (accessed 17 June 2020).

Pérez, M.C.C. (2018) 'Los lugares negados. Género y espacio público en Neiva', *Revista Academia Huilense de Historia*, 69, pp. 59–74.

Peters, B.G. (2019) *Institutional Theory in Political Science: The New Institutionalism.* Cheltenham: Edward Elgar Publishing.

Pfister, G. (2015) 'Sportswomen in the German popular press: a study carried out in the context of the 2011 women's football World Cup', *Soccer & Society*, 16(5–6), pp. 639–56.

Pielke Jr, R. (2013) 'How can FIFA be held accountable?', *Sport Management Review*, 16(3), pp. 255–67.

Pimenta, C.A.M. (2000) 'Violência entre torcidas organizadas de futebol', *São Paulo em perspectiva*, 14(2), pp. 122–28.

Pinheiro, L.B.S.P. (2018) *Mundos do Trabalho na Cidade da Borracha: Trabalhadores, Lideranças, Associações e Greves Operárias em Manaus (1880–1930).* São Paulo: Paco Editorial.

Pinheiro-Machado, R., de Freixo, A., Custódio, T., Maria, T.V., Miguel, L.F., Potin, F., Gallego, E.S., Guimarães, D.M., Flauzina, A. & Bianchi, A. (2019) *Brasil em transe: Bolsonarismo, nova direita e desdemocratização.* Rio de Janeiro: Oficina Raquel.

Pinochet, J. (2017) 'Abuso sexual, maltrato, desigualdad: lo que se sabe del escándalo que sacude al fútbol femenino en Colombia', *BBC News Mundo*, 1 March.

Piovezani, C. (2011) 'Sentidos dos nomes em campo: discursos sobre o futebol brasileiro', *Estudos Linguísticos*, 40(3), pp. 1231–40.

Piovezani, C. (2012) 'Identidades e metamorfoses na denominação dos jogadores de futebol no Brasil', *Esporte e Sociedade*, 7(19), pp. 1–17.

Pires, B. (2017) *A repentina demissão de Emily Lima, primeira mulher a comandar a seleção feminina de futebol.* [Online]. Available from: https://brasil.elpais.com/brasil/2017/09/22/deportes/1506100948_899758.html (accessed 7 June 2021).

Pooley, J. (2010) 'The consuming self: from flappers to facebook', in Aronczyk, M. & Powers, D. (eds), *Blowing Up the Brand: Critical Perspectives on Promotional Culture.* London: Peter Lang, pp. 71–92.

Prensafútbol (2019) 'Clásico universitario tendrá versión femenina como antesala'. *Prensafútbol.* [Online]. Available from: https://www.prensafutbol. cl/306193-clasico-universitario-tendra-version-femenina-como-antesala/ (accessed 27 March 2020).

Prieto, N. (2018) 'Jorge Enrique Vélez, presidente de la Dimayor, habla de la Liga profesional Femenina en Colombia'. *Fémina Fútbol.* Available from: https://feminafutbol.com/noticias/jorge-enrique-velez-presidente-de-la-dimayor-habla-de-la-liga-profesional-femenina-en-colombia-19314/ (accessed on 6 February 2019).

Pulzo (2018) *El beso con cerveza con el que Yoreli y su pareja festejaron la Libertadores.* [Online]. Available from: https://www.pulzo.com/deportes/yoreli-su-pareja-festejaron-con-beso-cerveza-titulo-libertadores-PP602427 (accessed 12 May 2020).

Quijano, A. (2000) 'Coloniality of power and eurocentrism in Latin America', *International Sociology*, 15(2), pp. 215–32.

Quintero, J. (2020) *Aumenta indignación por declaraciones de Camargo sobre el fútbol femenino*. *El Colombiano*, 20 February. Available from: https://www.elcolombiano.com/deportes/futbol-femenino/reacciones-a-declaraciones-de-gabriel-camargo-sobre-el-futbol-femenino-AX9909938 (accessed 12 May 2020).

Quitián, D. (2016) 'La voz académica del fútbol en Colombia: una lectura desde la violencia', in Rosa, S.G. & Rueda, M. (eds), *¿Quién raya la cancha? una lectura desde la violencia: visiones, tensiones y nuevasperspectivas en los estudios socioculturales del deporte en América Latina*. Buenos Aires: CLACSO, p. 77.

Radin, P. (1966) *The Method and Theory of Ethnology*. New York: Basic Books.

Ravel, B. & Gareau, M. (2016) '"French football needs more women like Adriana"? Examining the media coverage of France's women's national football team for the 2011 World Cup and the 2012 Olympic Games', *International Review for the Sociology of Sport*, 51(7), pp. 833–47.

Read, I. (2012) *The Hierarchies of Slavery in Santos, Brazil, 1822–1888*. Palo Alto, CA: Stanford University Press.

RedGol Chile (2018) *Pellejerías de la Conmebol: campeonas de la Copa Libertadores Femenina duermen en el suelo del aeropuerto*. [Online]. Available from: https://redgol.cl/youtube/Pellejerias-de-la-Conmebol-campeonas-de-la-Copa-Libertadores-Femenina-duermen-en-el-suelo-del-aeropuerto-20181205-0002.html (accessed 14 May 2020).

Restrepo, F.A.T. (2012) 'Los neivanos y huilenses como personas y ciudadanos, mirados desde fuera', *Revista Academia Huilense de Historia*, 63, pp. 123–32.

Rezende, A.J., Dalmácio, F.Z. & Salgado, A.L. (2010) 'Nível de disclosure das atividades operacionais, econômicas e financeiras dos clubes Brasileiros', *Revista Contabilidade, Gestão e Governança*, 13(2).

Rial, C. (2012) 'Banal religiosity: Brazilian athletes as new missionaries of the neo-pentecostal diaspora', *Vibrant: Virtual Brazilian Anthropology*, 9(2), pp. 128–59.

Rial, C. (2013a) 'El invisible (y victorioso) fútbol practicado por mujeres en Brasil', *Nueva Sociedad*, 248, p. 114.

Rial, C. (2013b) 'The "Devil's egg": football players as new missionaries of the diaspora of Brazilian religions', in Rocha, C. & Vasquez, M.A. (eds), *The Diaspora of Brazilian Religions*. Leiden: Brill, pp. 91–115.

Rial, C. (2014) 'New frontiers: the transnational circulation of Brazil's women soccer players', in Agergaard, S. & Tiesler, N.C. (eds), *Women, Soccer and Transnational Migration*. Abingdon: Routledge, pp. 86–101.

Ribeiro, M.G. (2016) 'Desigualdades urbanas e desigualdades sociais nas metrópoles Brasileiras', *Sociologias*, 18(42), pp. 198–230.

Ricatti, F. & Klugman, M. (2013) '"Connected to something": soccer and the transnational passions, memories and communities of Sydney's Italian migrants', *The International Journal of the History of Sport*, 30(5), pp. 469–83.

Rigo, L.C., Jahnecka, L. & da Silva, I.C. (2010) 'Notas etnográficas sobre o futebol de várzea', *Movimento*, 16(3), pp. 155–79.

Rocha, G. de F.F. (2021) 'A construção da cidadania indígena no Brasil e suas contribuições à Teoria Crítica Racial', *Revista Direito e Práxis*, 12(2), pp. 1242–1269.

Rodrigues, J.L., Sarmento, C.E. & Cruz, A.N. (2006) *A regra do jogo: uma história institucional da CBF*. Rio de Janeiro: FGV.

Rodrigues, M.S. & da Silva, R.C. (2009) 'A estrutura empresarial nos clubes de futebol', *Organizações & Sociedade*, 16(48), pp. 17–37.

Roland, R. (1995) 'Glocalization: time–space and homogeneity–heterogeneity', in Featherstone, M., Lash, S. & Robertson, R. (eds), *Global Modernities*. London: Sage.

Rookwood, J. & Pearson, G. (2012) 'The hoolifan: positive fan attitudes to football "hooliganism"', *International Review for the Sociology of Sport*, 47(2), pp. 149–64.

Rowe, D. (2013) 'The sport/media complex', in Andrews, D.L. & Carrington, B. (eds), *A Companion to Sport*. Oxford: Blackwell, pp. 61–77.

Rowe, D. (2015) 'The mediated nation and the transnational football fan', *Soccer & Society*, 16(5–6), pp. 693–709.

RT (2018) *Fury as women's Copa Libertadores winners forced to give $55,000 prize money to pay men's team debts*. [Online]. Available from: https://www.rt.com/sport/445668-copa-libertadores-women-prize-money-men/ (accessed 14 May 2020).

Saavedra, M. (2003) 'Football feminine – development of the African game: Senegal, Nigeria and South Africa', *Soccer & Society*, 4(2–3), pp. 225–53.

Said, E.W. (1978) *Orientalism*. New York: Vintage.

Salgado, A.L., Rezende, A.J. & Dalmacio, F.Z. (2008) 'Uma análise do nível de disclosure das atividades operacionais, econômicas e financeiras dos clubes Brasilciros', in Anais do Congresso Brasileiro de Custos-ABC. Available at https://anaiscbc.emnuvens.com.br/anais/issue/archive (accessed 17 July 2023).

Salvini, L. & Marchi Júnior, W. (2013a) 'Notoriedade mundial e visibilidade local: o futebol feminino na revista Placar na década de 1990', *Sociologias Plurais*, 1(1).

Salvini, L. & Marchi Júnior, W. (2013b) 'Uma história do futebol feminino nas páginas da revista Placar entre os anos de 1980–1990', *Movimento*, 19(1), pp. 95–115.

Salvini, L. & Marchi Júnior, W. (2013c) 'Velhos tabus de roupa nova: o futebol feminino na revista Placar entre os anos de 2000–2010', *Praxia: Revista On-line de Educação Fisica da UEG*, 1(2), pp. 55–66.

Sánchez, H.M. (2013) 'Conquista y creación del espacio urbano en la Provincia de Neiva, Timaná y Saldana', *Revista de historia regional y local*, 5(9), pp. 146–205.

Sánchez, L. (2018) *Con beso y cerveza celebró Yoreli Rincón el triunfo continental. La Nación*, 12 March.

Santiago Junior, J.R. (2917) *Iranduba, o Hulk da Amazônia, o maior alento do nosso futebol | JR Santiago*. [Online]. Available from: https://www.acritica.com/blogs/jr-santiago/posts/iranduba-o-hulk-da-amazonia-o-maior-alento-do-nosso-futebol (accessed 2 August 2020).

Santillán Esqueda, M. & Gantús, F. (2010) 'Transgresiones femeninas: futbol. Una mirada desde la caricatura de la prensa, México 1970–1971', *Tzintzun*, 52, pp. 143–76.

Santos FC (2020) *Muito Além do Futebol – Santos Futebol Clube*. [Online]. Avai
lable from: https://www.santosfc.com.br/en/muito-alem-do-futebol/ (accessed
5 August 2020).

Sapsford, R. (2006) *Survey Research*. London: Sage.

Sardinha, E.M. (2017) 'A estrutura do futebol feminino no Brasil', *HÓRUS*,
6(1), pp. 92–110.

Scharagrodsky, P.A. & Peréz Riedel, M. (2022) '"*Femina sana in corpore sano*"
(as long as they don't play football): football and womanhood in the 1920s'
Argentine capital', in Knijnik, J. & Garton, G. (eds), *Women's Football in
Latin America: Social Challenges and Historical Perspectives*, Vol. 2, *Hispanic
Countries*. London: Palgrave Macmillan, pp. 211–29.

Schmidt, V. (2010) 'Analyzing ideas and tracing discursive interactions in institutional change: from historical institutionalism to discursive institutionalism',
in APSA 2010 Annual Meeting Paper. [Online]. Available from: https://papers.
ssrn.com/sol3/papers.cfm?abstract_id=1642947 (accessed 27 March 2020).

Schmidt, V.A. (2002) *The Futures of European Capitalism*. Oxford: Oxford
University Press.

Schmidt, V.A. (2008) 'Discursive institutionalism: the explanatory power of ideas
and discourse', *Annual Review of Political Science*, 11(1), pp. 303–26.

Schmidt, V.A. (2010) 'Taking ideas and discourse seriously: explaining change
through discursive institutionalism as the fourth "New Institutionalism"',
European Political Science Review, 2(1), pp. 1–25.

Schwindt-Bayer, L.A. (2010) *Political Power and Women's Representation in Latin
America*. Oxford: Oxford University Press.

Schwindt-Bayer, L.A. (2018) *Gender and Representation in Latin America*. Oxford:
Oxford University Press.

Sciortino, M.S. (2018) 'Una etnografía sobre arreglos familiares, leonas y mujeres
superpoderosas', *Cuadernos de Antropología Social*, 48, pp. 55–71.

Scolari, C.A. (2015) 'From (new) media to (hyper) mediations: recovering
Jesús Martín-Barbero's mediation theory in the age of digital communication and cultural convergence', *Information, Communication & Society*, 18(9),
pp. 1092–1107.

Scott, J.C. (1990) *Domination and the Arts of Resistance: Hidden Transcripts*. New
Haven, CT: Yale University Press.

Selmer, N. (2021) 'Tivoli-Tussen and girls in football kits? Female fan cultures
in men's football', *Esporte e Sociedade*, 9.

@SemaforoDeporti (2018) *El premio que ganamos no es para nosotras, llega al
Huila masculino y el reconocimiento económico que tendremos nos lo dará nuestro
presidente y no es el premio que ganamos.* [Online]. Available from: https://
twitter.com/SemaforoDeporti/status/1069993784371544064 (accessed 14 May
2020).

Semana (2012) *¿Por qué banquearon a Yoreli Rincón?* [Online]. Available from:
https://www.semana.com/nacion/elecciones-estados-unidos/articulo/por-que-
banquearon-yoreli-rincon/262153-3 (accessed 31 May 2020).

Seráfico, J. & Seráfico, M. (2005) 'A Zona Franca de Manaus e o capitalismo no
Brasil', *Estudos avançados*, 19(54), pp. 99–113.

Shirky, C. (2011) 'The political power of social media: technology, the public sphere, and political change', *Foreign Affairs*, 90(1), pp. 28–41.

Silva, G.C. (2015) *Narrativas sobre o futebol feminino na imprensa paulista: entre a proibição e a regulamentação (1965–1983)*. PhD thesis. São Paulo: UFSP.

Silveira, R. da & Stigger, M.P. (2013) 'Jogando com as feminilidades: um estudo etnográfico em um time de futsal feminino de Porto Alegre', *Revista Brasileira de Ciências do Esporte*, 35(1), pp. 179–94.

Skidmore, T.E. (1974) *Black into White: Race and Nationality in Brazilian Thought*. Durham, NC: Duke University Press.

Sky Sports (2014) *Hodgson takes a tour of Manaus*. [Online]. Available from: https://www.skysports.com/watch/video/sports/football/competitions/world-cup/9171335/hodgson-takes-a-tour-of-manaus/more/30 (accessed 17 June 2020).

Soares, A.J. & Lovisolo, H.R. (2003) 'Futebol: a construção histórica do estilo nacional', *Revista Brasileira de Ciências do Esporte*, 25(1).

Soares, C. (2019) 'O Estatuto da FIFA e a igualdade de gênero no futebol: histórias e contextos do futebol feminino no Brasil', *FuLiA/UFMG*, 4(1), pp. 72–87.

de Souza, A., Salazar, V.S. & Feitosa, M.G.G. (2014) 'El Club 13 y el nuevo fútbol Brasileño: un análisis desde los campeonatos Baiano, Goiano, Paranaense y Pernambucano', *Revista Brasileira de Ciências do Esporte*, 36(1), pp. 103–22.

de Souza Gomes, E. (2012) *História comparada do esporte na América Latina: um olhar para a profissionalização do futebol no Brasil (1933–1941) e na Colômbia (1948–1954)*. Master's thesis. Universidade Federal do Rio de Janeiro.

de Souza Gomes, E. (2012) 'Caminhos da profissionalização: migração, política e nacionalismo na profissionalização do futebol colombiano (1948–1951)', Anais do XV Encontro Regional de História da ANPUH-RIO. [Online]. Available from: http://www.encontro2012.rj.anpuh.org/resources/anais/15/1338481367_ARQUIVO_Artigo.ANPUH-RIO.2012.pdf (accessed 27 March 2020).

de Souza Gomes, E. (2021) 'A chegada do profissionalismo: imprensa e dirigentes de futebol no Rio de Janeiro (1933) e na Colômbia (1948)', *Esporte e Sociedade*, 29.

de Souza Júnior, O.M. & dos Reis, H.H.B. (2010) *O canto das sereias: migrações e desafios de meninas que sonham ter o futebol como profissão*. Master's thesis. Available from: https://museudofutebol.org.br/crfb/acervo/654863/ (accessed 6 March 2020).

SoyReferee.com (2020) *Los 10 partidos de futbol femenil con mayor asistencia en el mundo | Referee*. [Online]. Available from: https://soyreferee.com/futbol/futbol-internacional/los-10-partidos-de-futbol-de-futbol-femenil-con-mayor-asistencia-en-el-mundo/ (accessed 29 June 2020).

Spaaij, R. (2006) *Understanding Football Hooliganism: A Comparison of Six Western European Football Clubs*. Amsterdam: Amsterdam University Press.

Suenzo, F., Boczkowski, P.J., Mitchelstein, E. & Mitchelstein, E. (2020) 'La crisis de la prensa escrita: una revisión bibliográfica para repensarla desde Latinoamérica', *Cuadernos.info*, 47, pp. 1–25.

Tato, E., Aon, J., Roman Lozano, J., Bramanti, M.B., Figueroa, M.J., Santino, M. & Korsakas, P. (2022) 'La nuestra fútbol feminista: a social experimentation and learning territory', in Knijnik, J. & Garton, G. (eds), *Women's Football in Latin America: Social Challenges and Historical Perspectives*, Vol. 2, *Hispanic Countries*. London: Palgrave Macmillan, pp. 77–94.

Taylor, L. (2020) *England women's and men's teams receive same pay, FA reveals. The Guardian*, 3 September. Available from: https://www.theguardian.com/football/2020/sep/03/england-womens-and-mens-teams-receive-same-pay-fa-reveals (accessed 13 December 2020).

Taylor, M. (2001) 'Beyond the maximum wage: the earnings of football professionals in England, 1900–39', *Soccer & Society*, 2(3), pp. 101–18.

Taylor, M. (2005) *The Leaguers: The Making of Professional Football in England, 1900–1939*. Liverpool: Liverpool University Press.

Taylor, M. (2013) *The Association Game: A History of British Football*. London: Routledge.

Taylor, M. (2016) 'History and football', in Hughson, J., Moore, K., Spaaij, R. & Maguire, J. (eds), *Routledge Handbook of Football Studies*. Abingdon: Routledge, pp. 23–33.

Taylor, M. (2017) 'The global spread of football', in Edelman, R. & Wilson, W. (eds), *The Oxford Handbook of Sports History*. Oxford: Oxford University Press, p. 183.

Taylor, T., Fujak, H., Hanlon, C. & O'Connor, D. (2020) 'A balancing act: women players in a new semi-professional team sport league', *European Sport Management Quarterly*, 22(4), pp. 1–21.

Taylor, T., O'Connor, D. & Hanlon, C. (2019) 'Contestation, disruption and legitimization in women's Rugby League', *Sport in Society*, 23(2), pp. 315–34.

Thorpe, H., Toffoletti, K. & Bruce, T. (2017) 'Sportswomen and social media: bringing third-wave feminism, postfeminism, and neoliberal feminism into conversation', *Journal of Sport and Social Issues*, 41(5), pp. 359–83.

Tiesler, N.C. (2016) 'Three types of transnational players: differing women's football mobility projects in core and developing countries', *Revista Brasileira de Ciências do Esporte*, 38(2), pp. 201–10.

Todorova, M. (2009) *Imagining the Balkans*. Oxford: Oxford University Press.

Toffoletti, K. (2016) 'Analyzing media representations of sportswomen: expanding the conceptual boundaries using a postfeminist sensibility', *Sociology of Sport Journal*, 33(3), pp. 199–207.

Toffoletti, K. & Thorpe, H. (2018) 'Female athletes' self-representation on social media: a feminist analysis of neoliberal marketing strategies in "economies of visibility"', *Feminism & Psychology*, 28(1), pp. 11–31.

Triana, R.E. (2001) 'Fuentes para la historia agraria e industrial de la provincia de Neiva', *Memoria y Sociedad*, 5(9), pp. 61–88.

Turow, J. (2011) *Media Today: An Introduction to Mass Communication*. London: Taylor & Francis.

Última Hora (2017) *Intoxicación aplaza la Libertadores femenina*. [Online]. Available from: https://www.ultimahora.com/intoxicacion-aplaza-la-libertadores-femenina-n1112223.html (accessed 30 March 2020).

Valdebenito, F. & Guizardi, M.L. (2015) 'Espacialidades migrantes. Una etnografía de la experiencia de mujeres peruanas en Arica (Chile)', *Gazeta de antropología*, 31(1).

Van Dijk, T.A. (1995) 'Power and the news media', *Political Communication and Action*, 6(1), pp. 9–36.

Vanguardia (2018) *Fuertes declaraciones del presidente del Tolima contra el fútbol femenino*. [Online]. Available from: https://www.vanguardia.com/deportes/futbol-colombiano/fuertes-declaraciones-del-presidente-del-tolima-contra-el-futbol-femenino-ICVL453568 (accessed 9 May 2020).

Vaz, A.C. (2017) 'A crise Venezuelana como fator de instabilidade regional', *Centro de Estudos Estratégicos do Exército: Análise Estratégica*, 3(3), pp. 1–7.

VBAR Caracol (2018) *'Liga Femenina sí vamos a tener': Jorge Vélez, presidente de la Dimayor*. [Online]. Available from: https://caracol.com.co/programa/2018/12/05/el_vbar/1543968571_142684.html (accessed 14 May 2020).

@VBarCaracol (2018) *Liga Femenina sí vamos a tener, nosotros podemos intervenir pero el tema no es masculino o femenino, que no se vuelva una guerra. Conmebol le paga a quien se inscribió.* [Online]. Available from: https://twitter.com/VBarCaracol/status/1070112930916696065 (accessed 18 May 2020).

Veja (2019) *Brasil registra a maior audiência do mundo para a final da Copa feminina.* [Online]. Available from: https://veja.abril.com.br/placar/brasil-registra-a-maior-audiencia-do-mundo-para-a-final-da-copa-feminina/ (accessed 9 March 2020).

Vélez, B. (1993) 'Sociología del deporte: algunos problemas teóricos y epistemológicos', *Educación Física y Deporte*, 14–15(1), pp. 65–72.

Vélez, B. (2001) 'La puesta en escena del género en el juego del fútbol', *Educación Física y Deporte*, 21(2), pp. 39–49.

Vergara, C.C.-C. (2019) 'Contra el fútbol del capital. Mercantilizaicón, sociedades anónimas deportivas y acción colectiva. El caso del Club Santiago Wanderers de Valparaíso y el movimiento "15 de Agosto"', *Deporte y Sociedad*, pp. 294–304.

Verón, E. (1982) *Construir el acontecimiento*. Barcelona: Gedisa.

Verón, E. (1987a) 'La palabra adversativa. Observaciones sobre la enunciación política', in Verón, E., *El discurso político. Lenguajes y acontecimientos*. Buenos Aires: Hachette, pp. 11–26.

Verón, E. (1987b) *La semiosis social: fragmentos de una teoría de la discursividad*. Barcelona: Gedisa.

Verón, E. (1997) 'Esquema para el análisis de la mediatización', *Matrizes*, 5(1).

Verón, E. (2009) 'El fin de la historia de un mueble', in Carlón, M. & Scolari, C.A. (eds), (AQ B4) *El fin de los medios masivos, el comienzo de un debate*. Buenos Aires: La Crujía, pp. 20–32.

Verón, E. (2013) *La semiosis social, 2: ideas, momentos, interpretantes*. Buenos Aires: Paidós.

Verón, E. (2014a) 'La mediatización', in Verón, E., *Semiosis de lo ideológico y del poder*. Buenos Aires: FFyL, pp. 39–112.

Verón, E. (2014b) 'Teoria da midiatização: uma perspectiva semioantropológica e algumas de suas consequências', *Matrizes*, 8(1), pp. 13–19.

Vieira, S. (2018) *O site 'dibradoras' como mídia de resistência ao preconceito machista no esporte*. Bagé thesis. Universidade Federal do Pampa.

Villoro, J. (2016) *God Is Round: Tackling the Giants, Villains, Triumphs, and Scandals of the World's Favorite Game*. New York: Restless Books.

Wade, P. (2012) 'Brazil and Colombia: comparative race relations in South America', in Bethencourt, F. & Pearce, A. (eds), *Racism and Ethnic Relations in the Portuguese-Speaking World*. Oxford: Oxford University Press, p. 35.

Wasser, N. & Lins França, I. (2020) 'In the line of fire: sex(uality) and gender ideology in Brazil', *Femina Politica – Zeitschrift für feministische Politikwissenschaft*, 29(1), pp. 27–28.

Watson, P.J. (2018) 'Colombia's political football: President Santos' National Unity Project and the 2014 football World Cup', *Bulletin of Latin American Research*, 37(5), pp. 598–612.

Watson, P.J. (2022) *Football and Nation Building in Colombia (2010–2018): The Only Thing That Unites Us*. Liverpool: Liverpool University Press.

Williams, J. (2006) 'An equality too far? Historical and contemporary perspectives of gender inequality in British and international football', *Historical Social Research/Historische Sozialforschung*, pp. 151–69.

Williams, J. (2007) *A Beautiful Game: International Perspectives on Women's Football*. London: A&C Black.

Williams, J. (2019) Introduction to the Second Special Edition of Williams, J., *Upfront and Onside*. London: Taylor & Francis.

Williams, J. & Hess, R. (2015) 'Women, football and history: international perspectives', *International Journal of the History of Sport*, 32(18), pp. 2115–22.

Wilson, E. (2021) *Love Game*. Chicago: University of Chicago Press.

WIN Sports (2018) *Yoreli Rincón: Soñamos la Copa Libertadores y aquí la tenemos*. Available from: https://www.winsports.co/futbol-colombiano/noticias/yoreli-rincon-sonamos-la-copa-libertadores-y-aqui-la-tenemos-104574 (accessed on 12 March 2020).

Wisnik, J.M. (2013) *Veneno remédio – o futebol e o Brasil*. São Paulo: Editora Companhia das Letras.

Wood, D. (2018) 'The beautiful game? Hegemonic masculinity, women and football in Brazil and Argentina', *Bulletin of Latin American Research*, 37(5), pp. 567–81.

Woodhouse, D., Fielding-Lloyd, B. & Sequerra, R. (2019) 'Big Brother's little sister: the ideological construction of Women's Super League', *Sport in Society*, 22(12), pp. 2006–23.

Zayas, E.R.C. (2020) 'Global Latin America in times of COVID-19 and hypermediations', *Journal of Latin American Communication Research*, 8(1–2), pp. 1–2.

Zouein, M.E. (2016) *A ideia de civilização nas fotografias, cartões postais e álbuns oficiais dos governos do amazonas e pará entre 1865 e 1908*. Rio de Janeiro: UFRJ.

Zúñiga Elizalde, M. (2014) 'Las mujeres en los espacios públicos: entre la violencia y la búsqueda de libertad', *Región y sociedad*, 26, pp. 78–100.

Appendix

Semi-Structured Interview List

Material for this book is drawn from semi-structured interviews which took place with the following players, managers and institutional figures (followed by dates and places):

At Santos FC

Alessandro Pinto	20 February 2019	Vila Belmiro Stadium, Santos
Angelina Costantino	27 February 2019	Vila Belmiro Stadium, Santos
Karla Alves	18 November 2018	Vila Belmiro Stadium, Santos
Kelly Rodrigues	31 October 2018	Meninos da Vila Training Facility, Santos
Marcelo Frazão	1 March 2019	Santos FC Business Centre, São Paulo
Maurine Gonçalves	28 February 2019	Vila Belmiro Stadium, Santos
Nicole Ramos	18 November 2018	Vila Belmiro Stadium, Santos
Rosana dos Santos Augusto	29 October 2018	Vila Belmiro Stadium, Santos
Sandrinha Pereira	18 November 2018	Rei Pelé Training Ground, Santos
Tayla Carolina Pereira dos Santos	26 October 2018	Vila Belmiro Stadium, Santos
Thais Picarte	29 October 2018	Vila Belmiro Stadium, Santos

At Esporte Clube Iranduba

Amarildo Dutra	9 February 2019	Arena da Amazônia, Manaus
Andressinha Machry	14 October 2018	Barbosa Filho Training Ground, Manaus
Camilinha Martins Pereira	14 October 2018	Barbosa Filho Training Ground, Manaus .
Driely Severino	18 November 2018	Barbosa Filho Training Ground, Manaus
Duda Pavão	9 November 2018	Barbosa Filho Training Ground, Manaus
Giselinha Teles	11 November 2018	Barbosa Filho Training Ground, Manaus
Lauro Tentardini	5 February 2019	Arena da Amazônia, Manaus
Mayara Andreia Vaz Moreira	11 November 2018	Barbosa Filho Training Ground, Manaus
Monalisa Belém	11 November 2018	Barbosa Filho Training Ground, Manaus
Renata Costa (Koki)	9 November 2018	Barbosa Filho Training Ground, Manaus
Rubi Pereira	14 November 2018	Barbosa Filho Training Ground, Manaus
Yoreli Rincón	8 February 2019	Barbosa Filho Training Ground, Manaus

At Atlético Huila

Carmen Rodallega	29 April 2019	player's house, Neiva
Daniela Narváez	30 May 2019	player's house, Neiva
Darnelly Quintero	29 April 2019	players' shared house, Los Cámbulos, Neiva
Fany Gauto	15 May 2019	player's house, Neiva
Gavy Santos	6 June 2019	Álvaro Sánchez Silva Sports Centre
Jennifer Peñaloza	29 April 2019	player's house, Neiva
Jorelyn Carabali	15 May 2019	player's house, Neiva
Levis Ramos	14 May 2019	player's house, Neiva

Maritza López	12 May 2019	player's house, Neiva
Nelly Córdoba	15 May 2019	player's house, Neiva
Paola Rincón	15 May 2019	player's house, Neiva

Management:

Albeiro Erazo	2 June 2019	manager's house, Neiva
Carlos Barrera	22 April 2019	club headquarters, Neiva
Diego Perdomo	23 May 2019	Perlun Company headquarters, Neiva

At CONMEBOL

| Romeu Castro | 4 December 2018 | Hilton Hotel, Manaus |

At CBF

| Vadão | 5 December 2018 | Arena da Amazônia, Manaus |
| Valesca Araújo | 21 January 2019 | CBF headquarters, Barra da Tijuca, Rio de Janeiro |

At DIMAYOR

Carlos Lajud Catalán	24 April 2019	DIMAYOR, Bogotá
Katherine Pimienta	24 April 2019	DIMAYOR, Bogotá
Vladimir Cantor	24 April 2019	DIMAYOR, Bogotá

At the Paulista Football Federation

| Aline Pellegrino | 22 February 2019 | Paulista Federation headquarters, São Paulo |

Index

Printed and bound by CPI Group (UK) Ltd, Croydon, CR0 4YY

16/04/2025

14658615-0002